Caribbean Religious History

Caribbean Religious History

An Introduction

Ennis B. Edmonds and
Michelle A. Gonzalez

NEW YORK UNIVERSITY PRESS
New York and London

NEW YORK UNIVERSITY PRESS
New York and London
www.nyupress.org

Library of Congress Cataloging-in-Publication Data
Edmonds, Ennis Barrington.
Caribbean religious history : an introduction /
Ennis B. Edmonds and Michelle A. Gonzalez.
p. cm.
Includes bibliographical references and index.
ISBN-13: 978-0-8147-2234-3 (cl : alk. paper)
ISBN-10: 0-8147-2234-2 (cl : alk. paper)
ISBN-13: 978-0-8147-2235-0 (pbk. : alk. paper)
ISBN-10: 0-8147-2235-0 (pbk. : alk. paper)
1. Caribbean Area—Religion. I. Gonzalez, Michelle A. II. Title.
BL2565.E36   2010
200.9729—dc22   2009050084

New York University Press books are printed on acid-free paper,
and their binding materials are chosen for strength and durability.
We strive to use environmentally responsible suppliers and materials
to the greatest extent possible in publishing our books.

Manufactured in the United States of America
c   10 9 8 7 6 5 4 3 2 1
p   10 9 8 7 6 5 4 3 2 1

To my grandmother, Florence Edmonds,
whose nurturing started me on the right path early in life,
and to my daughter, Donnisa Sara Edmonds,
for whom the future is wide open.
E. B. E.

To my sons, Byron Manuel and Michael,
Mis hombres, mi alma.
M.A.G.

Contents

Acknowledgments

Our appreciation and gratitude go to Jennifer Hammer, whose initiative, patience, and sharp editorial skills were crucial in shaping this project and producing the finished manuscript.

The direct and indirect assistance of a number of people has contributed to the bringing of this book to fruition. Therefore, I acknowledge and highlight the hard work and tenacity of my co-author and colleague, Michelle A. Gonzalez, whose constant urgings kept me focused and moving forward when taking it easy would have come more naturally. I am fortunate to have supportive colleagues in the religious studies department at Kenyon College, and so I thank them for their encouragements. Kudos to my wife, Donnaree, and my daughter, Donnisa, who supported me and kept me grounded throughout the whole process of producing this book.

E. B. E.

I would like to begin by thanking my co-author, Ennis Edmonds. Every research project is also a learning project, and I have learned very much from working with him. I am deeply grateful to the University of Miami for supporting this book through its Max Orovitz Summer Award in the Arts and Humanities and its Junior Faculty Research leave program. I would like to thank my colleagues in the Department of Religious Studies and the Program in Latin American Studies. I am indebted to UM's Cuban Heritage Collection for the wonderful resources I discovered there and to my research assistant, Jordan Adams. I want to thank my undergraduate students at UM, whose insights and questions constantly nourish my research. My family—Byron, Byron Manuel, and Michael—endured my hours at the computer with patience and love. Without them, none of my work would be possible.

M. A. G.

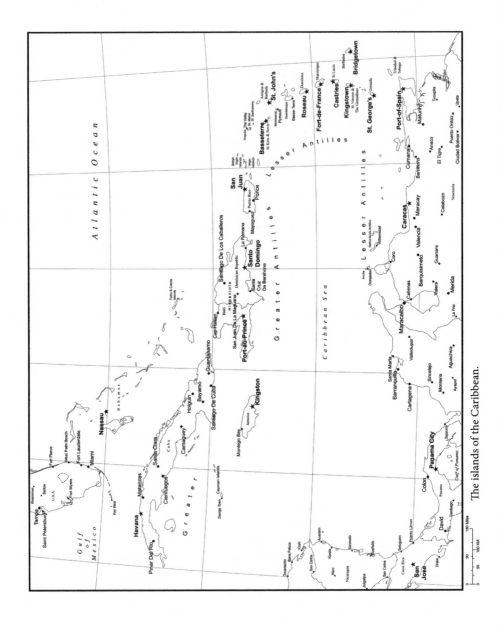

The islands of the Caribbean.

Introduction

Caribbean Crossroads: Historical
and Theoretical Considerations

The successful transatlantic crossing of Columbus and his crew in 1492 brought the Caribbean and the rest of the Americas into the mainstream of world history, initiating a process through which the area became an important arena in which European powers competed for political and economic dominance. This colonial experiment spawned the diversity of peoples, languages, and cultures that is the present reality of the Caribbean. An important part of this cultural mix is its variety of religious traditions. As these traditions encountered one another and their new environment, a process of accommodation, adaptation, and transformation began that has resulted in the character and diversity of religious beliefs and practices in the Caribbean today. This book traces the historical trajectory of the major (and some minor) religious traditions of the Caribbean against the broader background of Caribbean social history, paying particular attention to the historical events and processes that have shaped the religious experiences of the Caribbean people. To study the history of the Caribbean without serious consideration of the function and role of religion, we argue, is to miss a fundamental dimension of Caribbean cultures. The Caribbean is a microcosm of the world, where populations from around the globe have come together, with their cultures, traditions, and religions.

A Brief Profile of the Caribbean

In profiling the Caribbean, it seems apt to begin with geography, but we are immediately faced with the problem of delineating the area to be included under the designation "Caribbean." One way of posing the problem is to ask whether our definition of the Caribbean is going to be restrictive or expansive. The restrictive definition reserves the term for the islands in the

Caribbean Sea. These include the Greater Antilles, the large islands in the northwest Caribbean; the Lesser Antilles, the string of smaller islands in the eastern Caribbean stretching from the Virgin Islands in the north to the Grenada in south; and the southern islands of Trinidad, Aruba, Bonaire, and Curaçao, all off the coast of South America. In addition to the islands in the Caribbean Sea, the more expansive definition includes the Bahamas, which lie north of the Greater Antilles but are technically in the Atlantic, and such territories as Belize, Guyana, Surinam, and French Guiana, in Central and South America. The inclusion of these territories is usually based on historical and cultural ties that link these countries more strongly to the Caribbean than to the Latino history and culture of Central and South America. An even more expansive definition would include all the northern coast of Central and South America that is washed by the Caribbean Sea. In this book, we are following the more restrictive view of the Caribbean, not because we want to deny Caribbean identity to those traditionally linked to the history and culture of the islands in the more expansive definition but because it is a more manageable unit. We will make occasional references to places found outside this restrictive definition, but they will not be the focus of sustained discussion.

The Caribbean islands are home to close to forty million people of diverse ethnicities whose ancestors and cultural heritages originated in the Americas, Africa, Asia, and Europe. Probably an equal number of people living abroad, especially in North America and Europe, identify themselves as Caribbean. The Amerindians who occupied the islands when the Spanish arrived in 1492 were the Ciboneys, the Tainos, and the Caribs. The Ciboneys were a relatively small group residing mostly on the western tip of Cuba and probably in the southwest of Hispaniola. The Tainos occupied the large islands of Greater Antilles—Cuba, Hispaniola, Jamaica, and Puerto Rico— and the Caribs mostly resided in the islands of the Lesser Antilles. Within the first hundred years after the arrival of Columbus, a combination of European forced labor, massacre, and diseases killed most of the Amerindians. The Caribs who had intermarried with Africans who in turn had escaped from the Spanish resisted French and British encroachment into the late 1700s. The British eventually deported most of them to Roatán Island, off the coast of Central America. From there, they migrated into Belize, Honduras, and Guatemala, where they came to constitute the Garifuna people. Today a few small communities of Caribs have survived in Dominica, St. Vincent, and the Grenadines. Amerindian strains have also survived in various racial mixings, particularly in Puerto Rico and in Dominican Republic. People of darker hues in Dominican Republic, for example, are likely to refer to themselves as Tainos.

Today's Caribbean population is a result of repeated waves of immigrants since the late 1400s. These include Europeans, from northern and southern Europe, who migrated to the area in search of fortune or simply to better their lives. Though a numerical minority in most places, they exercised political, economic, and cultural dominance during the colonial era. Many European Jews also migrated to the Caribbean, fleeing persecution in Europe and/or pursuing business opportunities. Today, descendants of Europeans are a small minority in most places in the Caribbean. Official censuses in Puerto Rico and Cuba place whites/Europeans squarely in the majority, though scholars contest the validity of these censuses, arguing that Puerto Rico is a mestizo (mixed-race) society and that Cuba should be considered predominantly mixed race as well.[1] People of African descent and people of mixed African and European ancestry are the dominant ethnic groups in most of the Caribbean. However, significant numbers of Asians were brought to the Caribbean from the mid-1800s to the early 1900s. The most significant group was Indians—or South Asians (from India and Pakistan)—who were imported as indentured workers by the British after 1838. Between 1845 and 1917, more that 400,000 Indian indentures were transported to the Caribbean with the largest concentration setting in Trinidad and Tobago and Guyana. Today the number of their descendants is equivalent to the population of African descendants in Trinidad and Tobago, as well as in Guyana, and they form a substantial minority in Jamaica. Chinese also came to the Caribbean as indentured workers or as traders. They are a small minority in the Caribbean, mostly associated with commercial enterprises. Portuguese, Arabs, Syrians, and people of other ethnicities and backgrounds all add to the Caribbean mix, and miscegenation has produced a host of racial and ethnic mixings.

With the diversity of people comes a variety of languages. The major European languages—English, French, Spanish, and Dutch—are spoken. Various creole languages and dialects have also emerged in the Caribbean. Most Haitians speak Kreyol; Papimiento is the popular language in the Dutch Antilles; forms of French creole are spoken in the French Antilles and in Dominica and St. Lucia; and an English-based patois (patwa) is spoken in most former British colonies.

Modern Caribbean history may be divided into three periods based on European activities in the area. The first period stretches from exploration to emancipation (1492–1838) and covers most of the slave era. Though emancipation came at different times for different islands—Haiti in 1804 and Cuba in the 1890s, for example—the emancipation of the slaves in the British colonies in 1838 set the stage for the abolition of slavery throughout the Caribbean. The second period extends from emancipation to independence, 1838 through the 1960s. Again, independence did not come at once for all Caribbean islands. For example, for Cuba and Haiti emancipation and independence came together, while most of the larger islands that were former British colonies attained independence only after 1960. Other islands have maintained some form of dependent relationship with the European nations or the United States. The third period is from independence to the present.

Another way to characterize Caribbean history is to see it as composed of cycles in which the area alternates between taking center stage in world events and being peripheral to international interests and events. The Caribbean first burst onto the center stage of history between 1492 and the 1520s as it became the arena of Spanish exploration and colonization. Yet, it quickly became a kind of neglected backwater of the Spanish empire as the Spanish shifted their interest to Mexico and South America, where the precious metals of gold and silver were found in abundance. For most of the 1500s, the Caribbean became a mere staging area or filling station for Spanish ships on their way to and from what was seen as the Spanish mainland. As other European nations, especially France and England, challenged the Spanish monopoly in the Americas in the 1600s, the Caribbean became a main stage for the playing out of European conflicts. With the development of a plantation economy based on the growing of sugar cane, the Caribbean also became a main source of wealth for European powers. Successively, Jamaica, Haiti, and Cuba became the most economically prosperous colonies in the world from the early 1700s to the mid-1800s. With the waning of the sugar industry in the post-emancipation era, the Caribbean again became peripheral to metropolitan interests. During the Cold War that followed the Second World War, the Caribbean became an arena for U.S. and the Soviet Union geopolitics. Socialist revolutions in Cuba, Grenada, and Guyana and Jamaica's experiment with Democratic Socialism all fueled and were fueled by Cold War geopolitics in the area. With the fall of the Soviet Union and the rise of the global economy, the Caribbean lost much of its political and economic significance, remaining important mostly as a tourist playground. With the spreading of Chinese economic power in the Americas and with Russia seeking to reassert its influence, there are signs that the Caribbean may again be swept up in international power play in the early part of the twenty-first century.

With the evolving history of the Caribbean, political realities in the region have also undergone changes. Plantation societies during the slave era were dominated by Europeans, either through the agency of colonial administrators appointed directly from Europe or by local legislatures and assemblies of Europeans elected by and from the planter class. While the European interests and the planter class of European extract continued to dominate during the period bookended by emancipation and independence, the emerging local middle class, consisting predominantly of mixed-race people, and the working, mostly black, population, agitated for self-rule and eventually for independence. Emancipation and independence for Haiti resulted from the same struggle, the Haitian Revolution—which transpired between 1791 and 1804. Similarly, emancipation and independence in Cuba came out of a great effort that lasted from the 1860s to the 1890s. Independence in the Dominican Republic is somewhat complicated. That nation first became independent in 1821 as part of the general movement toward the independence of Spanish colonies in Latin America. Annexed by Haiti shortly thereafter, it regained its independence in 1884 but has experienced periods of foreign domination by Spain and the United States (1916–1924 and 1965–1966, respectively). Most of the larger English colonies became independent nations in the 1960s and 1970s. Other Caribbean islands maintain a variety of relationships with European nations and the United States.

Franklin W. Knight and Colin A. Palmer, both noted historians of the Caribbean, identify three types of political status in which most Caribbean island fall. First, most of the islands, with between 80 and 90 percent of the Caribbean population, are independent states: Antigua, the Bahamas, Barbados, Cuba, Dominica, Dominican Republic, Grenada, Haiti, Jamaica, St. Lucia, St. Kitts and Nevis, St. Vincent and the Grenadines, and Trinidad and Tobago. Second, a number of islands occupy the status of associated states of European nations or the United States. These include the French Overseas Departments of French Guiana, Guadeloupe, and Martinique and the Netherlands' self-governing territories of Aruba, Bonaire, Curaçao, Saba, Sint Maarten (island shared with the French territory St. Martin), and Sint Eustatius. Puerto Rico is a commonwealth, or dependency, of the United States, and the U.S. Virgin Islands of St. Croix, St. John, and St. Thomas are U.S. territories. Finally, a number of islands may still be considered colonies. These include the British colonies of the Cayman Islands, Montserrat, the Turks and Caicos Islands, and the British Virgin Islands of Tortola, Virgin Gorda, Anegada, and Jost Van Dyke. St. Barthélemy and St. Martin occupy a similar status under the French flag.[2]

For most of the region's modern history, the economy of the Caribbean has reflected the dominance of metropolitan interests, first of the European over-lords and then, increasingly, of the United States. The initial Spanish thrust into the area was stimulated by the search for gold and other precious metals, followed by an attempt to develop a plantation economy when these metals were not found in sufficient quantities. In the first half of the 1500s, most of the Spanish settlers headed to Mexico and South America, where gold and silver were found in substantial quantities, leaving those who remained in the islands to develop ranching and subsistence agriculture as the main economic activities. With the arrival of northern Europeans, mainly from France and Great Britain, tropical products for European markets came to dominate the economy in the Caribbean. The major crops included indigo, tobacco, sugar cane, cacao, and, later, bananas. Sugar was by far the most important product, dominating the economy of the Caribbean from the late 1600s into the 1900s. The contemporary Caribbean has a somewhat mixed economy. Sugar and bananas continue to be significant but are of diminish-ing importance in many islands. Manufacturing output has increased sig-nificantly since the mid-1950s. Much of the manufacturing is actually off-shore operations of multinational corporations, including the assembling of clothes, electronics, and baseballs. Exploration for bauxite (the raw material from which alumina is extracted), petroleum, and pitch add to the economic activities in the area. Increasingly, tourism has become the highest foreign exchange earner in the area. The Bahamas, Aruba, and Jamaica, for example, have long been recognized as world-class vacation spots. More recently, Bar-bados, Dominican Republic, Antigua, Puerto Rico, and even Trinidad and Tobago have developed robust tourism industries. Some smaller islands, famously the Cayman Islands, have become prosperous as off-shore bank-ing centers and tax havens. In most rural areas, subsistence farming and the rearing of cash crops remain the economic life line for many. Economists now credit drug trafficking and remittances from Caribbean people living abroad as substantial contributors to Caribbean economies.

Historically and currently, the Caribbean region has been marked by inter-nal fragmentation, resulting from the pattern of European involvement in the area. The present division of the region into Anglophone, Francophone, Hispanic, and Dutch Caribbean is a legacy of colonial conflicts and partitions of the islands by Europeans. This has created feelings of kinship based not on proximity but on language and former association with European powers. Jamaicans, for example, tend to feel closer and to have social and cultural exchanges with Barbadians and Trinidadians hundreds of miles away in the southeastern Caribbean, rather than with the Cubans, Haitians, and Dominicans in their own Greater Antilles neighborhood. Another expression of this fragmentation is that individual Caribbean countries tend to be oriented toward their former colonial powers instead of toward one another. Nowadays, the United States and, to some extent, Canada have replaced Europe as the object of the outward focus of Caribbean people. This shows up in travel and emigration patterns. Some observers have complained that it is easier to get to London, Paris, Toronto, New York, or Miami from any Caribbean country than it is to get from one place to another within the Caribbean.

In terms of public social institutions in the Caribbean, Europe still holds sway. Such institutions as politics, the economy, education, and the legal systems are either of European provenance or are adaptations of European institutions. On the cultural front there is a tension between what the Caribbean public intellectual and cultural scientist Rex Nettleford calls "the melody of Europe and the rhythm of Africa."[3] We see this tension between the official European languages taught in schools and the vernacular bending of grammar and vocabulary to African speech patterns. We also see this in the tension between the rational-ethical and confessional religious traditions from Europe and the vernacular religious traditions oriented more strongly toward ritual healing and expressive, emotional displays. As we will see, this tension in the religious sphere is finding some resolution at present in the growing, popular Pentecostal and charismatic churches. One of the ways of characterizing contemporary Caribbean culture[s] is to say that, while Europe rules in the official social institutions of politics, economic, education, and law, other ethnic groups, particular Africans, tend to rule in folk and popular culture, including religion, music, dance, and, increasingly, the visual and performing arts.

Social class is another issue that has evolved within the confines of Caribbean history. At first, the great divide was between white planters, traders, and colonial officials on one side and the mass of African slave laborers on the other. In some places, there were poor whites, but they tended to be identified with the white power structure. An intermediate group of mixed-race people emerged in most places through miscegenation between white males and slave women. Usually free, this group came to occupy a middle place between whites and blacks. Jews, Chinese, and Middle Easterners became grafted into the upper white class. When Indians (from India) first arrived, they were considered a special case outside the existing class construct. As they remained in the islands, particularly Trinidad, as poor rural agricultural workers, they were considered on a par with or below the masses of the black population well into the mid-1900s. Many have climbed the social ladder through educational, business, and professional success. Today, social class and social status in the Caribbean are much more complex. While race, color, and ethnicity remain important, education, economic success, and political power are more essential markers of socioeconomic status.

Theoretical Perspectives on Religions in the Caribbean

Theoretical consideration of the evolution and character of religion in the Caribbean falls within the broader discussion of how to account for the cultural traditions that have been forged in the Caribbean. In an attempt to explain the origin and character of Caribbean culture, scholars of the region have put forth three major theories: the plantation society theory, the plural-society theory, and the theory of creolization.

According to the plantation society theory, the legacy of the plantation slavery is the central determinant of life in the Caribbean. The Harvard sociologist Orlando Patterson and George Beckford, a prolific scholar of the Caribbean political economy, are the proponents of this view.[4] According to these scholars, the distinguishing features of plantation societies were coercion and exploitation, leading to a rigid system of domination and class and race stratification. The domination was not just political and economic but also social and cultural. The culture and heritage of the dominated—black slaves—were suppressed and strangled, and the ruling minority—white Europeans—imposed a new identity upon them. Some would even go so far as to agree with the African American sociologist E. Franklin Frazier, who argued that the horrors of Middle Passage (the slaves' journey from Africa to the Americas) and the brutality of plantation slavery erased the most significant features of African culture, including religion and family traditions, among African Americans and Afro-Caribbean peoples and that what we now identify as black culture is but a bastardized imitation of European culture.[5] A contemporary iteration of that thesis is that espoused by Prem Misir, Pro-Chancellor of the University of Guyana. He asserts that "Africans lost most of their African heritage to take on a creolized variant of European culture. This absorption process really is cultural assimilation at work where a minority group, either through force or voluntarily, surrenders its cultural tradition to become enveloped into a different and invariably dominant culture."[6] Advocates of this interpretation of Caribbean culture insist that the legacy of plantation society still persists in the economic and cultural dependency of the Caribbean on the metropoles of Europe and North America.

While the plantation society theory correctly highlights the coercion and oppression of plantation slavery and its continuing legacies in the Caribbean, it fails to acknowledge the abundant evidence produced by historians and social scientists of the survival of African cultural elements in Caribbean cultures, especially in musical and religious expressions. This theory also overlooks the cultural agency of the dominated to resist cultural imposition and to fashion cultural expressions to mirror their sense of identity. As we will see, in many cases in which Africans brought to Caribbean or their descendants accepted elements of European culture, they often deployed them in an African manner and employed them for their own purposes. For example, many Afro-Jamaicans accepted Christianity in the slave era but deployed it to resist their enslavement and to pursue liberation. Another example is the relationship of Afro-Cuban religion to the Virgen de la Caridad del Cobre, the indigenous patron saint of Cuba. Ostensibly a Catholic saint, she is understood by the devotees of the Afro-Cuban religion Santería as a manifestation of one entity in their spiritual pantheon, Oshun. Furthermore, plantation society theorists attribute too much to institutional and macro-level social forces and too little to vernacular cultural beliefs, ideas, and values. As the sociologist O. Nigel Bolland points out, this theory leaves the analysis at the institutional level, not accounting for the "values, beliefs and ideas of the various protagonists with the society."[7] While the plantation society theory gives all of the agency to the dominant class, much of what is distinctively Caribbean popular and folk culture has been fashioned by people on the lowest rung of the social ladder.

Moreover, the plantation society theory can quickly segue into a reductionist Marxian explanation in which culture is seen as the effluence of the underlying economic conditions. In other words, economic relationships are seen as the sole determinant of culture, including religious expressions. This explanation may have been espoused by some Marxist-oriented intellectuals from the 1960s to 1980s, but it has received no serious treatment in the sociological and anthropological literature on the Caribbean.

The plural-society theory of Caribbean culture was championed in the mid-twentieth century by the scholar M. G. Smith, of the University of the West Indies. According to Smith, Caribbean societies are made of "disparate parts" that emanated from elsewhere. These societies have no shared culture and no shared participation in common social institutions that could provide a precondition for social stability. With this lack of shared institutions and socialization, force is the only social mechanism that holds these societies together.[8] Thus, these societies are characterized by social pluralism in which "each cultural section has its own relatively exclusive way of life, with its own distinctive systems of actions, ideas, values, and social relations."[9] For Smith, these social divisions are based not on class distinctions but on cultural traits, though the history of the Caribbean has produced a correlation between race and culture.

If the plural-society theory has any merits, it is that it draws attention to the complexity of Caribbean culture and to the multiplicity of cultural influences vying for attention in the Caribbean public space. Admittedly, the Caribbean is a multicultural environment where diversity prevails. Though Smith concentrates on differences among the white, brown (mixed race), and black populations, he very well could have added the Indians, Chinese, Syrians, and Jews to the ethnic mix of the Caribbean. Smith also recognizes the fact that the historical relationship between groups has been determined by differential access to power. However, the glaring weakness of Smith's interpretation is that it is too static. Smith would have us believe that over the past five hundred years of Caribbean history, interaction between discrete groups has been minimal and cultural exchange has been nonexistent. Even if Smith is right, his theory is a simple classificatory scheme that does little to explain social and cultural change in Caribbean history.

Creolization or creole society theory has appeared in one form or another as an explanation for the social processes or dynamics that have produced various aspects of Caribbean culture. Such terms as syncretism, symbiosis, assemblage, bricolage, hybridity, and *mestizaje* have also been used to highlight aspects of the creolization process. The English word "creolization" has its roots in the French *creole* and the Spanish *criollo*. Quite early in the colonial history of the Caribbean, creole was employed to refer to "something or somebody derived from the Old World but developed in the New." Thus "locally born persons of non-native origin . . . of either African or European ancestry or both" were known as creoles.[10] In colonial Cuba, strict distinction was made between *criollos*, people of Spanish ancestry who were born in Cuba, and *peninsulares*, Spaniards who migrated to Cuba from Spain. On slave plantations, both masters and slaves maintained a distinction between creole slaves born in the Americas and African-born slaves (the African-born were more disposed to the plotting of uprisings). In time, "creole" came to refer not only to persons born in the Americas but also to social and cultural expressions and practices developed indigenously.

The Caribbean poet and historian Edward Braithwaite proposed the creolization theory in his famous study *The Development of Creole Society in Jamaica, 1770–1820*. Focusing on how European- and African-derived cultural elements contributed to the development of a distinct Jamaican culture that was neither European nor African, Braithwaite contended that the process of creolization is "based upon the stimulus/response of individuals to their environment and—of white/black, culturally discrete groups—to each other."[11] He goes on to point out that creolization in this instance resulted from an unplanned flow of influence emerging from co-presence and interaction in which there are mutual adaptations and imitation. The outcome is the evolution of shared cultural practices.[12] Rex Nettleford, an astute observer of Caribbean culture, joins Braithwaite in viewing creolization as the result of a creative interplay among transplanted cultures to produce a "new and rich phenomenon which is neither African nor European, yet embodying the two in unprecedented and creative modes of relationships."[13] In rather colorful language, Donald J. Cosentino, Professor of Culture and Performance at UCLA and editor of *Sacred Arts of Haitian Vodou*, describes creolization as "the process of furnishing a home with imported objects arranged according to the peculiar tastes and needs of the new owner."[14] In summary, creolization theory posits that the discrete cultural elements that have been transported to the Caribbean environment have undergone a process of transplantation, adaptation, and transformation to produce distinct cultural forms that reflect both the history and the social and geographic environment of the region.

Unlike the plantation society and the plural-society theories, creolization theory recognizes the dynamism of societies and cultures, highlights the importance of the agency of social actors and begins to articulate an explanation of societal change in Caribbean history. However, Bolland gently chides creolization theorists for not having adequately appreciated and articulated the dialectic relationship between the "mutually constitutive nature of 'individual,' 'society,' and 'culture,' and of human agency and social structure." Furthermore, creolization theorists do not foreground the conflictual nature of "social systems" and how such conflicts serve as "sources of social change."[15] Creolization theorists have not paid sufficient attention to the mutual influence of diverse elements of African heritage and have paid scant or no attention to the contributions of ethnic groups other than European and Africans to the dialectic of Caribbean culture. Some scholars, especially those of Indian descent, have expressed strong objection to the creolization model for understanding Caribbean culture and identity. Arguing that creolization is a process that involves the blending of Anglo and African cultures, often involving the subsuming or loss of African heritage, Misir contends that Indians in the Caribbean have maintained their own culture and their cultural and political bonds with India. He proposes that the concept of a mosaic better represents the multicultural reality of the Caribbean.[16]

Without directly taking on Misir's claims in detail, we point out that the choice between perceiving Caribbean culture[s] as preserving its multicultural mosaic or as erasing individuals' Indian, European, or African culture in the process of creolization is a false one. That there exists in the Caribbean a great variety of traditions reflecting various cultural backgrounds and maintaining a variety of cultural values and practices is undeniable. At the same time, most groups have made varying degrees of adaptations to the Caribbean environment. Even those that claim to preserve the pure African, European, Indian, or other traditions often show evidence of being shaped by the historical and cultural realities of the Caribbean. Thus, these traditions have not been static but have reflected the dynamism of the dialectic between change and continuity. The major theoretical perspective underlying this book is the conviction that religion in the contemporary Caribbean reflects a long history of encounter between various traditions and their adaptation to the presence of one another and to the physical, political, economic, and cultural realities of the Caribbean environment.

A particularly instructive inflection of the creolization theory is the notion of "nation dance" articulated by Patrick D. Taylor, a scholar and professor of Caribbean culture and religions. Inspired by Braithwaite's use of "nation language" to refer to the creole languages of the Caribbean, Taylor uses the imagery of dance to indicate the interplay among religious influences in the Caribbean social environment. Describing the Caribbean as a site of "difference, plurality, and transformation," he asserts that "the dispersed nations dance their separate dance in the same yard. They borrow from and influence each other, but the dancing of the different nations does not stop."[17] Informing Taylor's notion of Nation Dance and our approach to Caribbean religious history in this book are three concepts that capture the reality of cultural and religious creativity in the Caribbean: diaspora, crossroads, and liminality.

The Caribbean is a quintessential diasporic space traversed by a multiplicity of immigrants coming and going. From the first inhabitants encountered by Columbus to later African, European, Indian, and other populations, whether responding to the promise of the Caribbean or taken there under the duress of the slave trade or indentureship, repeated waves of diverse peoples have found their ways to its shores and transplanted themselves there. The present population of the Caribbean is composed of diasporic peoples who have moved into the region over the past five hundred years.

Implicit in the characterization of the Caribbean as a diaspora space is the idea of the crossroads. In Afro-Caribbean religions, the spiritual entity Papa Legba, or Elegguá, rules over the crossroads—the symbolic juncture between the human and the realm of the spirits, the pathway between present realities and the African past, the point that separates the present and the future, the place of ritual transformation and empowerment, and the site of decision and opportunity. In a historical and sociological sense, the Caribbean is a site where the meeting of diverse peoples and diverse cultures has opened up new opportunities for interaction, cultural innovations, and transformations. The meeting and cross-fertilization of various religious traditions have both given old traditions new inflections and created new, indigenous traditions.

Closely related to the idea of the crossroads is the notion of liminality. The renowned anthropologist Victor Turner describes liminality as the condition of being "betwixt and between."[18] He specifically uses this term to describe the status of people going through rites of passage. Having left their old status and standing, they go through a period in which the old no longer applies but the new has not yet arrived. Hence, one of the keys to liminality is indeterminacy. It is a dynamic situation that produces change and transformation. In the liminal spaces of the Caribbean crossroads, diasporic peoples have alighted, and, drawing on their cultural heritage and their historical, geographic, and social realities, they have fashioned cultural expressions and religious traditions that express their sense of self in the world.

This book investigates the diverse religious expressions that reflect the historical evolution of the Caribbean, the heritage of its diverse diasporic peoples, and the transformations, transmutations, and innovations in the dance of diverse religious influences in the same social space. Chapter 2 discusses Taino religions and the nature and results of the contact between their practitioners and the early Spanish settlers. Chapter 3 surveys the role of the Catholic Church in the Caribbean during the colonial era. Chapter 4 focuses on Protestantism in the Caribbean from the beginning of the northern European challenge to the Spanish monopoly in the region. Chapter 5 discusses creole African traditions, which have maintained many of their African elements even while being fused with elements encountered in the Caribbean. Chapter 6 investigates Afro-Christian traditions that have fused African and Christian elements to create new religious traditions, including the emergence and evolution of such groups as Revival Zion and Spiritual Baptists. In chapter 7 the focus falls on the role of the churches in the post-emancipation era and the emergence of the distinction between "mainline" churches (European-derived, with high status) and "clap-hand" churches (Evangelical and Pentecostal groups that originated mainly in the United States and are associated with lower classes). Chapter 8 surveys the growth of religious diversity in the Caribbean with the introduction of Islam, Hinduism, and the religious movement of Rastafari that emerged in Jamaica in the 1930s. The concluding chapter 9 offers a look at contemporary issues facing religion in the Caribbean today.

Amerindians and Spanish Catholics in Contact

The historical and archaeological evidence suggests that the islands of the Caribbean and the Bahamas have been continuously occupied since 4000 B.C.E. From that time on, repeated waves of migrations brought various groups to the area. Through interaction with one another and with their natural surroundings, these migrants made the Caribbean a dynamic and evolving social and cultural environment in which each wave of immigrants replaced or integrated with earlier inhabitants, adapted to the environment, and fashioned a coherent way of life. By the time Columbus arrived, in 1492, the Caribbean showed evidence of the dynamics of such migrations and interactions in the various groups living there. The earliest inhabitants, the Ciboneys, also called Guanahatabeys, had by that time been relegated to the western tip of Cuba and probably some enclaves in other locations of the Greater Antilles (Jamaica, Cuba, Hispaniola, and Puerto Rico). By far the dominant group, both numerically and culturally, was the Tainos, who likely migrated from South America and occupied the Greater Antilles in the northwestern Caribbean, the Bahamas, and probably the northern tip of the Lesser Antilles (an arch of smaller islands stretching from the northeast to the southeast and bordering the eastern Caribbean).[1] This group was by no means homogenous. As Irving Rouse, the famed archeologist of the Caribbean, observes, the Tainos of Hispaniola and Puerto Rico were more culturally and technologically developed than their counterparts in Cuba, Jamaica, and the Bahamas. Also within Hispaniola, linguistic and cultural differences prevailed. For example, the Ciqueyos (or Ciguayans) in the northeast spoke a distinct dialect.[2] The Caribs were the predominant people of the islands of the Lesser Antilles, but their religious outlook and their means of livelihood (cultivation and fishing) bore a great resemblance to those of the Tainos and may have been adopted from them. Moreover, these groups were in frequent contact, though the encounters seem to have been mostly of a hostile nature. Furthermore, the

Caribs made frequent raids on the Tainos, often capturing women whom they made their wives. Thus, many Caribs must have been part-Taino. For example, in the early 1500s, the leading *cacique* (paramount chief) of Maguana, a province of Hispaniola, was Caonabó, often identified as a Carib.

The Origins and Way of Life of Indigenous Caribbean People

The earliest settlers were Ciboneys, also called Guanahatabeys, who migrated to western Cuba some time before 1000 B.C.E., maybe as early as 4000 B.C.E. From there they spread out over the Greater Antilles. Neither the historical nor the archeological evidence provides any definite answer concerning their place of origin. They could have migrated from either the Yucatan Peninsula or Central America by boats or rafts, crossing the Yucatan Channel. Or they may have been related to the Amerindians in Florida, coming to Cuba across the Florida Straits. Another possibility is that they originated in the Oronoco Valley on the northeast coast of South America and their boats or rafts were carried to Cuba by the ocean current that flows from the southeast to the northwest in the Caribbean Sea. These early settlers were a hunting and gathering people. They left no evidence of having engaged in agriculture or the production of ceramics.[3] At the time of Spanish exploration and settlement, in the late 1400s and early 1500s, only a small number of these Ciboneys/Guanahatabeys remained in the Caribbean, mostly confined to western Cuba and to the southern peninsula of modern Haiti. Like their Taino counterparts, they soon became victims of the brutality and pressure of Spanish colonization.

Historians and archaeologists generally agree that the Tainos, the most numerous people that Columbus encountered in the Caribbean in the late 1400s, descended from the Arawaks of the Oronoco Valley. Rouse identifies Saladero in modern Venezuela as the region from which the Tainos' ancestors migrated. This conclusion is supported by the cultural similarities between the Tainos of the Caribbean and the Arawak people of South America. Among the evidence is the fact that they both engaged in similar types of agricultural production; they produced similarly styled ceramic with signature crosshatching, and representations of the flora and fauna of South America often appeared on their pottery and other artistic works; and the language of the Tainos is clearly related to that of the Arawaks.[4] Recent comparative DNA studies have confirmed the biological link between the Arawaks from Saladero and the Tainos of the Caribbean. During the first century of the Common Era, the Arawaks migrated, probably in repeated waves, into the southeastern islands of the Caribbean, and gradually, over the next 1000 years, they moved up the archipelago of the Lesser Antilles to settle mostly in the northwest islands of the Caribbean. They eventually displaced or merged with the earlier settlers to become the Taino people who occupied Cuba, Hispaniola, Jamaica, Puerto Rico, and the Bahamas at the time of the arrival of the Spanish explorers and colonists.

The Tainos ancestors were eventually followed into Caribbean by the Caribs, who originated in the same general area of the Oronoco Valley. Historians believe that the Caribs were at least partly responsible for gradually pushing the Tainos farther north and westward from the Lesser Antilles and into the Greater Antilles. When the European arrived in the Indies, the Caribs inhabited the islands of the Lesser Antilles. The Spanish had only limited, but violent, contacts with the Caribs, since the early Spanish settlements were concentrated on the large islands of the Greater Antilles, and by the mid-1500s the Spanish shifted their attention to Mexico and South America, where gold and silver were more abundant. The shipwreck, in 1635, of two Spanish vessels carrying slaves resulted in the settlement of a number of Africans on the island of St. Vincent. After initial hostility between the Caribs and the Africans, the two ethnicities eventually merged through intermarriages to create Black Caribs. When the northern Europeans—French, English, and Dutch—started to encroach on the Spanish monopoly in the Americas in the early 1600s, they colonized the islands of the eastern Caribbean and engaged in protracted wars with the Caribs. By the end of the 1700s, most of the Caribs (including Black Caribs) had been exterminated, with the exception of small groups in Dominica and St. Vincent. When the Caribs and Black Caribs of St. Vincent proved intractable, the British exiled most of them to the island of Roatán, off the coast of Honduras. From there, they spread into Honduras, Guatemala, and Belize and developed the Garifuna culture. Some Garifuna people migrated to the United States after World War II and now maintain active communities in New York, Los Angeles, and New Orleans.

Amerindian Economy and Social Structure

By the time Columbus appeared in the Caribbean, the Amerindians (a term we will use to refer to the indigenous people to distinguish them from Indians from India) had forged a way of life that enabled them to live in harmony with their environment. Combining agriculture with fishing and hunting, they were able to exploit the flora and fauna of the region without endangering their sustainability. They developed social conventions through which they governed themselves and regulated inter- and intragroup relationships. They also formulated ideas, expressed in their mythology, concerning the existential questions of their lives: how to account for their origin and the origin of their way of life; how to deal with misfortunes; how to align themselves with beneficent spiritual forces and how to stave off malevolent forces; and what happens to the dead and how to relate them.

Since, along with their culture, most Amerindians were exterminated within fifty years of the arrival of the Europeans, the data we have on the Amerindian way of life is limited to what we can glean from archeology and from the reports of the early explorers and settlers. Unfortunately, the European observers were looking not only with foreign eyes but with an attitude of superiority and, often, disdain for indigenous way of life. Nevertheless, the journals of Columbus, the proto-ethnographic reports of Fray Ramón Pané, a Spanish friar commissioned by Columbus to study the Tainos, and the writings of Bartholomé de las Casas, an avid advocate and activist for Amerindians rights, shed much light on the social and cultural aspects of the indigenous peoples of the Caribbean.

The Amerindian economy fell along a continuum ranging from basic hunting and gathering activities to sustainable agriculture to the weaving of cotton to interisland trading. The Ciboneys/Guanahatabeys developed no agricultural practice but lived by gathering fruits and plants from the rich vegetation, supplemented by hunting for animals and fishing for marine life. In contrast, Tainos and Caribs developed a form of subsistence agriculture called the *conuco*. The *conuco* consisted of series of raised mounds made with digging sticks, whose points were hardened in fire. In these mounds, crops such as corn, sweet potatoes, squash, peanuts, pineapple, and various beans were cultivated. By far the most important staple was the cassava, a starchy tuberous root, which was processed through grating and drying and then made into bread on clay griddles.[5] Christopher Columbus and Bartolomé de las Casas made repeated references to the Tainos of Hispaniola having storehouses stacked with cassava bread. Baked and dried in the sun, the bread could be stored for a long time. From these stores, they often supplied the early Spanish settlers. The Tainos also cultivated tobacco for recreational smoking as well as for the blowing of smoke over religious objects in their ceremonies. Fruit trees, both wild and cultivated, contributed to the edible fare of the Amerindians, and various herbs were grown and utilized for cooking and therapeutic purposes. Cotton was produced and woven into cloth and hammocks that were used for sleeping. Among the items traded with Columbus on his first voyage were huge balls of cotton.

The *conuco* system and agricultural production in general were particularly advanced among the Tainos in Hispaniola. According to some reports, they even utilized irrigation effectively in some places.[6] Such was their confidence in their system of production that a Taino *cacique* (chief), Guarionex, repeatedly proposed to Columbus that he and his people would cultivate enough food for the Spanish settlers as well as for all Spaniards remaining in Castile in Spain in exchange for the removal of the gold tribute imposed on the local people of Hispaniola. Of course, the Spanish obsession with gold and Columbus's need to repay the great expenditure that made his explorations possible led him to refuse the *cacique*'s proposal.[7]

Tainos and Caribs supplied their protein needs by hunting and fishing. For the efficient pursuit of these activities, they developed a number of appropriate technologies. The Spanish explorers and settlers were duly impressed by the size and buoyancy of the group's dugout canoes, which they used to ply the Caribbean Sea. The canoes of the Caribs were particularly impressive. Reports indicate that some of these vessels could transport as many as eighty to a hundred people.[8] On several occasions, Columbus encountered boats going from one island to another, sometimes with a single occupant (especially in the Bahamas). At other times, Amerindians in boats came to his ships or followed him from place to place. For hunting (and fighting), the Amerindians employed bone or stone-tipped spears (the Caribs had poisoned tipped arrows), traps, and clubs. The most sought-after species were birds (Columbus reported in his journals that these were in abundance everywhere in the Caribbean), rodent-like hutias, land and sea turtles, and large manatees or sea cows. For fishing, nets and lines, probably made from cotton or tree barks, were the most used devices.[9] Columbus also observed the Amerindians of Cuba using a sucker fish to catch other fishes and turtles.[10]

As hunters and gatherers, the Ciboneys/Guanahatabeys seem not to have developed any complex social and political systems. Unfortunately, none of the early explorers and settlers left any significant report about their way of life, except that their language was different from that of the Tainos. This lack of data is probably a result of the fact that the Ciboneys were among the first to succumb to the Spanish invasion. The best guess is that they lived and moved in small groups as they foraged for food.[11]

The Caribs of the Lesser Antilles had a more developed social structure, though they were still lagging behind many of their Taino neighbors in the Greater Antilles. Their basic units of social organization were all-male warrior bands. According to Rouse, they had no permanent leaders or chiefs; these were elected for individual raiding or trading ventures. Male members of Carib bands occupied the male house or houses in their villages from which they visited their womenfolk and children in their separate dwellings. The main activity of these bands of Caribs was to carry out raids on their Taino neighbors and later to defend their settlements against the encroaching Europeans. During these raids, villages were plundered, men were killed or taken captives, and women were taken as wives. Carib women, some of whom were obviously Taino, attended to the cultivation of vegetables, tubers and fruits. Women reportedly had their own language, probably the Tainos' language, representing the society from which many were kidnapped.[12]

Of the ethnic groups in the Caribbean, the Tainos had the most evolved political and social structure, with Tainos of Hispaniola exhibiting the highest level of development. Most Tainos lived in established villages, some consisting of as many as fifty houses and up to two thousand people.[13] Most houses consisted of a single room whose round frame was constructed of wood and lath (slender and narrow strips of board) made from the palm tree and whose roof was constructed of intricately intertwined palm fronds. The houses of the *cacique* and other dignitaries were usually larger and could be rectangular in shape, with several rooms. Typically, the whole village was laid out around a central plaza that was in front of the *cacique*'s residence. Hammocks were the main items of furniture in these houses. Used for sleeping, these were made of woven cotton and ropes fashioned from tree barks. In some cases, especially for the *caciques*, houses contained a raised platform for sleeping. Other items likely to be found in Tainos' houses were storage containers made of gourds or straw and ceremonial stools called *duhos* that were used by *caciques* as symbols of their status.

Each village was governed by a *cacique*, or chief, who exercised political, moral, and sometimes spiritual leadership and influence. Along with upholding the cultural traditions of the village, the *cacique* was responsible for defending the village against attacks and for maintaining diplomatic relationship with outsiders. In some communities, the *caciques* organized the production, storage, and distribution of food. In such cases, land was communally owned, and the *caciques* were responsible for economic welfare of all. In Hispaniola, individual villages were related to one another through a graduated system of *cacicazgos*, or chieftaincies. Villages were grouped into districts or regions, each under the supervision of a district or regional *cacique*, and districts were united into provinces, each governed by a head or paramount *cacique*, often referred to as a king or queen in early Spanish accounts. Alliances with other villages to form larger political units were essential for mutual defense against attacks as well as for the sharing of economic resources. Diplomatic relationship or agreement often existed between *cacicazgos*, and, in the Amerindians' struggle against the Spaniards, they often strengthened these alliances to resist Spanish aggression. A good example is the uniting of the *caciques* Guarionex and Mayobanex to resist encroachment by Bartolomé, Columbus's brother, who was in charge of Spanish settlers when Columbus returned to Spain after his second voyage. At the time of contact with the Spaniards, the Amerindians of Hispaniola were grouped into six *cacicazgos*. Marien in the northwest, where the earliest Spanish settlements of La Navidad and Isabela were located, was under the leadership of the affable and accommodating *cacique* Guacanagari. Maguana, in the south-central region, where the gold-rich area of Cibao was located, was governed by the *cacique* Caonabó, who was reported to be a Carib and who was one of the first *caciques* to resist Spanish occupation and domination. In the southwest, Xaragua was the prosperous province of the *cacique* Behechio and later the *cacica* (female *cacique*) Anacaona. Located in the southeast was Higuey, under the *cacique* Cotubanamá, whose rebellion was put down by Nicolas de Ovando, who became the Spanish governor of Hispaniola in 1502. In the northeast were two relatively small provinces, Magua and Ciguayo, under the leadership of the *caciques* Guarionex and Mayobanex, respectively.[14] Neither Jamaica nor Cuba seems to have developed the graduated system of *caciques* found in Hispaniola. Instead, local *caciques* governed their own villages or districts without owing allegiance to regional or provincial *caciques*. Puerto Rico had a graduated system but only one paramount *cacique*, Agüeybana.

While information on the social conventions governing succession to the position of *cacique* is somewhat sparse, the indication is that it was matrilineal and avuncular. That is, the lineage continued through the mother's family, and boys were raised by their maternal uncles, the eldest of whom would be the *cacique*'s successor. However, under some circumstances, women were elevated to the position of *cacica*. What those circumstances were is unclear, but at the time of contact with the Spaniards, Taino women were reported as occupying this position. The most illustrious of these *cacicas* was Anacaona, who succeeded her brother, the *cacique* Behechio, as ruler of Xaragua, a large and prosperous province. Apparently, Anacaona was also the wife of Caonabó, of the province of Maguana, and thus she embodied an alliance between the two provinces.[15]

Amerindians' social divisions followed gender and class lines. We saw earlier that for the Caribs, the basic social unit was a warrior band consisting of males who lived together and carried on visiting relationships with wives (some of whom were captured Tainos) and children who lived separately. Male activities revolved around planning and executing raids and sometimes trading ventures. Males may also have assisted in tilling the soil, but raising food crops and caring for children were the responsibilities of the women. While Taino men and women shared domiciles, they had a similar sexual division of labor. Men performed the tasks of hunting, fishing, and land preparation for farming, while women did the actual cultivation of *conucos*, performed the domestic work around the house, and reared the young. Women were also main creators of art and craft, fashioning various household utensils, including the much-used clay skillet on which cassava bread was baked, processing cotton from which cloth and hammocks were made, and creating and decorating objects of religious significance. Taino communities were divided into two distinct classes. The elites or upper class were *nitianos*, among whom were the *caciques* and their advisers. The *naborias* were the ordinary people who performed all the necessary labor for the communities. While women were generally subordinated to men, women, and especially *nitianios* women, could be very powerful, both influencing the choice of *caciques* and ascending to the position themselves.

Amerindian Religious Beliefs and Practices

In discussing the religiosity of the Amerindians, we will concentrate on the Tainos, because very little is known about the religion of the Ciboney/Guanahatabeys, except that they may have practiced some kind of ancestor veneration and that they left some petroglyphs (carvings on stones) that may have had religious significance; the less-developed traditions of the Caribs are similar to those of the Tainos. Columbus's first impression of the Tainos was that they had no religious tradition.[16] He soon discovered that they performed a kind of ritual (probably the *arieto*, or ceremonial dance) that he deemed to be religious, and that they believed in some kind of deity that dwelled in a celestial abode. Initially, Tainos believed that the Spaniards came from this abode, fulfilling a prophetic tale that circulated among them of white-bearded men arriving from the sky.[17] Though Columbus perceived the Tainos as very intelligent and morally upright, he attributed whatever religiosity he observed to superstition and expressed his desire to make them devoted Catholics and servants of Spain.[18] By the time Columbus returned to Hispaniola on his second voyage in 1493, he was eager to understand the Tainos' religious beliefs and practices so that he could formulate a strategy for evangelizing them. He therefore commissioned Fray Ramón Pané, a Spanish friar, to study the religious beliefs and customs of the Tainos of Hispaniola and provide him with a report. Pané lived in the villages of two principal *caciques*, teaching the Catholic faith and studying the religious customs and mythology of the people. Although somewhat confusing and laced with the ethnocentric glosses of a fifteenth-century Catholic, Pané's report provides valuable information about Taino cosmology and religious practices. Other fifteenth- and sixteenth-century observers and the work of archaeologists have corroborated much of what Pané observed and have provided further insights into the religiosity of the Tainos.

The Tainos conceived of their world as being controlled by cosmic forces. They recognized an eternal, invisible, supreme deity, called Yúcahu (the full name is Yúcahu Vagua Maórocoti, according to Pané). Yúcahu was complemented by his mother, Atabey or Atabeira (as well as other names).[19] As the name suggests, Yúcahu was associated with yucca or cassava, a main source of the Tainos' sustenance. He was also associated with the sea, the other main source of their livelihood. Associated with fresh waters, Atabey was a fertility goddess whose symbol of three-pointed stones was carried by women to encourage conception and successful pregnancy, and was planted in fields to ensure prodigious crop growth.[20]

While Yúcahu and Atabey were regarded in some sense as the supreme creators and sovereigns of the world, numerous spirits or supernatural forces, including the spirits of the ancestors, were believed to animate the world and to exercise direct control over natural and cultural forces. To the Tainos, these forces were often conflicting and sometimes downright malevolent. For example, Guabancex, "Lady of the Winds," assisted by Guatabá, representing lightning and thunder, and Coatrisquie, representing torrential rains, was greatly feared, given the frequency and destructiveness of tropical storms in the Caribbean.[21] Other Taino spirits or mythical beings included Baibrama, deity of the fertility of cultivation and especially of yucca; Opiyelguobirán, the spirit of the dog that liked to roam at night; Maquetarie Guayaba, the master of the Coaybay, the mythical paradise where the spirits of the dead lived in peace and happiness; Márohu, spirit of calm weather; Boinayel, the spirit of rain and the counterpart of his brother Márohu; and Inriri Cahubabayael, the mythical woodpecker responsible for creating males and females out of the asexual primeval humans.

Tainos employed the term *zemis* (or *zemes*) to designate these spirits as well as the plethora of images and other objects representing these spirits. *Zemis* are usually fashioned from wood, stones, clay, and other materials. Symbolic representations of *zemis* often appeared on ceramic vessels and artistic creations; often, such vessels were receptacles for the bones of dead relatives who were venerated by the living. According to Taino beliefs, *zemis* aided humans in the affairs of life. Some assisted with human fertility; some produced rain and ensured the bounty of the fields; others were responsible for ensuring good fishing and hunting and the successful pursuit of warfare. If not properly worshipped or venerated, the *zemis* could cause sickness or other misfortunes.[22] The wrath of Guabancex was frequently seen in the fierce Caribbean storms called hurricanes. Consequently, religious rituals were aimed at placating *zemis* or invoking their assistance for the health and well-being of the community and/or the individual.

Pané's account provides some insight into the mysterious and dynamic circumstances in which an object was transformed into a *zemi*. He describes how the wood or stones of which *zemis* were constructed often revealed themselves to their devotees. As reported to him, a person walking in the woods would see a tree whose roots were pulsating with life. In like manner, a stone might communicate to another person. The person involved would summon a *behique*, the Taino religious expert, to determine which *zemi* was communicating through the tree or stone. After inhaling an intoxicating substance called *cohoba*, the *behique* entered a trance state in which he spoke to the tree or stone to determine its identity and whether it wanted to be cut down, fashioned, and provided a house. If the answer was affirmative, the tree or stone was then taken and shaped into a representation of the *zemi*, who then received offerings from and provided good fortune to its devotee.[23]

The Tainos believed that human existence continued after death. The spirits of the dead went to a dwelling place called Coaybay, from whence they appeared among the living at night. The Tainos also believed that, in the afterlife, humans were rewarded or punished according to their deeds during their lifetime. The good could expect a paradisiacal existence within a pleasant environment with all the niceties they desired. The bad could expect only darkness and hardships. This belief is reflecting in the speech of an elder *cacique* to Columbus while he was visiting Cuba. As reported by de las Casas, the old *cacique* lectured Columbus in the following manner: "I want to tell that we believe in the life hereafter. Departing souls go in two directions: one is bad, full of darkness, where those who do evil to men go; the other is good and happy, and the peace-loving people go there. Therefore, if you feel you must die and believe that every man answers for his deeds after death, you will not harm those who do not harm you."[24]

Belief in the continued engagement of the spirits of ancestors in their lives was also an important component of Taino religiosity. Because of this, famous relatives often became *zemis* and were immortalized in images. Since bones were regarded as the repository of human vitality, the bones of dead relatives were placed in containers and hung in houses. In an effort to imbibe the spiritual vitality of dead relatives, Tainos seem to have practiced a kind of endo-cannibalism in which the bones of the dead were crushed and ingested in a drink.[25]

Like most other peoples, the Tainos told stories, or myths, that were meant to explain their sense of themselves in relation to the cosmic forces that impinged on their lives. In religious studies, myths are archetypical stories in which religious communities convey in narrative form their understanding of the world in which they live. These stories often narrate the beginning of the world or the group and the genesis of practices and traditions that are considered essential to community life. Unfortunately, not many of these stories were collected before the demise of the Tainos and their way of life. Pané's account is the best source we have, and it is flawed by his ethnocentricity, language deficiency, and lack of the understanding of the nature of myth and orality. He appeared to desire a literal reading of these stories; when he was treated to multiple tellings of the same stories with differing details, he assumed this was caused by the intellectual deficiency of his informants. Nevertheless, Pané's account gives us a window into the mythology of the Tainos. The stories reflect their Caribbean environment, their mode of production—gardening, hunting, and fishing—and their social and political arrangement, dominated by the *caciques* and the *nitainos*. They tell of how the physical environment and the cultural traits came to be through the creative activities of supernatural forces and cultural heroes.

Stories collected by Pané narrate the emergence of various aspects of the environment and social life. In these stories, the Tainos traced their origin to caves in a mythical mountain called Cauta.[26] Gradually, various aspects of nature and culture emerged through miraculous transformation. For example, the first cave dweller who ventured out was caught by the sun and transformed into a stone that stood at the mouth of the cave as a kind of guardian. This being, Maraocael, did not quite evolve to be fully human but remained close in essence to the *zemis* or gods. That may explain the view of stones, and especially the three-pointed stones, as containing vivifying forces believed to aid in the fertility of both soil and women.[27] Later, other cave dwellers decided to go fishing. Wandering too far from their subterranean abode, they were seized by the sun and transformed into trees, marking the beginning of vegetal life forms.[28] Another myth tells of the origin of the woodpecker and its role in the differentiation of men and women. At an earlier time, when children were apparently born asexually, as men and women were undifferentiated, a cave dweller set out in search of a plant called digo (used by Tainos in purifications rites), and was transformed into a singing woodpecker. When women-like shaped figures appeared in the trees and were captured by the men, they were found to be without vaginas. The cave dwellers tied the woodpecker between their legs; using its beak, it proceeded to carve the female sex organ.[29]

One of the more developed myths related by Pané tells about the creation of the ocean with its marine life, both important elements of Taino life. The story tells of a son, Yayael, who wanted to kill his father, Yaya. Knowing this, Yaya banished Yayael. When Yayael returned after four months, his father killed him, placed his bones in a gourd container, and hung it in his house. One day, Yaya had a strong urge to see his son and ordered his wife to open the gourd. To their amazement, his bones had turned into fish that they proceeded to eat. In another version of the story, it was Deminán, one of a quadruplet of four brothers, who visited the house one day while Yaya was away, took down the gourd, and, along with his brothers, started to eat the fish. On hearing Yaya returning to the house, Deminán rushed to replace the gourd, but, in his haste, he failed to anchor it properly on the hanging peg. The gourd fell to the ground and smashed, producing a deluge of water that covered the earth and swarmed with a multitude of marine life.[30]

This story reflects several elements of Taino cultural and cosmological understanding. The primary reference is to the creation of important elements of Taino livelihood—the ocean and its marine life that supplied much of their protein. However, José R. Oliver, an archeologist who researches Taino culture, finds implicit reference to the norm of matrilocality, in which boys lived with their maternal uncles to minimize conflicts in which sons want to usurp the authority of their fathers. Yayael's desire to kill his father and his refusal to stay banished contravened this norm and threatened the smooth transfer of power according to traditions, and thus he had to be dealt with. This story was a means of legitimating the social norm of matrilocality that governed the intergenerational transfer of power. Oliver also finds in this story a reference to the principle of impregnation and gestation. In his interpretation, Yayael's bones have phallic significance; their placement in the gourd, a mythic womb, is symbolic of impregnation, and the period they remained there speaks of gestation. The differing action of Yaya and his wife (unnamed) indicates a sexual division of labor: Yaya's putting the bones in gourd tells of his responsibility for impregnation, and his wife's taking them out speaks to her responsibility for giving birth. Closely related to impregnation and gestation is a reference to the cycle of life, death, and regeneration. Yayael having died, his bones became the source of new life that sustains the community. Finally, Oliver finds echoes of Taino funerary rites and ancestor veneration in this myth. As noted earlier, the hanging of the bones of the dead in houses was a Taino tradition for honoring dead relatives. The eating of Yayael's bones transformed into fish may be a veiled reference to the Tainos' endo-cannibalism, in which the crushed bones of relatives were mixed into a concoction and drunk in the belief that their spiritual vitality was thus imbibed.[31] Thus, this story and others provided religious explanation and legitimation for Taino social and cultural practices.

Along with the stories left by Pané, artifacts left by the Amerindians provide valuable insights into their mythology. Both eyewitness accounts and archaeological finds agree that Amerindian material culture was concerned with functionality, ornamentation, and religious representation. With regard to functionality, we have already made references to such elements of the culture as the digging stick used to cultivate the *conucos*, the clay griddle used to bake cassava bread, and the dugout canoes used to navigate the estuaries and the Caribbean Sea. Of course, the presence of these suggests, and archaeology has confirmed, the use of various tools for cutting, carving, shaping, and smoothing. These tools, such as axes, adzes, grinders, and drills, were fashioned from stones, wood, and bones or from some combination of these.[32] Amerindians also utilized various implements for preparing and serving food (calabashes) and for processing grains (metates) and cassava (a narrow straw basket and a press). In terms of ornamentation, body painting, gold nuggets worn in pierced nose or ears, and beaded necklaces and bracelets are repeatedly noted in early accounts. With regard to our focus on religious representation in Amerindian material culture, the evidence suggests that even the ornamental art and the functional implements were decorated with mythical representations or were used for spiritual purposes. The art of the indigenous Caribbean peoples was not simply aesthetic creation but a way to encode their mythology. Artistic creations were meant as "faithful translation of primeval mythology, that of the creation of the world, of animals, of the arrival of heroes who introduce cultural gifts," such as the cultivation of the land, the ocean with its fishes, or the power of the *cacique*.[33]

Probably reflecting their South American place of origin, pre-Columbian people of the Caribbean featured anthropomorphic, zoomorphic, and anthropozoomorphic figures in their ceramic art. Their carvings, engravings, and petroglyphs or pictographs also featured mythical representations. As the archaelogist Miguel Rodríguez observes, these depictions of mythical "personages, sacred animals, and fantastic creatures . . . suggest a complex system of supernatural and mythical representations."[34] Unfortunately, the meaning of a great number of these symbolic representations has been interred with the exterminated Amerindians. However, we do have a good idea of the signification of others. For example, the well-preserved three-pointed stones seem to represent the stages through which the cave people evolved to become humans with differentiated males and females. To quote Roget, "The three-pointed stones by nature of their material (stone), their triangular shape, and their decoration, as well as the leaf-shaped designs at their apex—or bird's beak—recall these stages." In other words, these stones represented the transformation of cave dwellers into the stone, representing the mineral kingdom, trees, representing the vegetable kingdom, and the woodpecker, representing the animal kingdoms.[35] These relatively small pieces of material culture are veritable texts of the myths behind Taino cosmology. They became associated with fertility and vital energy, especially the energy of the *zemis*, whose representations are often engraved on them. Three-pointed stones were buried in fields to promote crop yields, and, as we have seen, woman kept them in their possession to ensure fecundity.

A recurring motif in the pre-Columbian Caribbean art is the depiction of fruit-eating bats and tree frogs on ceramics and in petroglyphs. Roget interprets the depiction of the frog as a representation of Atabeira or Atabey, the mother of humankind, and of the bat as a representation of the masculine cultural heroes who created the cultural traditions and discovered the means of producing the goods that sustained the people.[36]

The *duhos*, wooden seats of the *caciques*, provide a good example of the blend of functionality and mythology in Taino art. The seats on which the *caciques* sat on official occasions represented their authority or power. However, some of these four-legged seats are carved with penises and raised tails like those of dogs, suggesting that they are representations of Opiyelgoubirán, known as the irrepressible, wandering dog deity. A Taino myth tells how this *zemi*, though tethered, escaped frequently, and on the arrival of the Spaniards it walked into a marsh and disappeared permanently.[37]

A variety of other artifacts of Amerindian material culture give us insights into the religiosity of the people of the pre-Columbian Caribbean. These include spatulas used to induce vomiting in cleansing rituals, trays and forked tubes used in the preparation and snuffing of a hallucinogenic substance called *cohoba*, and charms or amulets made of precious stones (amethyst, quartz, jade) and worn or kept to induce good luck and to provide protection from malevolent forces.[38] The carved stones that enclosed the ball courts called *bateys* have engravings of figures presumably depicting elements of Taino mythology.

Though the Tainos lacked a hierarchical religious organization comparable to European models, the Taino communities had the *behiques*, also called *bohutis*, religious functionaries who presided at ceremonial gatherings and provided therapeutic services to individuals in times of sickness. Their characteristic mode of operation was shamanistic in nature; that is, they served their communities and individuals by mediating contacts with the supernatural realm and providing healing. Apparently, some *caciques* possessed spiritual gifts that allowed them to double as *behiques*. Along with the *caciques*, *behiques* officiated at community ceremonies, including marriages, funerals, and preparation for, or celebration of, battles. The most important ceremony was the *arieto*, a dance celebration that featured a retelling or reenactment of the myths that undergirded the Tainos' sense of themselves. During the *arieto*, the *zemis* and ancestors were venerated and propitiated. An *arieto* usually began with fasting and a purification rite in which a spatula was used to induce vomiting. Central to the *arieto* and other ceremonies was ingestion of a psychoactive substance called *cohoba*. Prepared by crushing the seeds of an indigenous plant, sometimes mixed with tobacco, the *cohoba* was placed on special trays before the *zemis*. Using a forked snuff tube, the *behiques* or the *caciques* inhaled the substance, which brought on a hallucinogenic state in which they were able to communicate with the spirit world, presenting the concerns of the community and receiving messages from the *zemis* and the ancestors for the community. Offerings, especially of cassava bread and tobacco, were made to *zemis* during this ceremony, and the community celebrated with singing and dancing accompanied by drumming and the shaking of maracas.

Closely associated with the *arieto* was the *batey*, a ball game played on the central village plaza of the same name, as well as on other courts within and outside the village.[39] The game was played with a rubbery ball made of cotton fibers and resinous material from local trees. Striking the ball with most parts of the body, except the hands and feet, two teams of up to thirty players bounced the ball back and forth, trying to keep it in bounds.[40] The team that lost the ball out of bounds surrendered points to the opposing team. While the particular import of this game is uncertain, its association with *arieto*, the obvious religious motifs on protective belts of wood or stone worn during the game, and the mythical engravings on the stones that bordered the courts, suggest that it had religious significance.

Archaeological findings also suggest that the Tainos had developed an elaborate system of burial rites and a system of venerating their ancestors. Excavated burial sites reveal that bodies were buried in a squatting posture and accompanied by articles of pottery, food, stones, shells, necklaces, and beads. Most likely, this is indicative of the belief that the buried individuals needed these on their journey to or in the next life. At least some villages had designated burial sites.[41] As a gesture of honor, family members often retrieved some of the bones, especially skulls, of distinguished individuals, especially *caciques* and *behiques*, and kept them in calabashes hung in their houses; as we saw earlier, bits of these bones were sometimes crushed, mixed into beverage, and imbibed.

When sickness struck, individuals often resorted to the *behique* for the restoration of their health. Sickness was attributed to something eaten and/ or to the displeasure of a *zemi*, whom the sick the person failed to attend to properly. As part of the healing procedure, the *behique* took on the disposition of the sick person and partook of the same diet. Inhalation of the intoxicating *cohoba* powder by both the sick person and the *behique* produced a state of consciousness in which they spoke to and received messages from the *zemis*. The sick had to ingest a concoction of herbs that induced vomiting, thus cleansing the body. The *behique* also touched various parts of the body of the sick person and sucked on them as though to pull something out of the body. Eventually, he was likely to produce a stone or bone fragment supposedly drawn from the body of the sick, declaring it to the cause of the illness.[42] In cases where the sick persons died in spite of the efforts of the *behique*, family members of the dead sometimes accused the *behique* of contributing to the death. To find out if this was the case, they fed the dead, through the mouth and nose, the juice of an herb called *güeyo*, while asking questions. If the dead answered clearly, implicating the *behique* in his death, the family, if it was powerful enough, would exact revenge against the *behique* by wounding or even killing him.[43]

Obviously, the Tainos lived in a world that made very little, in any, distinction between the sacred and the secular. Their everyday lives were informed by their understanding of a sacred past in which the materials in their environment and the elements of their way of life came to be. Cultivating the soil, going on a fishing expedition, and playing a ball game all had religious resonance. Unfortunately, the arrival of European settlers heralded the end of their way of life and their very existence.

Spanish Colonization and the Subjugation

Columbus first approached the Spanish Crown in 1485 seeking funds for exploration that he believed would take him to Asia if he sailed west from Europe. He spent six years trying to persuade the commission that Queen

Isabella appointed to study the feasibility of his proposal. Receiving numerous rejections and subjected to dismissive ridicule from the experts of the day as a man of fertile and fanciful imagination in search of riches, status, and honors, Columbus decided to try his luck elsewhere. Apparently, his brother Bartolomé had already been dispatched to pitch Columbus's plans to the sovereigns of England and France. Before Columbus could depart for France, persons close to the Spanish Crown intervened on his behalf. Columbus himself in his letters to Isabella and Ferdinand names a prominent friar (a member of a mendicant order), Fray Antonio de Marchena, as his greatest supporter and the most persuasive influence on the Queen.[44]

Bartolomé de las Casas, who became an ardent campaigner for Amerindian freedom, emphasizes the roles of the cleric Fray Juan Pérez in securing Columbus an audience with the Queen, and of Luis Santángel, the queen's treasurer (Keeper of the Privy Purse), in impressing upon Isabella what was at stake. They emphasized the prospects for salvation for many and the growth of the Church, the prosperity for Spain and the Crown, and the extension of the Spanish domain. In a moving speech that invoked the courageous and daring ventures of such monarchs as Ptolemy and Alexander the Great, they urged the Queen to be bold, pointing out the minimal cost of the venture even if it was unsuccessful and the enormous rewards should the enterprise prove fruitful. Santángel raised the stakes by impressing on Isabella how personally disappointed she would be, and the derision she would face from friends and enemies, should Columbus meet success under the sponsorship of another sovereign. Santángel even volunteered to loan the Crown the funds needed to outfit Columbus for the journey. With Isabella persuaded, court officials were dispatched to track down Columbus and bring him back to the court, where the necessary documents were executed formalizing Spain's sponsorship of Columbus's western venture.[45]

After a lengthy and fitful transatlantic crossing during which his men were sometimes on the brink of mutiny, Columbus sighted land and established contact with indigenous people of the Caribbean on an island he named San Salvador. Believing he had reached islands on the outskirts of India/Asia, he declared that he had reached "the Indies." Between mid-October of 1492 and mid-January of 1493, Columbus and his crew visited several islands in the Bahamas and explored the northeast coast of Cuba and most of the northern coast of the island he named Hispaniola. During his journey, he renamed islands and other land forms, mostly giving them names associated with his faith and the Spanish Crown (San Salvador, Fernandia, La Navidad). Early on, he conscripted several Amerindians as his guides, and, along the way, he forcibly took others he desired to convey to Spain to demonstrate the success of his travels.

Columbus's journal is replete with his first impressions of the people he encountered. Though somewhat taken aback by their nakedness or near-nakedness (some wore only a covering over their genital areas), he was duly impressed by their physical features, describing them as handsome and well built. He was also of the opinion that they had excellent native intelligence, since they were adept at learning to communicate with the Spaniards by signs and even quick to learn Spanish words. Ever the crafty admiral, he quickly noted their apparent defenselessness, since they had only wooden spears tipped with stone or fish bone and no arms made of iron. In his estimation, they would make good servants and could be subdued easily by relatively few Spaniards with European weaponry. What impressed Columbus most about these people was their peaceable disposition, kindness, and eagerness to assist. Though he noted their conflicts with their neighbors from the east, he repeatedly remarked on the state of tranquility and the atmosphere of generosity that prevailed among them. The *cacique* Guancanagarí was a great example of the peaceful and generous disposition of these Tainos. He was very solicitous of Columbus, providing whatever he needed and showering him with various gifts of gold and honorific treatment. He comforted Columbus when his ship, the Santa Maria, ran aground and was wrecked on Christmas day. He provided housing and food for him and his crew. He supported the building of La Navidad, the first settlement and fort, constructed from the wreckage of the Santa Maria.[46]

Ever the faithful Catholic with a desire to spread his faith, Columbus made a diligent effort to perceive and understand the religiosity of the newly encountered people. Initially, as we have seen, he perceived no religious traditions, commenting, "I do not know of any creed they have."[47] He later wrote to Santángel that "they know neither sect nor idolatry, with the exception that all believe that the source of power and goodness is in the sky, and they believe very firmly that I, with these ships and people, came from the sky, and with this belief they everywhere received me."[48] From these observations about their religiosity and his perception of their amiable disposition, Columbus concluded that the Amerindians could be quickly and peaceably converted.[49] Pursuing his ultimate goal of a peaceable conversion of indigenous people to the Catholic faith, Columbus pursued a course of action meant to ingratiate himself with them. To this end he gave them gifts and forbade his men to take anything forcibly or to hurt the locals in any way. He wrote in his journal, "I, in order that they might feel great amity towards us, because I knew that they were a people to be delivered and converted to our holy faith rather by love than by force, gave to some among them some red caps and some glass beads, which they hung around their necks, and many other things of little value."[50] His commitment to peaceful persuasion quickly dissipated when Columbus returned to Hispaniola in 1493 to find that all thirty-nine men he had left at La Navidad were dead and the fort burnt to the ground.

Columbus's journal entries show that lively but unequal trading went on between the two groups everywhere Columbus landed. Repeatedly, the Spaniards traded useless Spanish items, such as beads and broken crockery, for Tainos valuables, such as balls of cotton fiber and pieces of gold. Of course, Columbus's overwhelming preoccupation was to find gold. His journal entries contain extensive records of repeated efforts to get the indigenous people to tell him where he could find it or to lead him to its source, especially after he encountered locals with gold nuggets in their noses. When told of Cuba, he assumed it was Japan (Cipangu), the place where he would find all the gold he desired. His exploration of the northeastern coasts of Cuba brought great disappointment because no abundant supply of gold was discovered.

After spending three months in the Caribbean, Columbus sailed for Spain, taking with him the Amerindians he had captured, a quantity of gold received through trading or as gifts, and specimens of the Caribbean flora and fauna, including birds, plants, and wood. On reaching Spain, he was accorded a hero's welcome that included a parade through Castile in which he showed off the captured Amerindians and other specimens from the islands he had visited. De las Casas describes the throngs of people who lined the streets to get a glimpse of Columbus and the New World novelties everywhere he traveled. He also records how Columbus was received with tears of joy and jubilation by the King and Queen and a host of Spanish nobles.[51] As was agreed in the documents authorizing the Columbus's first journey, he was granted the titles "Admiral of the Sea and Viceroy and Governor of the islands which have been discovered in the Indies."[52] Columbus reported to the Crown and nobles on the beauty of the numerous islands with their abundance of people who demonstrated a gentleness of spirit that he believed would dispose them to an eager acceptance of the Christian religion. He spoke of the mainland he was convinced was close to the islands and spoke about the abundance of gold and other riches to be derived from these lands.

Quite telling were the religious sentiments that bathed the reactions and response to the success of Columbus's venture. Both Columbus and the Spanish Crown attributed the success of his undertaking to God's having chosen him, giving him the keys to unlock the darkness of the Atlantic and beyond. According to de las Casas, it was all part of a divine plan to bring salvation to the people of the Caribbean, since they "were eminently ready to be brought into the knowledge of their Creator and to the faith."[53] The Spanish Crown was convinced that the New World discoveries were a mark of divine favor. The fact that Spain, and not other Christian nations, had been granted this gift was seen as evidence that it had been specially chosen by God to receive this bounty, as well as to bear the responsibility of Christianizing the inhabitants of the Indies. In granting Columbus what was necessary to make the second voyage and to establish Spanish settlements in the Indies, the Spanish sovereigns made clear that it was their top priority to bring the indigenous people into the Christian fold: "showing with words and actions that their principal source of pleasure was having such favor in the eyes of God as to have been allowed to support and finance . . . the discovery of so many infidels ready for conversion."[54]

Alexander VI, the presiding Catholic pope, acted with exigency in confirming Spain's claim on the newly explored territories. He justified this claim by invoking a Catholic doctrine first articulated by Cardinal Bishop Henry of Susa in the thirteenth century. According to the cardinal, when Christ came into the world, he divested all heathen powers of their authority and became the sole sovereign over humankind. Before returning to heaven, Christ passed this authority on to Peter, the first pope, and to succeeding popes, who are Christ's representatives on earth. Popes therefore have the authority to assign jurisdiction of any territory to "Christian princes." Acting on this premise, Pope Alexander VI issued a papal bull assigning all newly discovered land beyond an imaginary line in the Atlantic to Spain, giving it the right to occupy, govern, and profit from these lands, as well as the responsibility to Christianize the local peoples.[55] The same bull gave Portugal the rights to lands discovered east of that imaginary line. A year later, on June 7, 1494, the Treaty of Tordesillas moved the dividing line to 370 leagues west of Cape Verde, giving Portugal the rights to Brazil when it was later explored.

The preparation for Columbus's second voyage and for the establishment of Spanish settlements in the Caribbean paid special attention to the need to convert the Amerindians. The Tainos taken by Columbus to Spain were baptized with much fanfare, with Ferdinand and Don Juan, son of Ferdinand and Isabella, serving as their godfathers. The Crown ordered that they be fully instructed in Catholicism so that they could aid in the conversion of their fellows back in the Caribbean. Among the personnel sent with Columbus on the second voyage to establish settlements were clerics under the leadership of Fray Bernardo Boyl (or Buil), a priest commissioned to oversee the conversion of the Amerindians. The Crown gave orders that every effort be made to convert the indigenous people to the Catholic faith. In a personal letter, Isabella urged Columbus to make sure that the people of the newly discovered lands were treated well to facilitate their conversion and to punish those Spaniards engaged in abusive behavior toward them.[56]

Columbus returned to Hispaniola in September 1493 with a convoy of seventeen ships, a host of settlers, numerous animals, plants and seeds, and whatever supplies and equipment were deemed necessary to establish Spanish settlements in the Caribbean. The early efforts at establishing a settlement were fraught with many difficulties: the unpreparedness of the Spaniards for the kind of work required; the preoccupation with the search for gold and the desire for quick wealth; the distance between the Caribbean and Spain and the difficulty of obtaining supplies in the needed quantities; Spanish resentment of Columbus and his brothers for their Italianness; and the growing intransigence of the Tainos. The relationship between the Spanish and the Tainos quickly degenerated, extinguishing the initial idealism about converting the Tainos and ultimately leading to their extermination.

When Columbus returned to Hispaniola on his second journey, he discovered that all thirty-nine Spaniards whom he had left at Fort La Navidad were dead and the fort had been burned. According to the local people, the settlers had perished from a combination of infighting among themselves and attacks by a neighboring *cacique* called Caonabó, who had burned the fort, probably because he became infuriated by the Spaniards' taking multiple Taino women and pestering the locals for food and gold. Some Spanish officials wanted Columbus to arrest the local *cacique*, Guanangarí, though he proclaimed his innocence in the death of the Spaniards. Columbus refused on the grounds that he did not have enough evidence on which to proceed and that such action would sully his relationship with the indigenous people and make the mission of settlement and evangelization more difficult, if not impossible.[57] However, when Columbus decided to explore the interior of the island to search for gold and to establish another fort for defense, he did so in military formation, with the aim of instilling fear in the local people in order to discourage any aggressive action they might have contemplated against the Spanish settlers. On his march into the interior, "he ordered his men to proceed in military formation, with their banners displayed, with their trumpets sounding, and perhaps firing guns, [as a result of which the Indians would be sufficiently frightened]. He did this in every village he came to on the journey, both on entering and departing."[58]

Fort St. Thomas, constructed in the rugged mountain region of Cibao during the exploration of the interior, was intended to facilitate the Spanish exploitation of this gold-rich area and to serve as a safe retreat should the Spanish come under attack from the locals. However, this fort quickly became the catalyst for a rapid decline in the relationship between the settlers and the indigenous people and started the spiraling violence that led to the decimation of Taino population over the next fifty years. When advised by Pedro Margarite, whom he had left in charge of the fort, that the Tainos were abandoning their villages and that the *cacique* Caonabó was plotting to attack, Columbus sent in reinforcements under the leadership of Alonso Hojeda. He specifically instructed the reinforcement troops to spread terror among the local population to make them submissive. Hojeda proved to be an effective agent of terror. Entering a Taino village, he captured the local *cacique*, his brother, and his nephew and sent them in chains to Columbus. Capturing another man, he ordered his ears cut. He did this in response to the *cacique*'s failure to punish men who had abandoned a group of Spaniards midstream instead of conveying them to the other side of the river as they were supposed to do. Columbus heightened the terror by proclaiming that the prisoners were to be publicly decapitated. In response to the pleading of a neighboring *cacique* and his promise to prevent future offense, Columbus stayed the execution of these men. But the Rubicon had been crossed. From here on, the Tainos were subjected to Spanish domination and brutality that hastened their demise.[59]

Commenting on this series of incidents, de las Casas laments, "What a reputation for Christians who had been held but a short while back to be men come from Heaven! This was the first injustice committed against the Indians under the guise of justice and the beginning of the shedding of blood which was to flow so copiously from then on all over the island."[60] De la Casas proceeds to argue that the Indians had every right to attack the Spaniards, since the Europeans had come to the island uninvited, trespassing and acting menacingly toward the local population. Las Casas further argues that universal practice and natural law dictated that the Tainos act in self-defense against the Spanish incursion and menace. Conversely, he excoriated Columbus and the Spanish settlers in general for operating on the assumption that the use of fear and force was the best way to achieve success in the Indies. He claims that "this is contrary and inimical to the way those who profess Christian benignity, gentleness and peace ought to negotiate the conversion of the infidels."[61]

Conflicts with the elite class of the Spanish settlers and the problems of establishing a successful settlement dogged Columbus during his tenure as governor of the Indies and eventually led to the erosion of his reputation and his humiliating arrest by Francisco de Bobadilla, who was sent by the Crown to Hispaniola in 1500 to investigate complaints against Columbus and his brothers. Though Columbus was promptly released after his conveyance to Spain, he was never able to regain his authority or restore his reputation. He made a fourth voyage to the Americas from 1502 to 1504, during which he explored the northern coast of Central America. Spanish officials in the Caribbean treated him shabbily, refusing him entrance to Santo Domingo even though his ships needed repairs, and refusing to come to his aid while he was stranded in Jamaica for a year. After returning to Spain in 1504, Columbus lived in relative seclusion, battling illness and contending with the Crown to receive the 10 percent of the riches of the Indies he had been promised in the documents that authorized the first voyage of exploration. He died in 1506.

Estimates of the number of number of Amerindians in the Caribbean at the time of initial contact with Europeans vary greatly, from more than twelve million to fewer than 100,000. While early chroniclers tended to give larger numbers, these were not based on census figures. What is more, these chroniclers were often passing on secondhand the impressions and guesses of a few observers. Recent scholarship has produced more modest estimates of between 200,000 and 500,000. For the Greater Antilles, the general agreement is that Hispaniola was the most populous, followed by Jamaica, Puerto Rico, and Cuba. The Bahamas and the Lesser Antilles had significantly smaller populations.[62] What is not in dispute is the rapid decline of the indigenous population and the essential extermination of the Tainos in Hispaniola. This rapid decline of the local population was replicated in Puerto Rico, Jamaica, and Cuba, so that by the 1550s only a few Tainos remained in scattered remote villages. Others, especially women, were absorbed into the colonial society through intermarriage. The major factors in this disaster were the brutality of Spaniards in subjugating the local population, the local's susceptibility to European and, later, African diseases, and the de facto enslavement of the Amerindians and the disruption of their way of life by the *encomienda* system, the policy of apportioning Tainos and their land to Spanish settlers.

Though Columbus was initially desirous of peaceful coexistence with the Tainos, he was prepared to use violence, and, when the relationship deteriorated between the two groups, the Spaniards were quick to use brutal methods in subjugating the locals to their authority. In retaliation for the slightest offense, disrespect, or show of resistance, the settlers would go on an indiscriminate killing rampage without regard for the guilt or innocence of those being killed. Using their military advantage, they wreaked havoc on the local population in the name of subduing them. Their swords, lances, and cross-bows far outmatched the Tainos' spears and clubs. Most fearsome were the ferocious dogs let loose to hunt and tear locals to pieces and the horses used to charge crowds, mowing down and trampling some and sending others into flight.

The catalogue of atrocities against the Tainos is large, but perhaps the most egregious involved the hanging of Anacaona and the massacre of her people. The *cacicazgo* (chieftaincy) of Xaragua in southwest Hispaniola was revered for the dignity, courage, and generosity of its leaders and people. Infuriated by the frequent demands for food and the threatening behavior of Spaniards who settled in the area in the early 1500s, the locals often resisted them or threatened them with violence. Of course, any resistance to the Spaniards was deemed a revolt by Spanish authorities. Hearing of such resistance, Nicolas de Ovando, who became governor of Hispaniola in 1502, decided to pay a visit to Anacoana. Like Columbus before him, he marched into the territory with a great show of force. On news of Ovando's approach, Anacoana and a retinue of local leaders with crowds of local people went out to greet him, cordially invited him to her compound, and treated his great company with much generosity. Anacoana held a reception for Ovando, replete with music, dancing, and all the edible delicacies that the area afforded. As the reception neared its end, Ovando informed Anacoana that he was going to put on a show (jousting of men on horses) and asked her and the dignitaries to step outside with him. Once outside, he gave a prearranged signal to his men (touching his gold pendant). Drawing their swords, they proceeded to bind Anacoana and her retinue. Most of the local dignitaries were hounded into a house that was set of fire, and Anacoana was hanged "as a mark of honor." The foot soldiers and horsemen then rampaged through the village, killing and maiming indiscriminately. That is how Ovando subjugated the Xaragua territory.[63]

Along with the violence that accompanied subjugation, the Amerindians experienced disruption of their way of life from the presence and demands of the Spaniards. To pay the debt incurred by his voyages, Columbus instituted a tribute of gold (at least a hawk's bell full and more in some areas) every three months to be paid by every Taino over fourteen. The settlers made constant demands for food and even pressed the locals into forced labor to satisfy their voracious appetites. They disregarded the social conventions of Tainos and treated their leaders and people of high rank with the utmost disrespect. Worst of all, the colonizing Spaniards were indiscriminate in taking and abusing the local women for sexual pleasure.[64]

Although the Spanish Crown never sanctioned the enslavement of the Amerindians and, in fact, eventually took a strong position against it, acts of enslavement started with the initial contact and became widespread as the Spaniards became more entrenched in the Caribbean. The unofficial practice of pressing the Amerindians into the service of the Spanish took on somewhat greater formality in 1499 with the practice of *repartimientos*, the distribution of land and Amerindians to Spanish settlers. This morphed into official policy under the *encomienda* system instituted under the governorship of Ovando with official sanction of Queen Isabella. Ovando had been sent to the Caribbean by Isabella with the charge to preserve order in response to reports that settlers were behaving lawlessly. He was to facilitate the conversion of Tainos to the Catholic faith by gentle persuasion and not by force, to make sure their wives and possessions were not expropriated by the settlers, and to secure the labor of Tainos in their majesties' services with the appropriate compensation but not through enslavement.[65]

Once in Hispaniola, Ovando discovered that the provisions coming from Spain were insufficient to sustain the settlers. Furthermore, efforts to get the Tainos to stay in permanent settlement and provide the labor necessary for the economic success of the settlers were unsuccessful. As a result, starvation, disease, and death were rampant among the settlers. To alleviate the food crisis as well as to provide labor for the mines, Ovando wrote to Ferdinand to secure permission to force the Tainos to settle in one place and provide labor to the settlers. Ovando argued that the freedom that the Tainos enjoyed was inimical to their conversion as well as to the economic development of the colony. He described how they roamed freely, refused to work for the Spaniards, and generally fled from the presence of Spanish settlers. In such a situation, he claimed the priest had no opportunity to teach "them our holy Catholic Faith."[66] The Crown acceded to Ovando's request, arguing that, since the conversion of locals was their priority, they should be forced into a situation where they could be instructed.

Under the *encomienda* system, as indicated earlier, land was distributed to settlers along with a number of Amerindians who were to provide labor for the cultivation of the land. In turn, the settlers were responsible for the religious instruction of the Tainos who were committed to them. While they were not technically slaves, the Amerindians were subjected to hard labor and brutal treatment, while hardly any efforts were made to Christianize them. Starvation caused by the destruction of their cultivated land, despondency (often leading to suicides, infanticides, and abortions), and the scourge of European diseases wreaked havoc on the Amerindian population. De las Casas estimates that during the eight-year governorship of Ovando, 90 percent of the Tainos living on Hispaniola were wiped out. The extension of the *encomienda* system to Cuba, Jamaica, and Puerto Rico occasioned a similar extermination of the local population.[67] With the decimation of the Tainos of Hispaniola, the settlers initiated raids against the Amerindians of the Bahamas and the coastal areas of northern South America to satisfy their labor demands.[68]

Conversion and Protection of the Amerindians

The colonial undertaking was intertwined and suffused with religious sentiments and convictions. Columbus, the prime mover and central character in the Spanish exploration and colonization of the Caribbean, certainly perceived himself as undertaking a divine mission, and, when he succeeded, he never failed to recognize the workings of the divine on his behalf. Bartolomé de las Casas portrayed Columbus as deeply committed to the Catholic Church and devotedly observant of Catholic religious practices. Closely related to his desire to bring wealth and distinction to Spain was his desire to secure the devotion of the Amerindians to the Christian religion.[69] Although the conversion of the indigenous population was among the stated purposes for the exploration and colonization of the Indies, with the destruction of the initial Spanish settlement at La Navidad and the need to secure the Amerindian submission to his authority, Columbus eventually resorted to violent means to subdue the Tainos. Despite the directives from the Crown to Christianize the Amerindians and treat them humanely, the early settlers had no qualms about crushing the Amerindians in the pursuit of their goals. The religious instruction of the Tainos was low on their list of priorities.

For the priests and friars who came with the explorers and settlers, the establishment of the Catholic Church in the Caribbean was made difficult by the frontier conditions, the apathy and unchristian behavior of the settlers, and the disinclination of the Amerindians to trust the Spanish in light of the poor treatment they had received. In the face of these difficulties, some clerics became disillusioned and returned to Spain. Fray Boyl, mentioned earlier, who came on Columbus's second voyage, made a quick exit. Even after the Catholic Church was fairly well established in Cuba with the creation of an archdiocese in Santiago de Cuba, Bishop Juan de Ubite and later Bishop Diego Sarmento resigned their charges because of the intransigence of the Spanish settlers. Even more problematic was that many of the missionaries had neither the training nor the inclination to carry out the work for which they had been sent. Others, more interested in enriching themselves, joined in the general corruption that characterized colonial officials. For example, Miguel Ramirez, a bishop in Cuba, joined in the avariciousness of his fellow settlers and colluded with colonial officials to enrich himself by gaining possession of large tracts of land.[70]

The problems notwithstanding, some clerics, including the aforementioned Ramon Pané, carried out conscientious missionary work among the settlers and the indigenous population of the Caribbean. Some of the most dedicated and effective missionaries belonged to the mendicant Franciscan order instituted by Francis of Assisi in the 1200s and to the Dominican order founded by Saint Dominic around the same time to preach the gospel and combat heresy. With the work of these clerics, the Catholic Church was able to establish a foothold in the Caribbean in the early 1500s. The Franciscans established their first monastery in Hispaniola in 1502 and were followed by the Dominicans in 1509. In 1504, Pope Julius II designated three dioceses, administrative units supervised by bishops, but these did not come into being because of Spanish objections. In 1511, he created two dioceses in Hispaniola and one in Puerto Rico under an agreement with Spain that they would be supervised by the archbishop of Seville. Cuba's first diocese was created in Baracoa in 1517, but it was moved to Santiago de Cuba in 1522. The Franciscans founded a monastery in Cuba in the 1520s.[71]

Concerned about the debilitating effects of the *encomienda* system, some friars gathered Amerindians into mission villages where they were taught the basic beliefs and practices of Catholicism, plus agricultural and artisanal skills that would better prepare them for life in Spanish colonial society. As was done elsewhere in the Americas, some missionaries removed children from their homes to the mission villages, where they were imbued with Catholic religion and Spanish culture. Despite the work of some dedicated missionaries, the Catholic evangelization of the Amerindians met with very little success. Although there were reports of converts who worked with the missionaries and although missionaries conducted numerous baptisms, these were accompanied by neither a clear understanding of the Christian faith nor the lifestyle changes that indicated the acceptance of Christian ethics. Furthermore, within a half-century of Columbus's arrival, only pockets of Tainos remained in the Greater Antilles. Those who were not exterminated were absorbed in to the Spanish population, starting the emergence of the mestizo (a person of mixed race) that is so characteristic of Hispanic societies in the Americas.[72]

In the first half of the 1500s, two Spanish clerics stood out as prophetic voices against the harsh treatment of the Amerindians and advocates for their freedom and human rights: Antonio de Montesinos and Bartolomé de las Casas. The Dominican friar Antonio de Montesinos was the first to raise his voice in open condemnation of the Spanish settlers for their treatment of the Tainos. During an Advent sermon in 1511, he excoriated his listeners for the sins they had committed against the defenseless local people. Portraying himself as "the voice of one crying in the wilderness," he bemoaned the "aridity in the desert of the Spanish conscience" and informed his listeners of the impending divine punishment that they must face because of the gravity of their ill treatment of the Tainos. His listeners, instead of acknowledging their ill deeds, were mostly infuriated, and the colonial administrators and colonial elites sought to muzzle the friar and extract an apology from him. With the support of his superiors in the order, Montesinos stepped up his condemnation of the treatment of the Tainos in his subsequent sermons, and the Dominicans instituted a policy of not hearing confession from or performing extreme unction for those who refused to give up the land and the Tainos apportioned to them under the *encomienda* system.[73]

De las Casas, another Dominican, came to Hispaniola in 1502 with a group of settlers led by Nicolas Ovando. Because of his education, he had been recruited as a teacher to instruct the Tainos in the Christian religion. Initially, he seemed more preoccupied with subduing the locals and pursuing his own economic interests. In Hispaniola, he was awarded an *encomienda* and exploited the labor of its Tainos in the fields and in the gold mines. In pursuit of ministry credentials, he traveled to Rome to be made a deacon, becoming the first priest to be ordained in the Indies in 1512. From Hispaniola las Casas traveled to Cuba with Diego Velásquez, who led the Spaniards in subduing and colonizing the island. In Cuba, he was granted an *encomienda*, and, although he exploited the labor of Tainos in both mining and farming, he reportedly treated them with a measure of kindness.[74]

De las Casas eventually came to the conclusion that enslaving the Amerindians was morally wrong. He signed over his charges to Pedro de Renteria, his business partner, and embarked on a career of advocacy on behalf of the Amerindians. He started by preaching against the unjust and brutal treatment the Amerindians by his fellow settlers in Cuba. After becoming ordained as a Dominican friar, he traveled throughout the Spanish colonies in the Americas and to Spain, agitating for enactment and enforcement of laws to protect the Amerindians from the greed and brutality of the colonialists. Along the way he was appointed bishop of Chiapas, Mexico, and earned the honorific titles "Apostle of the Indies" and "Protector of the Indians."[75]

Though de las Casas shared the contemporary European view that the Amerindians were spiritually destitute and culturally backward, he argued that many great nations were at one time backward, lacking knowledge of Christianity, but were eventually led by divine providence to accept the gospel and to improve materially, socially, and culturally. In the same vein, the Tainos had been prepared providentially for the message of the gospel and were to be won to the church by gentle persuasion. He saw the Spanish settlers as having acted selfishly, dishonorably, and without charity in disrupting the lives of Tainos by dismantling their political system, destroying their livelihood, and forcing them into slavery.

Despite the early hope of economic success in the Caribbean and the vision of peaceful conversion of the Amerindians, the early days of colonization were marked by difficulties and setbacks for the Spaniards. The quantity of gold was much smaller than expected; the work of growing food and export crops did not gel with the temperament of many and challenged the fortitude of others; rebellious Amerindians tested their forbearance, and tropical diseases wreaked havoc on their health; and the Amerindians died more rapidly than they could be converted. To fill the labor void left by the death of Amerindians, the Spaniards started importing African slaves in early 1500s. Though the Church showed very little initial interest in evangelizing these newcomers, some of them adopted Christianity; others maintained their African beliefs and practices; yet others blended elements of Christianity with both their African religions and practices they adopted from the Amerindians. Despite the challenges, the ministries of committed clerics, the establishment of monasteries (especially by the Franciscans and Dominicans), the creation of dioceses, and the establishment of educational institutions set the stage for the gradual growth of the Catholic Church in the Caribbean during the 1500s.

Early Colonial Catholicism

The history of the Roman Catholic Church in the colonial era is marked by the Church's complicity with and support of Spanish colonial domination and exploitation of indigenous and African peoples throughout the Caribbean. This was a chapter in the Catholic Church's history in which the Church and the state remained united in their efforts to conquer the Americas, territorially, spiritually, and culturally. While Spanish Catholicism was not unilateral in its support of the conquest and the transatlantic slave trade, voices of dissent were the exception and not the rule. While one finds various clerical voices that argued for and defended the rights of indigenous and African peoples, as an institution the Roman Catholic Church remained heavily aligned with the Spanish colonial government.

The Church's close relationship with the Spanish Crown during the colonial era had a significant impact on the role of institutional Catholicism in the region once former colonies gained their independence from Spain. The case of Haiti is singular in this regard, for, after its independence from France was gained in 1804, the Vatican cut all ties with the new country between 1805 and 1860. On other islands, in spite of the Church's close ties with colonial power, however, as an institution it remained relatively weak, in large part because of the relatively small number of clergy present in the Caribbean; furthermore, most of these were located in urban settings, where they did not reach the large African populations living in rural areas. The lack of institutional presence led to a Catholicism in the Caribbean that was not defined by the doctrines, sacramental life, and clergy of European Catholicism but was instead much more reflective of a mixture of European folk Catholicism, indigenous beliefs, and African religion.

This distinction between institutional and lived religion is not intended to imply that the more popular-based faith of Caribbean Catholics today is in any way in tension with or opposed to institutional Catholicism. Similarly, our focus on the lived or vernacular religious practices of Caribbean Catholics is not meant to downplay the role of the institutional Church. However, history teaches us that, although Catholicism has saturated the culture and religious worldviews of Caribbean peoples, the institution has not had a similar impact. When attention is paid to the institutional Church, it tends to be with regard to its interaction with non-Christian religions in the region and the role it played in Caribbean cultures broadly. By focusing on Caribbean colonial Catholicism, with special attention to the lived religion of Caribbean Catholic communities and their interaction with non-Christian religions in former Catholic colonies, we can get a sense of the religious life of Caribbean Catholics.

Spanish Catholicism

Any study of Caribbean Catholicism must begin with the Catholicism that arrived with the Spanish. The conquest of the Americas occurred during the exact historical moment of the reconquest of the Iberian Peninsula from Muslim invaders. For eight hundred years, ending in 1492, Moors occupied the Iberian Peninsula. Medieval Spanish Catholicism had a distinctive flavor, marked by heavy aesthetic expression that remained relatively unscathed by the 1545–1563 Council of Trent, which sought to deemphasize these devotions. This aesthetic emphasis is found in the strong presence of processions, devotionals, and performative rituals. The historian Laura De Mello de Souza argues that the absence of Trent reforms contributed to the popular religious landscape and syncretism so predominant in Brazil. As she notes, Trent took time to root itself even in Europe. She writes, "During the seventeenth century, two different religions cohabitated in Europe—that of theologians and that of believers—despite the elites' intensified efforts to crush archaic cultural features that had for centuries survived in the hearts of these Christianized masses."[1] Regarding the religion of everyday believers, De Mello de Souza notes, "This religiosity was imbued with magic belief, more inclined to images than to what they represented, to external aspects more than to the spiritual."[2] Trent would not be truly felt until the eighteenth century. She argues, however, that this inclination toward images and processions was not necessarily Iberian (Spanish and Portuguese) but in fact European. Her comments on Brazil can be applied to Latin America and the Caribbean as a whole. The regulation of individual rituals and devotions that Trent instituted were not in place when Catholicism sailed across the Atlantic. However, this regulation was not an outright rejection of popular devotions. As highlighted by the religious historian Anthony Stevens-Arroyo, "The council did not wish to accept the Protestant rejection of devotion to Mary and the saints, but it instituted a set of reforms that were designed to control excesses. . . . Local devotions had to be approved before they could share the benefits of indulgences, and theologically correct prayers had to be composed with ecclesiastical approbation."[3] Local devotions were transformed into devotionalisms. There was a movement to control the religion at the popular level, which was not characteristic of Spanish and Portuguese colonial Catholicism in the Americas.

The sixteenth century was marked by the Church's efforts to direct institutionally certain local religious practices, as local religious customs were placed under diocesan control. Trent attempted, for example, to institutionalize the verification of miracles; rather than leaving it up to local communities to declare that a miracle had occurred in their locale, the Council decided that miracles would have to be verified by the institutional authority, thus imposing institutional control over local customs. However, these reforms, among others, left local religion relatively unchanged. Regional devotions were not exclusively the devotions of the poor. As the medieval Spanish historian William Christian argues, class was not a factor in terms of local religion; both rich and poor shared these devotions, though the practices of the two classes differed in style. He argues, "In the villages, towns, and cities of Central Spain (and, I suspect, in most other nuclear settlements of Catholic Europe) there were two levels of Catholicism—that of the Church Universal, based on the sacraments, the Roman liturgy, and the Roman calendar; and a local one based on particular sacred places, images, and relics, locally chosen patron saints, idiosyncratic ceremonies, and a unique calendar built up from the settlement's own sacred history."[4] The local church is the most significant for our consideration of the manner in which African Diaspora religion came into contact with and appropriated the symbolic worldview of Catholicism.

It is important to note that this local religion represented not a pure Catholicism but instead a Catholicism that had been mixed with folk religion. Too often, studies of Caribbean religion present Catholicism as if it had been untouched by other religious phenomena prior to its encounter with African and indigenous religions in the Americas. This is far from the case. The Catholicism that arrived in the Americas was one that had been thoroughly influenced and shaped by other European and African religious worldviews. This influence would materialize in the folk religion of the Americas, for example in the common belief in evil eye and in Espiritismo, a religious philosophical system that believes in communication with the dead, which continue to characterize Latin American and Caribbean religious worldviews even today.

In addition to being a medieval Catholicism that remained relatively unin-fluenced by the reforms mandated by the Council of Trent, the Christianity that arrived in the Americas was one branded by Spain's reconquest of the Iberian Peninsula from the Moors. The colonization of the Americas, there-fore, must be seen in light of this broader project of recovering Catholic lands and spreading the gospel. For the Spanish, these were one and the same, as we have seen in Columbus's and the Spanish Crown's emphasis on convert-ing the indigenous peoples to Catholicism. One cannot understand the con-quest and the slave trade without contextualizing them in light of Catholi-cism's struggle to regain Spain and Portugal. The year in which Columbus set sail across the Atlantic was the year in which the Iberian Peninsula was reclaimed as a Catholic land.

The same tactics were often employed by the Church in both Europe and the Americas. One of the most common was the conquering of sacred space by Christianity. Beginning at the turn of the sixteenth century, churches sprang up across Spain, and many of these were on sites that had previously been Muslim sacred spaces. Mary became a key figure in this re-Christianizing of the Iberian Peninsula, and large churches were named after her. In rural areas, "some sacred spaces also become linked with stories—sometimes describing apparitions—about the discovery of her images."[5] The historian Linda B. Hall argues that the eleventh, twelfth, and thirteenth centuries were a time of a Marian surge. Worship of Mary came to replace local devotions to saints, who were not so readily acces-sible under Muslim rule, and her name began to appear more frequently in ecclesial documents. As noted by the historian Angus McKay, "The late medieval frontier was a Mariological one."[6] She was intimately associated with Spain's Catholic, military conquests.

The prominence of Mary in medieval Spanish Catholicism should not be surprising, given her later prominence in the Americas. The medieval Mari-ological frontier became a colonial Latin American and Caribbean frontier. The site of Our Lady of Guadalupe in Mexico, built after what is the most well-known Marian apparition and where she requested the construction of a shrine, is on the sacred mountain of the Aztec goddess Tonantzin. The Marian frontier becomes a useful tool for spreading Spanish Catholicism among indigenous and African peoples in the Americas. It was well received by these populations, as contemporary devotion to Mary attests. The promi-nence of Mary is one of the hallmarks of Caribbean Catholicism and, as we will see, a site for the encounter and co-mingling of European and African religious worldviews.

Caribbean Catholicism

While Caribbean Catholicism shares some broad features, including elements that characterize the lived or popular Catholicism across the various colonies, each nation also has its distinctive manifestations of religiosity. As we will see, the religious practices and devotions of Cuba, Haiti, and the Dominican Republic evolved out of their particular contexts.

Patronal Festivals

One characteristic of Caribbean Catholicism that is found in Latin America as a whole is the significance of patronal festivals, which are linked, in turn, to the prominence of the cult of the saints. Patronal festivals are most often celebrated in the town or region that bears the name of a saint, known as its patron saint. Since the second century, Christians have in some way venerated and offered intercessory prayers to saints. Saints, in this formal sense, are individuals who have been canonized by the institutional Church. In the New Testament, however, the term "saint" refers to anyone who was baptized in the Church. The veneration of saints implies that these are individuals who have a special closeness to God and are enjoying eternal life.

Patronal festivals were a way of recognizing and commemorating the patron saint of a particular region. These festivals serve to cement Catholicism within the daily life and rhythm of Caribbean daily life, creating a Catholic calendar to mark time and space. They are usually public festivals and often reflect the different textures of Caribbean Catholicism. In the town of Loíza, Puerto Rico, the festival to Santiago Apóstol (Saint James) is not only the largest public festival but also the clearest expression of black Puerto Rican identity and religion. In addition to regional patronal festivals, there are also particular saints whose devotion comes to involve a nation as whole. In Cuba, the feast day of La Caridad del Cobre (Our Lady of Charity) is one example of this. The public communal festivals were in part a response to the individual, interiorized spirituality affirmed by the Protestant Reformation.

Some popular feast days that occurred throughout the Catholic Caribbean include Holy Week, Corpus Christi, and the Innocents. The feast day of Corpus Christi was particularly rich, for, in addition to processions, it often included the performance of an auto-sacramental, a type of play. "The autos derived from medieval religious theater, which was still pervaded with ancient ceremonies and pagan festivals. These sacred mysteries, accompanied by games and pantomimes, were performed in the atriums of churches."[7]

Often, Greek mythology was used in Spanish dramas in the "Siglo de Oro" (sixteenth and seventeenth centuries). The plays were used as catechisms, to educate Catholics and to fortify their beliefs. The auto-sacramental always ended with the triumph of the Eucharist over the misery of life.

Local patronal festivals were often organized by *cofradías* (confraternities), powerful lay organizations that are fundamental for understanding Caribbean Catholicism. These *cofradías* filled a vacuum caused by clergy shortages, particularly in rural areas. The *cofradía* was a religious brotherhood whose structure was imported by the Spanish during the conquest. The head of the *cofradía* was called the mayor (*alcalde*), who in some areas served as the actual mayor of a town or region. *Cofradías* also functioned as mutual aid societies and could have male and female members.

Cofradías and Cabildos

A significant percentage of the population of Cuba and the Dominican Republic belonged to one or more *cofradías*. These lay organizations often had their own chapels or worship spaces, which might or might not be dedicated to the organization's patron saint. A fundamental dimension of Caribbean Catholicism, linked to the *cofradía*, was the *cabildo* system. These brotherhoods of Africans date to as early as the late sixteenth century. Their predecessors were the Andalusian *cofradías*. The Cuban ethnographer Fernando Ortiz traces the origins of African *cabildos* to fourteenth-century Seville, arguing that they were a Spanish institution transplanted into the Afro-Cuban context. In Andalusia, the term "*cabildo*" often referred to a religious brotherhood, although throughout the rest of Spain it referred to a city council.[8] While noting the Sevillian roots of *cabildos*, the Afro-Cuban scholars Jorge and Isabel Castellanos offer an alternative theory of the of the of the origins of *cabildos* in Cuba. They posit that their origins were in the Americas.[9] Beginning with the informal gatherings of Africans on feast days, *cabildos* were most often organized around African nations (ethnicities). The original intent behind the formation of the *cabildo* system was the desire of Spanish colonists to keep the African population divided, united exclusively by nations and/or languages. This "divide and conquer" strategy was a method of preventing a widespread slave insurgency throughout the island.

Cabildos raised funds, acquired lands and houses for their gatherings, organized parties and processions, participated in carnival, took care of their sick, paid for funerals, and even bought the freedom of some of its members. In a sense, "it was the cabildos rather than the parish churches which were the principal organizations for the religious life of urban Afro-Cubans up until the twentieth century."[10] The most significant *cabildo* activity was the *baile*, or dance, which included extensive drumming. These dances were religious rituals, though in the eyes of Spanish authorities they were merely social gatherings. Whites ignorantly assumed that these gatherings were solely recreational. Those outsiders who witnessed the dancing, drumming, and singing did not fully comprehend the true meaning of these practices.

The initial Spanish disregard for *cabildo* activities allowed Africans to preserve significant aspects of African religious practices under the noses of Spanish authorities. In Cuba, Afro-Cubans would disguise their devotion to African deities, known as *orishas*, under their devotion to Catholic iconography. The Santería scholar Rafael Ocasio situates the *cabildo* as a colonial site for the preservation of African religiosity.[11] Either under the guise of Catholic devotion, or blatantly following old practices in front of a Spanish population that did not know better, *cabildos* were a space where the Afro-Cuban population could gather, worship, and preserve its religious identity. In the late nineteenth century, the activities of *cabildos* began to be severely restricted, and a series of laws was passed that limited the nature and number of *cabildo* gatherings. Eventually black *cabildo* activities were outlawed; the organizations were forced to affiliate with Roman Catholic parishes in 1884, and, in 1894, musical celebrations during carnival were banned. *Cabildos* slowly evolved into *casas de santos*, the house temples that were the center of Santería worship in Cuba. Little is known about this eventual development, but it is clear that in the late nineteenth and early twentieth centuries, Afro-Cuban religions became more institutionalized, and houses of worship began to emerge throughout Cuba.[12] It was under the *cabildo* system that African *orishas* were able to survive in Cuba, facilitating the broad retention of African cultures, religions, and languages throughout the Caribbean.

The Institutional Church

The flourishing of *cofradías* and *cabildos* was in large part a result of the weak institutional presence of the Catholic Church. In this vacuum, lay leadership emerged. Linked to this development was an overall apathy on the part of clergy in the Americas toward evangelizing African populations. This led, in turn, to the Africanization of Catholicism in the Americas. As noted by the historian Joan Cameron Bristol, "While civil and ecclesiastical authorities expected Africans to practice Christian ritual in an orthodox fashion, by and large these authorities put very little energy into African's religious education."[13] This ecclesial evangelical apathy existed despite the fact that, early on in the conquest of the New World (1518), King Charles I stipulated that all slaves must become Christian upon arrival there. The definition of Christian, however, varied. Sometimes this stipulation was interpreted as requiring only baptism; at other times, it seemed to call for some sort of religious instruction.

As highlighted by Bristol, there were three paths through which Africans arriving in the New World came in contact with Christianity. First, some Africans had been aware of Christianity even prior to their enslavement because of missionary activity in Africa. This occurred primarily in Western Africa, particularly in the Congo region. As noted by Bristol, often their conversions were voluntary. A second route was the baptism of slaves at trade posts in Africa, sometimes forcibly, though this was technically against canon law. Often these slaves received no exposure to Christian education prior to their baptism, and they were not asked if they wanted to be baptized. These forced coastal conversions created an African Christian population in the Americas that knew little about Christian doctrine, ritual, and practice. A final and less common avenue of conversion to Christianity was actual religious instruction after the slave's arrival in the Americas. It often fell on slave owners to provide the time and means of religious instruction. Owners were required by the Crown to have a church on their plantation and to allow slaves to attend religious services. The slaves were supposed to receive Eucharist and participate in religious instruction. The Crown saw Christianization as a means of controlling slave unrest.[14] Ultimately, the Catholic Church legitimized its role in the transatlantic slave trade by arguing that, through enslavement and conversions, souls were being saved.

Marian Devotion in the Caribbean

A foundational feature of Caribbean Catholicism was the prominence of Marian devotion. As we have seen, this was also a clear hallmark of the Spanish Catholicism that was brought to the various islands. There is often a direct connection between a particular Marian devotion in the Americas and its Spanish counterpart. As noted by the religious historian Irene Wright, there exists a Lady of Charity in Spain that is the twin to the Cuban patroness.[15] Also similar to the Spanish reconquest of the Iberian Peninsula was the creation of a Marian geography in the Caribbean, naming various ports and cities in her honor. As Terry Rey, a religious scholar of Haiti, highlights,

In naming the first two Hispaniolan bays in which they anchored Puerto María and Puerto de la Concepción, the Columbus expedition, who had sung the Salve Regina nightly during their voyage, reflected this Spanish understanding that the entire colonial endeavor was the work of the Virgin Mary. Obviously this lent forceful sanction to the brutal conquest and exploitation of indigenous and imported peoples that would ensue. Marianism was thus a central feature of the Catholic basis of Spanish colonialism in the New World, and the Mary cult flourished in conjunction with the establishment of the colonies and the expansion of transatlantic Iberian imperialism.[16]

This Latin American Marianism in which conquered territories of the Caribbean were renamed as Marian space was a strategy of the Counter-Reformation Catholicism that the Church employed in Europe and its new colonies in response to the Reformation. Mary became the great defender of the Catholic faith both in Spain and abroad. Similar to the geographic Marianism was her ecclesial presence. The first church built in the Americas, under the orders of Queen Isabella, was the Church to the Immaculate Conception on Hispaniola, built in 1503. Mary was replaced in 1842 by Our Lady of Perpetual Help, who was credited with ending a smallpox epidemic in 1882 after a painting of her arrived on the island. Her arrival was seen as a way of shedding Marian association with Vodou, which connected her to the African *loa* Ezili (a Vodou devotion that became associated with this Roman Catholic image), and reasserting Catholic orthodoxy. In other words, it is clear that Mary's prominence in the Catholicism of the colony of St. Domingue translated into her iconographic prominence among practitioners of African religions on the island. Monsignor François-Marie Kersuzan, bishop of Cap-Haïtian (Haiti), who "had Perpétuel Secours' image placed in his insignia when he was promoted to bishop, regarded the propagation of the new cult as the opening of a new front in the war against Vodou."[17] As was the case with all the Catholic devotions that become prominent throughout the Caribbean, their appropriation by African traditional religions became a major concern for the institutional Catholic Church.

Specific Catholic Contexts

While the practices of adherents of the Roman Catholic Church in the Caribbean as a whole have some shared characteristics, local Church practices on each specific island or nation have developed their particularities. Quite early on, the Catholic Church in the Caribbean became independent of Spain. In 1511, two sees (the seat or center of authority for a bishop) were created: one on Hispaniola, the other on Puerto Rico. In 1517, a diocese was established in Cuba. The province of Santo Domingo was established in 1546, composed of Puerto Rico, Cuba, Venezuela, Colombia, and Honduras. Though at first it answered to Seville, by the late 1540s the Church in the Americas had become independent and no longer answered to Spain.

Cuba

Though the Dominican Juan de Witte was named the first bishop in Cuba in 1518, it was not until the second half of the sixteenth and the seventeenth centuries that the Church in Cuba became consolidated. The seventeenth century was marked by an increase in clergy vocations and by Catholicism's growing influence on Cuban culture as a whole. A 1689 ecclesial census reports that there were 225 diocesan priests, 205 members of religious orders, and 100 women religious on the island. Ramón Torreira Crespo, a Church historian, contends that the period between 1697 and 1837 marked the high point of the Church's control over the island; it owned a third of its riches and controlled the educational system, ultimately becoming a key component of colonial exploitation.[18] By the end of the eighteenth century, Cuba had more than seven hundred priests, and in 1795 it was divided into two dioceses: Santiago de Cuba and San Cristóbal de La Habana. The 1820s marked a turn in the Church's presence on the island, as the Spanish government struggled to suppress brewing independence movements. In 1836 and 1838, the government passed laws suppressing religious orders and confiscating all their property in Cuba and in Puerto Rico and shutting down convents. The given reason was the supposed "secularization" of the clergy.[19] This action led to a drastic reduction in pastoral agents, and by 1840 the number of clergy was reduced to fewer than 150.

The Church then moved into "survival" mode, doing anything and everything it could to maintain some power. The strategy it used was to align itself with Spanish colonial rule and to support Spain's efforts to squash independence movements in Cuba. Part of this project was the Church's support of the transatlantic slave trade. The Church was rewarded with the recuperation of some of its land. While the Church in the latter half of the nineteenth century seemed more Spanish than Cuban, some members of the clergy supported independence struggles. The Manifiesto del Clero Cubano Nativo was a group of native-born Cuban priests who took a stand against the Spanish clergy and expressed solidarity with independence movements. They linked their struggles against Spanish clergy to the island's attempt to overthrow colonial rule and argued for a Cuban national Church liberated from Spanish control.[20]

Dominican Republic

Santo Domingo was the first city in the Americas founded by Europeans and the first Catholic diocese. The first cathedral in the Americas, La Catedral de Santa María la Menor (1521–1540), was built in Santo Domingo. In 1503, the Cofradía de la Pura y Limpia Concepción de Nuestra Señora was founded in Santo Domingo. Its charitable focus was the San Nicolás hospital.[21] This *cofradía* is an excellent example of the unity of spirituality and charity that defined these lay organizations. The *cofradía* had its chapel in the very hospital it helped build. Other *cofradías*, such as the Cofradía de Nuestra Señora de los Remedios del Carmen y Jesús Nazareno, played similar roles on the island. Ecclesial documents reveal that these *cofradías* were extremely active in public liturgy, sponsoring and leading Holy Week and Corpus Christi processions and patronal events. Members of *cofradías* accompanied clergy to take communion to the sick and helped plan masses.

It is in Santo Domingo that some of the most fascinating demographic data have been recovered about the origins of slave populations. As the historian Carlos Larrazabal Blanco observes, "from the first years of the foundation of the city of Santo Domingo [1496] there existed slaves. The [very] first slaves—whites, Berbers or blacks—must have been imported illegally." Later, by way of Cape Verde, came "jolofos, mandingas, branes, zapes, biafaras"; from Sao Tome arrived "minas, popos, barbas, falas, araraes, lucumies, carabalies"; and from Luanda, "congos y angolas." These different African tribes or nations represent the diversity of the slave populations throughout the Caribbean. "In Santo Domingo, as elsewhere in the New World, Africans either took or were given ethnic or place-name designations as surnames. Thus, we read of Pedro Angola, married to Victoriana Angola; Francisco Biafra, the husband of Luisa Manicongo; Lucia Arara, the wife of Pedro Congo, and so on. There are numerous examples of this naming pattern."[22]

There was a clear distinction in the Dominican Republic between slaves in rural areas and those in urban centers. The latter received more institutional religious instruction, interacted more frequently with whites, and thus absorbed a more institutional type of Catholicism; the former maintained their African religious beliefs much more strongly. The Dominican ecclesial historian José Luis Saez argues that parochial records reflect a commitment to the evangelization of slaves. Cathedral records in Santo Domingo reflect the baptism of 11,516 slaves and 1,765 freed men and women between 1590 and 1882, among the 40,007 persons baptized on the island during that period. Records even reflect the religious orders that were in charge of the doctrinal instruction of certain slaves.[23] He nonetheless recognizes that the situation was quite different for rural slaves.

Early on, African slaves and the indigenous populations attempted to organize against the Spanish. *Ladinos* (Latinized Africans who were brought to the Iberian Peninsula and converted to Christianity) were the first slaves to be brought to the Americas, first arriving in Santo Domingo in 1502. However, they organized with the local Arawak population, and the Spanish ceased their importation.[24] Nonetheless, within the Dominican Republic one finds evidence of the colonial Church's solidarity with persecuted populations. A 1528 law required all indigenous and African slaves to go to Santo Domingo for religious instruction. This mandate was not warmly received by the colonists, and slaves did not receive the institutional evangelization that they appeared to receive if one looks only at the legal history of Catholicism in the Dominican Republic. There were moments when the Church took a stand against the colonial government and attempted to undermine its authority. Churches and monasteries became safe havens for runaway slaves and those fleeing persecution. In 1532, Emperor Charles V of Spain put a limit on the number of individuals allowed to seek shelter in ecclesial institutions. Almost two hundred years later, Archbishop Isidoro Rodríguez y Lorenzo limited the number of safe haven churches to one, San Nicolás in Santo Domingo.[25]

Unlike in other Latin American nations, in the Dominican Republic many priests struggled and died on behalf of Dominican independence. The Church therefore maintained certain privileges in the early years of the Dominican nation, though by 1854 power struggles between the Church and the government led to the revision of the constitution to give the government greater control over the Church. After Spain annexed the Dominican Republic in 1861, the Church sought to revive itself, mainly through use of Spanish manpower. Spanish rule was short-lived, and in 1865 Spain abandoned the Dominican Republic. With the departure of the Spanish came an exodus of Spanish clergy. Between 1865 and the U.S. occupation of the Dominican Republic in 1916, a result of political instability in the region, the Dominican Republic had fourteen constitutions, and power was transferred forty-nine times.[26]

As in the rest of the Catholic Caribbean, despite the Church's low level of involvement in the rural Dominican Republic, the culture was clearly shaped by a Catholic ethos. Johannes Meirer, a historian of the Caribbean Church, outlines a list of official feast days in early seventeenth-century Santo Domingo that included no fewer than forty dates. In addition, cities had their own set of feasts, not limited to the patronal celebrations.[27] Marian celebrations abounded, the most popular being Nuestra Señora de Altagracia. Yet another prominent devotion in the colonial Dominican Republic was El Cruz del Santo Cerro (Cross of the Holy Hill). The cross at the center of this celebration was said to have been erected by Christopher Columbus; it was eventually moved to the cathedral in Santo Domingo and is routinely displayed in religious processions and venerated.[28]

The Catholic Church in both Cuba and the Dominican Republic was marred by a weak institutional presence. Neither Church had enough priests to minister to the slave populations. In addition, the Church, while making a sincere effort to evangelize the indigenous population, neglected the slaves; clergy, for example, did not learn African languages. The Catholic Church supported the status quo and was completely silent in the face of colonial injustices; many Church groups, in fact, owned sugar plantations that depended on slave labor. John Kirk, a scholar of Cuban Christianity, notes that there are two schools of thought regarding the Church's relationship to slavery and the treatment of indigenous people. "The 'apologist view' admits that some abuses did take place and that some clergy did ignore the plight of the wretched slaves but claims that, for the most part, the church supported the slaves with spiritual solace and looked after their moral well-being." The second school, he suggests, "takes issue with the concept that heavenly rewards recompense the centuries of suffering imposed upon slaves, and . . . regrets the absence of clergy like las Casas and Varela to condemn these practices. Representatives of this position accuse church people of both a sin of omission in not condemning slavery and a sin of commission in taking advantage of it."[29]

When we move to the context of Haiti, the picture becomes quite different. Recent scholarship demonstrates that the divisions between European and African, Catholic and non-Catholic are not quite as easy to categorize in that nation.

Haiti

The Roman Catholic presence in Haiti was markedly different from its role in the colonies already discussed, partly because Haiti became independent earlier, in 1804. Colonial and postcolonial Haiti was ecclesially distinct not only in this sense but also because of the Vatican's break with the newly founded republic between 1805 and 1860. At the time of the most successful slave rebellion in the Americas, the colony of St. Domingue was under French Catholic rule. The transition from European colonialism to African self-governance was not smooth, for often it was the lighter-skinned, racially mixed Haitians who came to have economic and political power in the new republic. The hierarchy of European colonizer, mixed or light-skinned free blacks, and African slave that marked the colonial era became translated into a pigmentocracy in independent Haiti that assumed the racial stratification of its colonial past. There were three social groups on the island: grands blancs, petits blancs, and gens de couleur. The first two were plantation owners and merchants, and the latter were slaves and mixed-blood individuals.

The Spanish controlled Hispaniola until 1697, when Haiti was ceded to France in the Treaty of Ryswick. The French first began to settle on the western portion of Hispaniola in search of gold, and eventually spread across the island. The first priests arrived at the turn of the sixteenth century, initially Franciscans and Dominicans, two religious orders that played a pivotal role in the evangelization of not only Africans but also the indigenous populations throughout the Spanish-speaking Americas. From 1697 until independence in 1804, the French colony was named St. Domingue. Priests on the colony owned slaves, and the transatlantic slave trade was legitimated by religious imperialism under the guise of saving indigenous and African souls. Arguably, "the Church actually owned three-fourths of all slaves in the colonial French Antilles."[30]

While the Spanish had imported slaves to St. Domingue, the French rapidly and aggressively accelerated the slave trade to the colony. In 1690, it was estimated that there were two thousand enslaved Africans on the island. That number jumped to 600,000 by 1789. These slaves were primarily from the Congo, Dahomey, and Nigeria.[31] These groups' religious traditions (Fon, Yoruba, and Congo) intermingled and became the foundation of a new, African-derived religion, namely Vodou, which also draws on Catholicism and indigenous religion. In 1683, the *code noir* was passed to affirm the orthodoxy of Catholicism on the island. The clergy wholeheartedly supported the Code and in addition passed various rulings to squelch African "superstition." The police rulings of 1758 and 1777 prohibited the slaves, "under penalty of death," from meeting "during the night or day," especially in the absence of a Catholic priest, under the pretext of celebrating weddings or grieving over the body of a departed friend. Also in 1758, it was stipulated that slaves could not gather either near their master's house or anywhere else, for that matter. Slaves could not play drums, certain items (linked to religious rituals) could not be sold, and slaves could not leave their plantations.[32] These laws represent the concentrated efforts of the French to efface and control African religious practices.

At the time of the Haitian revolution, in 1791, Haiti was the world's leading producer of sugar. Some estimates calculate that the ratio of slaves to Europeans on the island was ten to one. Maroon communities made up of runaway slaves often attacked plantations, but it was not until the voodoo priest François Mackandal unified these groups in 1751 that a cohesive resistance was formed. However, it was not until 1791 that a massive uprising of slaves initiated the revolution. For the next decade, power struggles marked the island, with the French consistently promising the abolition of slavery but never delivering. Instead, the slaves delivered their own emancipation in 1804. It took thirty years for France to recognize Haiti as an independent nation. The Vatican took longer, waiting fifty-six years to reinstate ties with the new republic.

Colonial-era documents reveal that African slaves did not abandon their religious beliefs upon arrival in the Americas but instead "mixed" them with Catholicism. This practice continued in independent Haiti, for as the religious scholar Hein Vanhee points out, "After the Haitian Revolution, the scanty historical documentation we have, points to a continued process of an appropriation and a reworking of rituals, texts and objects drawn from Roman Catholicism—yet in the relative absence of regular priests and missionaries."[33] An important factor that Vanhee emphasizes is the presence of Catholicism in Haiti, imported by slaves who were brought to the island. As he rightly points out, Portuguese and Italian missionaries were extremely active in the Congo region beginning in the fifteenth century. As part of their missionary enterprise, they employed *maestros de igrejas*, lay assistants who served as catechists and at times even held political offices. These lay African missionaries, who are estimated to have numbered in the thousands, traveled to remote areas and instructed potential converts.[34] Individuals traveled great distances to be baptized. The French followed with heavy missionary activity in the Congo region in the eighteenth century.

King Nzinga, a Nkuwu of the Congo, was baptized voluntarily in 1491 by Franciscan priests, though he did not place a heavy Christian emphasis upon his leadership and the kingdom's identity. Though his rule was short-lived, his son Afonso, who ruled from 1506 to 1543, affirmed Christianity as central to the Congo kingdom. This led to the conversion of the elite, who nonetheless remained strongly influenced by indigenous Congolese religion. Jason Young, a religious scholar and historian, argues that "Kongolese converts regarded Christian missionaries in much the same way as they did indigenous Kongolese ritual experts."[35] Missionaries adopted Congolese ritual language to name and categorize Christian rituals, erasing the linguistic distinctions between Congolese religion and Christianity.[36] In the mid-seventeenth century, the Congo kingdom dissolved, and local noble elites bartered with Europeans for slaves. Young maintains that baptism became a form of "protection" from enslavement for villagers. This rural Christianity, often practiced in the relative absence of priests, was vastly different from the formal, catechized Christianity of the elites. "In this way, one notes the establishment of two rather distinct negotiations with the Christian faith in Kongo between the sixteenth and eighteenth centuries: one headquartered at central court and radiating outward through provincial lords and nobles and a second that operated in the rural and outlying regions of the state and was practiced by those who, as a response to the exigencies of the transatlantic slave trade, saw opportunities for protection and status in the ritual of baptism."[37] The reasons for conversion to Christianity were thus very different for the elite and for rural populations. However, Young argues, in both cases the conversion to Christianity did not involve a radical change in one's religious worldview. Baptism did not lead to the end of one's indigenous religious beliefs.

Missionaries in the Congo region seemed to have accepted the inevitable association of Catholicism with traditional Congolese religion. The existence of Catholicism in the Congo region in the early sixteenth century is well documented. Indeed, the African historian John Thornton argues that the demise of Catholicism in the region resulted in part from the Church's definition of authentic Roman Catholicism, which led to an actual decline in the number of Catholics. "Its apparent disappearance in the nineteenth century was not due to a lack on the part of Kongo, a resurgence of suppressed local religion or a failure on the part of the clergy. Instead it was caused by a changing definition among European clergy (including Rome) as to what constituted Christianity, coupled with more chauvinistic attitudes towards non-Western (and especially colonial) peoples that arose after 1850."[38] In other words, Congolese Christianity itself did not change, only the manner in which Europeans defined Christianity.

Catholicism thus became a part of the Congolese religious worldview not through the transatlantic slave trade in the Americas but instead through the conversion of its leaders: "Christianity 'conquered' Kongo peacefully—but at the cost of adapting itself almost wholly to Kongolese conceptions of religion and cosmology."[39] Young argues that Thornton perhaps pushes the point too strongly and suggests that the Congolese religious core remained, thereby challenging the authenticity of rural Congolese Christianity.

Catholicism in the Congo maintained its Congolese cosmological foundation. "In fact, when the effort of the missionaries in Kongo is compared with efforts made elsewhere, it is fairly clear why the Christianity of Kongo fitted so smoothly into the country's own cosmology. Missionaries who went to Kongo carried with them what might be described as an inclusive conception of the religion, as opposed to an exclusive concept, such as was applied in the Spanish colonies in the Americas."[40] Unlike in the conquest of the Americas, Catholicism was welcomed by Congo royalty. Many Congolese embraced Catholicism without changing many of their core Congolese religious values, and Catholic priests were accepting of this practice. "Willing to accept this Kongo definition of religious belief on theological issues, the priests concentrated on placing recognized religious actors in control of all religious functions, and in suppressing practices which were considered sinful in Europe (primarily polygynous marriage or concubinage). These twin goals explain the two most common activities of priests: burning of 'fetishes' and exhortations regarding marriage."[41] It appears that Catholic missionaries were much more concerned with religious practices than with the actual theological beliefs of their Congolese converts.

Thornton's scholarship offers a fresh way of viewing the encounter between Catholicism and traditional Congolese religion by reminding us that it did not occur initially in the Americas. His scholarship undermines the notion that the retention of African religious beliefs (sometimes substantial, other times barely a trace) resulted from a lack of attentiveness by the clergy and from shortages of clergy in general. Thornton instead argues that there was a particular Christianity that developed in Africa prior to the transatlantic slave trade. There existed in the Congo kingdom, and in parts of Western Africa, an African Catholic Church that became the philosophical foundation of the evangelization of slaves in the New World. "The clergy in America, overworked and lacking opportunities to engage in substantial teaching in any case, found African Christianity acceptable, while Africans who came from non-Christian parts of Africa found it comprehensible and adapted it easily."[42] Thornton argues that clergy in Western and Central Africa in the sixteenth and seventeenth centuries were much more tolerant of syncretism than clergy today. As an example, he cites a 1658 Spanish catechism approved by the Inquisition that allowed the Fon word for God, "Vodu," to be used for the Christian God and the Allada word "Lisa" to be used for Jesus Christ. "Lisa" formed a pair with "Mawu," a bipartite deity similar to the tripartite Christian Trinity. In Central Africa, priests referred to themselves as *nganga*, the local term for priest.[43] African Christians were often instructed by their own people who were converted African catechists, rather than by European clergy. The clergy's role was purely sacramental. Catechists were in charge of daily life and of instruction in Christianity, and this practice contributed to the mixing of Christianity and traditional African religion.

These missionary efforts came to shape the religious iconography of the Congo region which included images of saints, crosses, and crucifixes, either imported from Europe or crafted by local artisans. In addition, Hein Vanhee emphasized that there is documented knowledge of Catholic prayers and songs by the Congolese, both in Spanish and in Kikongo, from the eighteenth century. By that time, "As virtually all Kongolese were baptized Catholics … thousands of African Catholics would reach St. Domingue in the eighteenth century."[44] This accords with colonial accounts of Congo groups in St. Domingue inappropriately mixing Roman Catholic rituals and beliefs with traditional African religion. Vanhee's work is extremely important for understanding Catholicism in Haiti, for it debunks the myth that Catholicism arrived on the island exclusively through European missionaries. This is far from the case. Missionary activity in Haiti was scant; often missionaries employed Africans who had arrived on the island already converted to catechize others. As Terry Rey affirms, the Congo kingdom, whose people accounted for half of the slave imports to St. Domingue, had been Catholic for more than one hundred years.[45]

Rey's research documents the influence of specifically Congolese Catholicism on Haitian Catholicism. He argues that if scholars are going to claim that traditional Congolese religion had a huge impact on Haitian Vodou, then a similar claim must be made about Congolese Catholicism's influence on Haitian Catholicism. Too often scholars have created a polarity of Vodou and Catholicism, Africa and Europe, denying or erasing African Catholicism's role in Caribbean Catholicism as a whole. Instead, Catholic influences are depicted as remnants of slavery that existed within contemporary Vodou. Rey proposes the "radical" idea that "Africans and diaspora Africans might have taken a genuine interest in Christianity."[46] K\Congolese Catholicism is marked by devotion to St. James the Greater and Mary, saint cults that also became dominant in Haiti. In Haiti, Saint James is associated with Ogun (the *loa* associated with war and iron), and his festival is one of the largest in the nation. Supporting Rey's thesis is the fact that during the Vatican's refusal to send priests to Haiti, we find the "crystallization" of Vodou as more Catholic than it was during the colonial era. In the absence of official Catholic leadership Haitians continue to attend mass, embrace Catholic ritual life, and integrate it with Vodou. The realization that Congolese Catholicism predated the transatlantic slave trade is fundamental to understanding Catholicism in Haiti. While the Spanish were the first to introduce Catholicism on the island institutionally, it is also clear that Africans themselves brought Catholicism with them as well. This African Catholicism, with its underlying African worldview at its core, set the stage for the creation in the Americas of religions such as Vodou that draw from both African and Catholic worldviews.

Institutional evangelization in Haiti encountered many of the roadblocks that the Church as a whole faced throughout the Caribbean, where the labor of slaves was valued over the conversion of their souls. "Although the Spanish had been responsible for the introduction of Catholicism on the island, their missionary endeavors in western Hispaniola were actually rather limited, with very few genuine converts being won. The first French missionary orders in the Caribbean, mainly Dominicans and Capuchins, were only marginally more successful than the Spanish had been."[47] The Jesuits were more successful, learning African languages and attempting to engage in dialogue with Africans and the indigenous population. Franciscans arrived in 1505 and Dominicans in 1512. In 1547, Santo Domingo became the center of ecclesial power in the West Indies. Accounts of early missionary activity in Haiti are scarce, though in 1639 Pope Urban gave permission to four Dominican missionaries to visit the island. The 1652 Council of Martinique required that slaves not work on Sundays or on Catholic feast days. "The government also stated that masters, regardless of their personal religious beliefs, must not prevent their slaves from attending Mass on Sundays and Feast Days. Further, they were to send them to Divine Service and catechism. Disobedience of this regulation carried a fine of 120 pounds of tobacco. Masters were additionally ordered to provide baptism and marriage for their slaves, and baptism of all infants growing out of these marriages."[48] Failure to administer these sacraments also resulted in fines.

The Church historian George Breathett presents the Jesuits as thorough and dedicated in their missionary activity from the mid-sixteenth century until their expulsion in 1763. "Outstanding Church Fathers such as Le Pers, Larcher, Margat and Boutin added much to this chapter of Jesuit history, and the writings of Fathers Margat and Le Pers give some of the best descriptions of missionary activity among the Negro slaves."[49] The Jesuits were responsible for the evangelization of close to half the slaves on the island—until 1762, when they were accused of corruption of the faith and insubordination to the Crown. The Capuchins and the Trinitarians were brought in to replace them. Colonial accounts by clergy document their ownership of slaves and their general apathy toward evangelization, resulting in a population that was institutionally disaffiliated and open to other religious traditions. At the end of the nineteenth century, the Haitian Church became extremely aggressive in its critique of both Vodou and Protestantism. In 1896, Bishop Monsignor François-Marie Kersuzan started the Catholic weekly *La Croix*, which became a vehicle to denounce both Vodou and Protestantism. In his writings, Kersuzan castigated Vodou to Haitians as a dishonor that was an impediment to Haiti's being regarded as a civilized nation. He called upon Haitians "1) To combat, by all means in their power, all superstitious practice, all commerce with bocors, chapiteurs, devineurs, etc.; 2) To never hesitate to bring justice against the faiseurs de caprelatas; 3) To denounce to the authorities, and, when necessary, public opinion, by means of newspapers, all public practices of vaudoux, and the existence of all places consecrated to vaudoux meetings."[50] The paper published the names of Vodou *oungans* (male priests) and *manbos* (female priestesses), as well as the locations of Vodou rituals. Campaigns by the Church against superstition, undertaken in 1896, 1913, and 1941, directly targeted Vodou practitioners and sacred sites. President Fabre Nicolas Geffrard (1859–1867) negotiated the 1860 Concordat with the Vatican that ended its schism with Haiti. As the anthropologist Kate Ramsey rightfully argues, the Church's primary role became to combat superstition. After the signing of the Concordat, popular religious practices in Haiti declined, and the Church instituted numerous sanctions against those who participated in any "magical" practices.[51]

The Catholic Church struggled to negotiate the various challenges of colonialism in the Caribbean. The Church's association with Spanish colonialism often hampered the reception of Catholicism in the newly independent nations of the region. Its participation in the slave trade made it an ambiguous institution in the eyes of Afro-Caribbean peoples. In spite of its weak institutional presence, however, Catholicism became a hallmark of the Caribbean cultures where it was part of the colonial enterprise. Because of the lack of clergy, Catholicism was reinterpreted by enslaved peoples and, in this transformed state, embedded itself in Caribbean culture. While the Church struggled to control Roman Catholicism, the everyday faith of Caribbean Catholics that emerged was shaped tangentially by the institutional church.

For God and Nation

Protestantism in the Colonial Caribbean

As we saw with Spanish colonialism, the entrance of northern Europeans into the Caribbean region was inspired by a combination of religious and political motives. Thus, the challenge to the Spanish monopoly in the Caribbean was at the same time a challenge to the dominance of Catholicism. As much as the English and the Dutch wanted to break the political and economic stronghold of the Spanish in the region, they also wanted to open new territories in which they could spread their "superior" Protestant faith.

Challenge to Spanish Monopoly

By the second half of the 1500s, the English were deluged with national propaganda that challenged the authority of the pope to give a monopoly over newly discovered territories to the Catholic nations of Spain and Portugal. In addition, propagandists were instructing the nation that it had a moral responsibility to establish colonies in the Americas, where it could spread pure religion, instead of allowing the Catholics to dominate the area with its corrupt form of Christianity. One of the foremost propagandists was the Anglican clergyman Samuel Purchas, whose treatise was dedicated "to the glory of God and the good of my country."[1] Even the French Huguenots (Protestants) who raided Spanish settlements and attacked Spanish ships conceived of their undertaking as not only a way of plundering for economic spoils but also as acts of resistance against oppressive Catholicism.[2]

During the 1500s, the challenge to the Spanish monopoly was accomplished chiefly through illegal trading and plunderous attacks on Spanish territories and shipping. Since the Spanish colonies were poorly supplied in the early colonial era, illegal traders found ready markets for their commerce. The English and the Dutch were particularly successful at this.

In the mid- to late 1500s, the notorious John Hawkins and Francis Drake traded their cargoes, including slaves, in the Caribbean islands and on the coast of Central and South America. The Dutch trade became so entrenched that traders became known at the "foster parents" of the Spanish colonies, because, without their illicit trade, many of those colonies might not have survived. Trading was soon accompanied by pillage. During periods of war between Spain and its rivals—and these were frequent—these rivals would authorized privateers (private operators) to plunder Spanish colonies and attack Spanish shipping, taking whatever booty on which they could lay their hands. During times of peace, these privateers turned into pirates and operated on their own. The French privateers and pirates led the way in the first half of the 1500s. For example, in 1523 they captured part of the Spanish fleet that was transporting the treasures that the Spanish had fleeced from the palace of Emperor Montezuma of the Aztec Kingdom in Mexico. By the 1550s, they had pillaged numerous Spanish colonies and ships.[3] One of the most amazing plunders was carried out by Francis Drake in 1572, when he transformed his trading mission into a pirate heist. The capture of the Spanish mule train ferrying Peruvian silver across the Panamanian Isthmus to the Caribbean coast made Drake and all his sailors "rich for life," even though they left behind tons of silver for which they had no room on their ships.[4] The Dutch capture, in 1628, of an entire Spanish fleet, with its rich cargo of silver, gold, and a host of tropical products, signaled the approaching end of the Spanish monopoly in the Caribbean.[5] By the early 1600s, the Netherlands, England, and France had begun their lasting encroachment on Spanish sovereignty in the Caribbean by starting to establish permanent settlements in the region. By this time, it had become the accepted doctrine that claim to a territory must be accompanied by effective settlement. Since the area it claimed in the Americas was so extensive, Spain could not effectively settle all parts of it. The Netherlands, England, France, and even Denmark all moved into the region and started to establish colonies in areas peripheral to the Spanish enterprise. The nations of the Netherlands, England, and France all attempted to plant colonies along the northeast coast of South America; the Netherlands was the first to achieve some measure of success, in 1616. Though the Dutch were more concerned about trading than settlements, the Netherlands eventually occupied a number of southern islands off the coast of South America—Aruba, Curacao, and Bonaire—as well as the small islands of Saba, St. Maarten (shared with France), and St. Eustatius in the eastern Caribbean. The first English foothold in the Caribbean came in the 1620s with the joint colonization, with the French, of the small island of St.

Kitts (St. Christopher). In the same decade, the English added Barbados and Nevis to their settlements, and in the next decade they planted colonies in Antigua and Montserrat. In 1655, England captured Jamaica from the Spanish after failing to seize the prized but more robustly defended Santa Domingo (Hispaniola). From St. Christopher, the French colonized Martinique, Guadeloupe, and Dominica in the 1630s. French settlers also started to settle in Tortuga, and from there they moved into the western areas of Hispaniola. By the end of the 1600s, the French were so entrenched in the western third of Hispaniola that the Spanish ceded it to them in the Treaty of Ryswick in 1697. The French renamed it St. Domingue.

Christianity in the Dutch Caribbean

The islands of Aruba, Bonaire, and Curaçao (the ABC Islands) became Spanish possessions in 1499, when they were visited by the Spanish explorer Alonso de Ojeda and the Italian Amerigo Vespucci, after whom America was named. Because of the aridity of their climate and the fact that no precious metals were found there, the Spanish found these islands unattractive for extensive settlements. However, the Catholic Church took an interest in evangelizing the local population of Caiquetios (Arawaks). The Catholic mission was directed by the diocese of Coro (Venezuela) until it became part of the diocese of Caracas in 1638. Because priests were seldom present on these islands, lay persons played a crucial role in advancing Catholicism among the Caiquetios, who readily accepted the basics of Catholicism and fused it with their local traditions.[6]

Responding to their expulsion from St. Maarten by the Spanish in 1633, the Dutch captured Aruba, Bonaire, and Curaçao in the mid-1630s. Curaçao became the administrative and commercial center from which the Dutch West India Company plied its illicit trade with Spanish colonies. Slaves from the Guinea coast of West Africa were the most important commodity that the Dutch traded. They were exchanged for colonial products that were then sold in Europe. On the ABC Islands, the Dutch developed a colonial society of plantation owners, traders, and colonial administrators who were served by a slave population. The white elites included Jews who came to the islands from Holland and elsewhere. While slaves performed agricultural, domestic, and other services, their significance to their masters was not so much their productive capacity but the social prestige that their ownership bestowed on the masters. Of course, they were of great economic value and were often sold for ready cash in economic hard times. Curaçao was one of the few places in the Caribbean where the slave population increased naturally because slaves there were not victims of the overwork that jeopardized slaves' lives in many slave societies. Because of the cash value of the slaves, the owners were also keen on having them increase through procreation.[7]

Though the Dutch took political control of Curaçao in the mid-1630s, they allowed the Catholic Church to continue its mission among the Caiquetos. Over the next two hundred years, the slave population introduced by the Dutch and the emerging colored (mixed race) population were also converted to Catholicism. Between 1638 and 1767, the Catholic mission in the ABC Islands fell under the auspices of the diocese of Caracas; in 1767, the ABC islands came under the direct supervision of the Vatican, and the Vatican committed the affairs of the mission to Franciscans from Holland. In 1842, these islands were upgraded to the status of apostolic vicariate—a provisional diocese administered by representative of the pope—and Matinus J. Niewindt was elevated to serve as vicar general. Under his leadership, Catholic religious ethos and structure became entrenched in the islands. He organized parishes, schools, and social service organizations.[8]

Though the Catholic Church had the numerical dominance with its Caiquetios, African, and colored parishioners, it nevertheless lacked power and prestige in the ABC Islands. It was stigmatized because members of the powerful Protestant ruling class brought their prejudices against Catholics with them from Europe and because it was associated with people considered racially inferior.[9] To some degree, the Catholic Church became a kind of haven for slaves. Since social gatherings of slaves were prohibited by law, Catholic church services provided their only legitimate means of coming together and experiencing a sense of solidarity. The Catholic clergy also became strong advocates for and defenders of the legitimacy of slave marriages. Throughout the pre-emancipation period, Catholic priests were in constant conflict with the local Dutch authority over their consecration and recognition of slave marriages in contravention of the law requiring that religious marriages be performed only after the marriage had been conducted by civil authorities.[10] Toward the end of the slave period, the issuance of baptismal certificates was another cause of conflict between the Catholic Church and Dutch authorities. Some slaves believed that these documents granted them freedom. To complicate matters, the Spanish had stipulated that slaves who embraced the Catholic faith and who sought refuge in its colonies should be granted haven. Slaves from the ABC Islands, especially Curaçao, often fled to Venezuela, where they presented their baptismal certificates as proof of their freedom. A

Catholic priest, Father Ten Oever, ran afoul of Dutch authorities in Curaçao for allegedly baptizing too many slaves and was declared persona non grata in 1785, resulting in his having to leave the island.[11]

Despite its advocacy for the humanity and the dignity of slaves, the Catholic Church nevertheless supported their human bondage. In fact, it could be argued that the Dutch ruling class tolerated the Catholic Church because of its usefulness in placating the slaves and discouraging them from militant activities. The social elites, fearing the potential for slave conspiracies created by large gatherings of slaves in Catholic services, insisted that Catholic priests stress the Christian virtues of submission, obedience, and loyalty to their congregants. The priests willingly complied. Even on the eve of emancipation in the mid-1800s, the venerable Bishop Niewindt (elevated from vicar general) sought to suppress slave uprisings, owned a plantation with twenty-three slaves, and, even when he became convinced of the inevitability of emancipation, argued for a gradual approach on the grounds that slaves were mentally and culturally unprepared for freedom.[12]

The Dutch Reformed Church was established by Dutch settlers in conjunction with the Dutch West India Company in 1635. The first church building in Curaçao was in Fort Amsterdam, and the company director was named president of the church council, signaling the ties between civil and religious authority. For the most part, this was the church of the Dutch elite. Despite urgings from the Church leaders in Holland (official communication in 1741 and 1821), local church leaders failed to pay attention to the religious instruction of coloreds and blacks, freed or enslaved. In the mid-1700s, a minister of the Dutch Reformed Church, Pastor Wigbold Rasvelt, cited the masters' opposition to religious instruction for slaves and the common knowledge that slaves were Catholics as justification for his inaction in extending the ministry of the Reformed Church to them.[13]

The Dutch had also encroached on Spanish territories on the northeast tip of South America, establishing settlements in Surinam, Berbice, Demerara, and Essequibo. Shortly after Surinam was ceded to the Dutch by the Treaty of Breda, in 1667, the Dutch Reformed Church was established as the official religion of the colony. In the first half of the 1700s, the Dutch Reformed Church was similarly established in Berbice and Essequibo. Since many of the Dutch settlers were Lutherans, they eventually organized congregations in the colonies, beginning with Surinam in 1741 and Berbice in 1743. Unlike the Dutch Reformed Church, which received support from the colonial government, the Lutherans had to raise their own financial support. This fact, along with theological differences, created some tensions between these two groups. However, they suppressed their differences to present a united front in the maintenance of the plantation system based on slave labor.[14]

The frontier nature of these colonies presented several challenges to the churches. One of the most important was securing ministers to conduct worship and other services. In fact, in the 1600s, not too much attention was paid to religious matters, and when the colonists turned their attention to religious concerns, they struggled to attract and retain competent clergy. For example, though the Lutheran church in Berbice was organized in 1743, the first pastor, Johan Henrik Faerkenius, arrived in 1752.[15] A second challenge for the churches was the issue of maintaining moral discipline among the colonists. Both the Reformed Church and the Lutherans espoused rather strict moral codes. However, in the frontier conditions of the colonies, these were often difficult to uphold and enforced. One particular prevalent problem was sexual promiscuity. With very few European women in the colonies, the settlers depended on sexual liaisons first with native women and later with slave women to satisfy their sexual needs. Race and class prejudices precluded legal and religious marriages to these women.[16] Another formidable challenge was how the churches should relate to the slave population. Like their counterparts in Curacao, both groups neglected the conversion and religious instruction of slaves. What is more, not only did ministers own domestics slaves, but the Lutheran Church in Berbice operated an estate with slave laborers in order to support the ministry of the church. The result was that slave hostility against slavery was accompanied by antipathy for Christianity. Thus, Cosala, a leader in the Berbice slave rebellion of 1763, declared that the aim of the uprising was to purge the colony of the cruelty of Christians and whites.[17] Only the arrival in the late 1700s of the Moravians, a pietistic and missionary-minded Christian group founded in Bohemia (in the present Czech Republic), brought religious instruction to slaves.

Church of England in the British Caribbean

The British eventually proved to be the most formidable challengers to Spanish dominance in the Caribbean. By the mid-1600s, they were firmly ensconced in St. Kitts, Nevis, Barbados, Antigua, Montserrat, and Jamaica. From the various wars and treaties of the 1700s and the early 1800s, Britain emerged with most of the spoils, taking Grenada (1763–83), St. Vincent (1763–83), Dominica (1763), St Lucia (1814), and Tobago (1814) from the French; Trinidad (1802) from the Spanish; and Berbice, Demerara, and Essequibo (renamed British Guyana) from the Dutch (1803). Various British settlements (as well as pirate hideouts) were established in the Bahamas in the 1600s, but these islands did not become an official British colony until 1717.

The Church of England (also called the Anglican Church) arrived in the Caribbean as an integral part of the colonial venture, reflecting the situation in England, where civil and ecclesiastical authorities were closely allied. Settlers and governors were enjoined to preserve the integrity and authority of the Church. In some colonies, certain religious observances such as church attendance, the religious education of children, and even family devotions (Barbados) were legally mandated.[18]

Though the preoccupation with making the colonies profitable and defending them from attacks from the Spanish and the Caribs at first limited the attention settlers paid to the creation of religious institutions, by the 1700s, the Anglican Church was well ensconced in the British Caribbean. Following the English pattern, the colonies were divided into parishes that served both as civil administrative and as ecclesiastical units. Each parish was administered by a vestry that performed such civil functions as collecting taxes and such religious functions as building and maintaining churches and paying for the upkeep of the ministers. Ministers were recruited from England and were salaried partly from grants from the royal treasury and partly from local taxation. However, from the very beginning, the social and political conditions of the Caribbean colonies militated against the ability of the Church of England to assert its authority and to accomplish its ministry.

Though, in the early days of the colonies, the Church of England sought to suppress other religious groups, especially Catholics, the religious diversity of the settlers migrating to the Caribbean short-circuited any kind of orthodoxy that the Anglicans wished to impose. In admitting people to the colonies, the need for productive and defensive manpower took precedence over religious orthodoxy, and thus people of diverse religious persuasions were allowed to settle. Religious nonconformists such as the Quakers and the Puritans often sought refuge in the islands; Scottish and Irish Catholics were among the early settlers; and both French Catholics and Huguenots settled in English areas of St. Kitts. Jews fleeing persecution in Europe were allowed to settle, exempted from attending Anglican worship, and permitted to establish synagogues, but they had to pay taxes that supported Anglican establishment. The acquisition of former French and Spanish settlements in the second half of the 1700s and in the early 1800s greatly complicated this situation by adding colonies with predominantly Catholic populations. Hence, from the early days, the colonies tended to be more religiously tolerant than England. Orders from the Colonial Office directed that only colonial officials be required to belong to the Church of England and that freedom of conscience be allowed to prevail as long as such freedom was exercised peacefully.[19] Political allegiance to the colonies and to England took precedence over religious conformity. The Act of Toleration promoted by William and Mary and passed by the British Parliament in 1689 also granted some measure of tolerance to religious groups in the colonies, though political and ecclesiastical authorities sometimes argued that the law did not apply to the colonies.[20]

A lack of an overarching ecclesiastical organization and clerical leadership in Caribbean contributed to the ineffectiveness of the Church of England. No local ecclesiastical body or person of authority directed or oversaw the works of the individual rectors or priests. Theoretically, the Caribbean was a mission field under the jurisdiction of the bishop of London. In addition to the fact that the bishop was too far removed to exert any significant power, when he tried, he faced opposition from local planters and colonial officials who wished to maintain their independence of ecclesiastical power. Toward the end of the 1600s, the bishop of London sought to assert his authority in the Caribbean by appointing commissaries as his representatives in the colonies. The commissaries were resident clergymen who were responsible for the maintenance of discipline among clergy and parishioners. The colonial civil authorities staunchly resisted the power of these commissaries. For example, when the Anglican clergyman William Gordon was appointed commissary in Barbados and sought to set up a Church court to deal with moral laxity and abuse of power by the local parishioners, the Barbados Assembly voted that the bishop of London and his representative had no authority to judge the behavior of lay people. They could pass judgment on the behavior of the clergy, but the behavior of the laity was regarded as a strictly civil matter. The Jamaican Assembly was even more resistant to Episcopal powers, ruling that ecclesiastical representatives could not issue or enforce any penalty in that colony.[21]

What is more, when the authority of the bishop of London over the Caribbean was challenged, no official records conferring such authority could be found. Only in the early 1800s did the British Crown and the Anglican hierarchy grant official status to the authority of the bishop of London over the Caribbean Church. Thus, for almost the first two hundred years of the British Caribbean colonies, the most effective power that the bishop of London exercised was that of issuing licenses for clergy heading to the colonies. The effective authority over the churches of the colonies was in the hands of the governors: they, along with local legislatures, organized parishes; requested clergy from England and installed them when they arrived; recommended "worthy" colonists for ministerial licenses; had the power to suspend or revoke the charge of priests and rectors when the occasion warranted such action; and granted marriage licenses. In the exercise of such power in ecclesiastical matters, some governors allegedly resorted to making appointment as personal favors and even for financial gain.[22]

Thus dominated by the local planters, Anglican clergymen were either constrained in what measures they could take to deal with the ecclesiastical and spiritual issues in their cures or had to pander to or ingratiate themselves with the powerful in their midst. Of course, this suited many ministers, who were more invested in personal gain than in pursuing effective ministry.[23] The outcome was that there was little courageous opposition to the greed and moral laxity of the planters, who engaged in pervasive, promiscuous sexual liaisons with their female slaves. Furthermore, despite directives from England ordering the clergy to engage in the evangelization of the slave population, resistance from the planters stifled any effort to do so.

The state of the clergy itself was a major hindrance to the progess of the Anglican Church in pre-emancipation Caribbean. Throughout this period, clergymen were trained, licensed, and sent to the colonies at the request of governors. Historians point out that these were probably not the most promising men, but mostly those who had very little prospect of rising through the ranks of the Church hierarchy in England.[24] An observer in the mid-1700s opined that "such worthless and abandoned men should not be sent" to the colonies.[25] Persons born in the colonies sometimes aspired to the office and went to England with the recommendations from the governors and other persons of repute to be licensed by the bishop of London. Alfred Caldecott, the nineteenth-century Anglican historian, claimed that "a few unsuccessful planters, merchants, and ex-military officers" opted to go to England to receive ministerial licenses and returned to islands to partake of the charmed lifestyle of priests in the Caribbean.[26] Most of these men often lacked the requisite professional training but received appointment as gubernatorial favors or because of their social connections.

Often bemoaned was the poor quality of clergy with regard to their intellectual abilities and training in divinity, their conduct of their ministries, and their moral behavior. Since they were rather secure in their positions and had little or no room for promotion, they lacked any incentive for diligence and excellence, and thus many went about their duties in the most perfunctory manner. Alcoholism, sexual promiscuity, and gambling were some of the vices that were attributed to many of the clergy. To complicate the issue, absenteeism was a pervasive problem, with priests and rectors leaving their charges and returning to England for extended periods while still collecting salaries. Of course, as Caldecott points out, some members of the clergy distinguished themselves by the diligent performance of their duties and by their personal moral virtues.[27]

A major problem with the Church of England in the Caribbean was that it had too few clergymen, who numbered only about fifty in the early 1800s.[28] Many parishes had neither rectors nor churches. Add to these issues the scattered nature of the settlements and the primitive means of transportation, and even if there were rectors for all the parishes, they could not have effectively ministered to all their far-flung parishioners. But even where there were rectors and priests, church morale and interest in spiritual matters among the parishioners were very low. As late as 1800, church attendance in some colonies was appallingly low. Jamaica, the largest colony of the British Caribbean with a population of 400,000 (blacks and whites), had only twenty houses of worship for Anglicans, and average attendance each week was only three hundred.[29]

Education, which in England had traditionally come under the umbrella of the Church, was woefully lacking in the British Caribbean before emancipation. Unlike the North American colonies, which quickly founded colleges for ministerial and liberal arts education and in some places set up public schools for secondary and elementary education, the colonies of the British Caribbean paid very little attention to education. Through the 1700s, a few grammar schools were founded.[30] Most schools were the result of endowment by individual benefactors. A revealing fact is that in many cases the number of available endowments for schools far exceeded the actual number of schools, with many bequests lying dormant for years or lost because they were not taken up. For example, a report to the Jamaican Assembly showed more than two hundred bequests left for the founding of schools between 1667 and 1736, yet only three such schools existed in Jamaica at the time of the report.[31] As the historian Edward Long observed disapprovingly, even when bequests for schools were acted upon, poor management minimized the effectiveness of the education that resulted.[32] Most planters, merchants, and colonial administrators sent their boys to England for education; most girls had to make do with music and dancing lessons when tutors were available. Boys from the upper and middle classes who were not sent to England were taught by private tutors, mostly from the clergy. With the exception of a school on the Codrington estate in Barbados established by the bequest of Christopher Codrington III, who was a Barbadian planter and governor of the Leeward Islands in early 1700, and probably a school of the Christian

Faith Society in Antigua, no provision was made for the education of slave children.[33]

Like their counterparts in the British colonies in North America, the members of the Church of England in the British Caribbean and their supporters at home attributed the weakness of Church of England to the absence of a bishop and made repeated representations to the civil and religious authorities in England to create an Episcopal diocese in the Caribbean. The authorities in England did not heed such requests for such representation until 1824. The troublesome issue of the intertwining of political and ecclesiastical powers may have been at the root of the reluctance to send a bishop to the colonies. Local political bodies that wanted to remain independent of Church power persistently rejected such a religious authority. People of other religious persuasions, many of whom had left England because of religious persecution directed by bishops of the Church of England, were even more adamantly opposed to the appointment of an Anglican bishop in the Caribbean.[34] The secession of the thirteen North American colonies to form the United States of America and their institutionalization of the separation of church and state showed how ecclesiastical power could be separated from political power. Shortly after the American Revolution and the Episcopal Church's (as the Church of England was renamed in the United States) installation of its own bishop, the Church of England became more opened to the appointment of bishops in British overseas territories. Eventually, two bishops were appointed and inducted in the Caribbean in 1824.[35]

One serious attempt to address the ecclesiastical issues facing the British Caribbean came from Governor Christopher Codrington of the Leeward Islands. Disenchanted by the quality of the clergy sent to the islands and by their lack of effort to Christianize the slave population, Codrington made a bequest of his estate in Barbados to the Society for the Propagation of the Gospel (SPG), a missionary organization that supported the work of the Anglican Church in the British colonies. The bequest stated that the properties and their slave population were to be kept in perpetuity and that the earnings of the estate were to be used to establish a theological college to train local ministers to undertake the mission of converting the slaves.[35] The SPG struggled for years to bring Codrington's vision to fruition. Receiving much opposition from the local planters and clergy, the SPG was able to achieve some success in converting some of the slaves but, under pressure, it abandoned efforts to teach them to read and write. Instead of establishing a theological college, the SPG went along with local wishes and established a grammar school for local white children in 1745. Only on the eve of emancipation, in 1830, was a theological college eventually established.[36]

Another issue that bedeviled the Church of England during the pre-emancipation period was the religious instruction of the African slaves in the colonies. In theory, part of the justification for colonization and the slave trade was the opportunity they provided for bringing heathens to Christianity. And, while the British had no official code governing the treatment of slaves and their religious instruction (like the *code noir* of the French and the *siete partidos* of the Spanish), the colonial office called for their instruction in the Christian faith.[37] Even the Jamaican slave code of 1696 specifically called for the evangelization of the slaves and their instruction in the principles of Christianity. Despite these expressed calls, the planter class resisted any extension of the services of the church to the slave population, and, for the most part, the clergy acquiesced to its wishes.

Several factors seem to have informed this opposition to slave conversion and religious education. One was the widely held belief that Christians should not be kept in a state of perpetual enslavement. This reflected the European practice of not enslaving fellow Christians and may have generated the feeling that having Christian slaves was immoral even if there was no explicit legal prohibition against it. Citing the British tradition of the incompatibility of being a Christian and a slave, Barbadian planters refused to instruct a slave who expressed a desire to become a Christian.[38] So, fearing that Christian conversion conferred greater status if not equality on the slaves, the colonists opted for not evangelizing them. The Barbados legislature went as far as prohibiting any form of religious education for the slaves. The withholding of religious instruction was also predicated on the belief that Africans were too uncivilized and too uncultured to be able to become Christian. Planters argued that slaves lacked the intellectual capacity and the cultural development to embrace Christianity and that they preferred their native "superstitions." Some even posited the notion that the Africans belonged to an inferior race despite their having a human appearance. They found support for this in the contentions of ethnologists of the period who argued that the Africans were of another species that was inferior to that of the Europeans. Furthermore, in a jab at what was perceived as "forced" conversion in Catholic colonies, and in a strange defense of individual liberty, the British colonial administrator and historian Edward Long argued, in the late 1700s, that not proselytizing the slave was in line with good Protestant principles that abhorred forced conversions. Thus, the planters and the clergy refused to evangelize the slave population and resisted those who dared to try, such as the Anglican missionaries of the Society for the Propagation of the Gospel on the Codrington estate and nonconformist missionaries who started to arrive in the mid-1700s.[39]

The Nonconformist Challenge to Anglican Dominance

"Nonconformist" was the label attached to groups of British Christians who disagreed with the theology, liturgy, and polity of Church of England and who refused to submit to its authority, especially after the "Act of Uniformity" passed the English Parliament in 1662. One of the characteristics that distinguished the Nonconformists was their rejection of the liturgy of the Church of England, which they saw as smacking of Catholicism and as too formal and perfunctory. They advocated instead the simplicity and spontaneity of the worship they perceived in the New Testament. The authority of Anglican bishops and their political clout, especially in suppressing dissent, reminded the Nonconformists of the irksome high-handedness of the Pope. Some Nonconformists viewed members of the Church of England as being only nominally or culturally Christian and as lacking any vital or genuine Christian experience. Also objectionable to the Nonconformists was what they perceived as the moral laxity and the ethical failings of the both the clergy and laity in the Church of England.

Members of these dissenting groups were among the early settlers in the British Caribbean. However, they posed very little challenge to the religious status quo on the issue of the religious instruction of slaves. Having become successful planters, some of the dissenters, especially the Puritans, dropped their nonconformist views and returned to the Anglican fold. Reportedly, even successful Jews became members the Church of England.[40] In the Caribbean, the Presbyterian Church, which was established in Scotland, was regarded as a sister church to the Church of England, received official support, and in turned supported the status quo. In the first hundred years of British colonialism in the Caribbean, the Quakers were the most likely group to challenge the planters and the Church of England, particularly with respect to its refusal to extend the Christian ministry to slaves. In Barbados and the Leeward Islands, the Quakers acquired a reputation for belligerence in their refusal to abide by local ordinances and to participate in the defense of the colonies.[41] However, the activities of the Quakers were severely restricted by local laws and violent intimidation. Most other dissenters held their opinions privately as long as they were not disturbed by the established Church. By the mid-1700s, however, the evangelizing impulse sweeping Europe brought

Nonconformist missionaries to the Caribbean with the expressed purpose of instructing blacks, slave and free, in the principles of the Christian religion.

The Moravians or United Brethren (*Unitas Fratrum*) were the first organized group of Nonconformists to arrive in the Caribbean. In 1732, they made their appearance in St. Thomas, one of the Danish Virgin Islands (now U.S. Virgin Islands). The first missionaries were sent out under the patronage of Count Zinzendorf, a German nobleman converted to the pietistic movement. After learning of the plight of the African slaves in the Danish colonies from Anthony Ulrich, an enslaved African whom he met in Copenhagen, Zinzendorf returned to his estate and dispatched Leonard Dober and David Nitchmann to St. Thomas with the express mission of seeking the conversion of the slave population. Though Nitchmann soon returned home and was followed by Dober some time later, other Moravians arrived to carry on the mission they had started. Opposition by the slave owners to the Moravians' missionary activities among the slaves was fierce. The missionaries endured violent attacks from the planters and imprisonment by the local authorities. In fact, some of the early missionaries might have perished in jail had not Zinzendorf arrived to check on the progress of their ministries. Informed that they were imprisoned, Zinzendorf was able to secure their release. Over time, the Moravian missionaries secured a foothold in St. Thomas and spread their mission to other Virgin Islands, St. John and St. Croix. Within the next hundred years, the Moravians admitted more than 18,500 persons into their fellowship.[42] Since the Moravian missionaries were self-supporting, they eventually bought their own plantations, which they cultivated with slave labor. Though they were known for their humane treatment of their slaves, their Christian witness was tainted by their participation in this fundamentally cruel institution. In the Virgin Islands, they continued their embrace of slavery until emancipation was proclaimed by the governor in 1848 to stave off violent uprising by the slaves, who seemed to have interpreted an amelioration measure, proclaimed by the Danish government and scheduled to go into effect that same year, as the granting of freedom.[43]

The Moravians arrived in Jamaica in 1754 at the behest of two absentee planters, John Foster Barham and William Foster, who were English converts to the Moravian faith. Convinced that Moravian ministry to the slaves would be beneficial, these planters sponsored missionaries to go to Jamaica to minister to the slaves on their estates in the parish of St. Elizabeth.[44] When the resident managers of these estates resisted the missionaries, the planters replaced them with an attorney who was Moravian. Eventually, the Moravians established five stations from which they ministered to the slave population, but efforts over the first fifty years garnered minimal success, baptizing only about a thousand converts. Disagreements among missionaries, opposition from the planter class, natural disasters, the illness and death of missionaries from tropical diseases, and the missionaries' support of slavery were among the factors putting constraint on the success of their ministries.[45] At first, they sought to support themselves by establishing estates with slave labor. Though they avoided the cruelty of the general slave system, they may have failed to win the favor of the slaves because of their support for and their practice of slavery. Over the next half-century, especially after they sold their estate in 1823, their ministry met considerable success. By the 1854 celebration of their one-hundredth anniversary in Jamaica, they had amassed a membership of more than thirteen thousand people and were operating scores of schools that educated the children of those emancipated from slavery. The Moravians were also involved in purchasing vast tracts of land and subdividing it among their members to create the free villages in which many former slaves lived after emancipation.

In Barbados, the Moravians were strongly resisted by the English planters and the Church of England. In the pre-emancipation era, they had very little success, numbering only forty slaves in their congregations for their labors from 1665 to 1695. Their ministry in Antigua, which started in 1756, showed much greater success, securing a membership of almost nine thousand persons in their fold by 1812.[46]

Methodism, which was started by John and Charles Wesley as a movement within the Church of England and which emphasized "warm hearted" religion and ministry to the poor, was introduced to the Caribbean by Nathaniel Gilbert, who was the speaker of the colonial assembly in Antigua. Apparently, Mr. Gilbert had read some of John Wesley's writings and decided to travel to London to have a conference with him. In England, Mr. Gilbert and the two slaves he had taken with him were converted to Methodism after meeting with Wesley. On his return to Antigua in 1754, Gilbert started a Methodist class meeting on his plantation in which he instructed his slaves in the teachings of Methodism, converting some two hundred of them. After his death in 1661, two slave women converts seem to have assumed leadership of the class until John Baxter, who came to Antigua to work on the docks, succeeded Gilbert in leading the Methodists on the islands.[47]

The spread of Methodism throughout the Caribbean received tremendous impetus from the chance arrival of the notable Dr. Thomas Coke in Antigua in 1789. Coke was in charge of Methodist mission work and was on his way to North America when bad weather caused his ship to lose its way and land in Antigua in 1786. This was auspicious for Methodism in the British West Indies because Coke spent the next four years visiting various islands, establishing Methodist societies, and stationing missionaries in a number of British colonies, including St. Kitts, Nevis, and Jamaica. In Antigua, the Methodists found success mostly among the slave population, garnering 6,570 members by 1793, but some colored and a few whites joined the societies, as well.[48] Methodism in St. Kitts experienced immediate and sustained success, gaining a membership of two thousand by 1800. By this time, the Methodists were operating a Sunday school and a day school for the instruction of the children of slaves. The Methodist missionary there indicated that if more preachers were available, the Methodists could enjoy an even more remarkable success.[49] In Jamaica, the work was initially restricted to urban areas and among coloreds and free blacks, among whom the Methodists gained a following of about six hundred by the early 1800s. Because of the strength of the established Church of England, the Methodists made very little headway in Barbados. By 1812, they were able to assemble only a mixed group of adherents numbering about thirty people.[50]

Probably because of Wesley's known opposition to slavery, the Methodists experienced stiff opposition from the colonists. In Jamaica, for example, the colonists instigated a riot in opposition to the building of a Methodist meeting house in Kingston, and the local assembly passed a measure that prohibited Methodist missionaries from preaching after dark, effectively curtailing the ministry to the slaves, who were otherwise occupied at other times of the day. In Barbados, a mob destroyed a Methodist chapel in Bridgetown, and a jury refused to find the perpetrators guilty.[51] As late at 1816, a planter who was disposed to have other religious groups minister to his slaves adamantly refused access to Methodists.[52] Despite their initial confinement to town areas and the severe opposition of the planter class, Methodists were eventually able to extend their ministry to slaves. In this, they received the assistance of influential people in the colonies. Interestingly, even in the pre-emancipation era, the Methodists were able to establish a few congregations in which blacks, whites, and mixed race people worshipped together.

The Baptist presence in the British Caribbean was occasioned by the arrived of George Liele (also Lisle), an African American, who came to Jamaica in the early 1780s with a loyalist British officer, fleeing from North America after the British defeat in the American Revolution. Liele had been set free by his master at the onset of the Revolution. After his former master was killed in battle while fighting on the side of the British, Liele, to avoid re-enslavement, took refuge in Savannah, Georgia, which was occupied by the British. Converted to the Baptist faith while he was still a slave, Liele felt a strong call to spread the gospel to his fellow slaves. To this end, he was ordained by the white Baptist church in which he was converted. For several years, Liele ministered to the slaves on plantations along the Savannah River. Along with two of his notable converts, David George and Andrew Bryan, he established the first black Baptist congregations and churches in Georgia around the time of the American Revolution. For some reason, Liele became indebted to a white supporter, Colonel Kirkland, who took Liele with him to Jamaica as an indentured servant for a period of two years as a means of discharging his debt.[53]

After fulfilling his indenture with Colonel Kirkland, Liele started preaching to free blacks and slaves in and around Kingston. His earnest, emotional preaching and lively worship services garnered a growing following. Soon he established a church on property that he had purchased. Though he had obtained the requisite preacher's licenses from the colonial authorities, Liele was repeatedly arrested and incarcerated for violating the terms of his preaching license, but, along with his assistants, he established the first Baptists congregations in the islands. Through the work of Liele, a number of assistants, and the movement of converted slaves from one plantation to another (through sales), the Baptist faith quickly spread across the Island. For example, one of Liele's assistants, Moses Baker, was invited by a planter from the western end of Jamaica to minister to his slaves. Baker's ministry there led to the establishment of a Baptist church near the Adelphi plantation in St James. By the beginning the 1800s, Liele was reporting some 350 members in his church, including a few whites and former Methodists.[54] Liele even organized a school where free blacks, both children and adults, learned to read and write. So rapid was the growth by the early 1800s that the Jamaican Baptists felt that they needed assistance and invited the newly formed Baptist Missionary Society of London to provide missionary oversight. The society responded by sending John Rowe to Jamaica in 1814 to take charge of the work there.[55] He was followed by others such as Thomas Burchell, William Knibb, and James Phillippo, who became almost legendary for their ministry to the black population leading up to and after emancipation. The Baptists concentrated their efforts on the evangelization and education of the slave population. They were often suspected and accused of inciting rebellion among the slaves in the years leading up to the emancipation in 1834. Most famously, they were the objects of the ire of the planters after the "Baptist War" around Christmas of 1831, in which a black Baptist deacon, Sam Sharpe, led a rebellion on plantations in western Jamaica that involved more than fifty thousand slaves. More than three hundred blacks and about fourteen whites died in the ten-day conflict, and damage to the plantations was estimated at almost £1.2 million or more than $3 million U.S. Sharpe and his co-conspirators were executed; Knibb was arrested and later released. Burchell, who ministered in the area of rebellion, was apprehended and jailed; after his release, he had to flee the island temporarily to avoid the wrath of the planters. Baptist churches and chapels were ransacked and destroyed by mob activities in retaliation for the uprising.[56]

For the most part, Nonconformist missionaries acknowledged the humanity of the slaves and conferred on them a sense of dignity by addressing them as brothers and sisters. The more able and more committed slaves were often appointed to positions of leadership by the missionaries. Those thus appointed were responsible for maintaining Christian discipline and conducting services in the absence of the missionaries or assisting them when they were present. Generally, the worship services conducted by the Nonconformist missionaries were more informal and participatory, extending to the attendees more avenues of self-expression, especially in singing and testifying.[57]

In some cases, the Nonconformists were accorded courtesies and allowed by sympathetic planters to preach to slaves. However, for the most part, they were resisted by most planters and relegated to urban areas, where they ministered to free blacks and persons of mixed race. These limits were imposed because Nonconformists contravened the longheld opposition to the conversion of the slaves and to teaching them to read and write. Planters also opposed the Nonconformists because of their evangelical British counterparts who supported the amelioration measures (to be discussed later) enacted by the Parliament and who were often activists in abolitionist cause. Of course, the colonial authorities feared that the activities of these missionaries among the slaves could give cover for subversive activities, especially after the Haitian revolution from 1791 to 1804. The growing restlessness and uprisings among the slaves in the early 1800s seemed to justify their fear. They blamed the Moravians, the Methodists, and the Baptists for fomenting unrest among the slave population by elevating some of their converts to leadership positions in their churches.[58] After the "Baptist War" of 1831, the leader of the rebellion, Sam Sharpe, who had been a deacon in the Baptist church, was pointed out as exhibit A of the danger of converting slaves and bestowing leadership position on them.

To counter the perceived danger posed by the Nonconformists, colonial authorities resorted to a number tactics. Some assemblies enacted measures that restricted Nonconformists' activities. These included a ban on preaching after dark, a prohibition on preaching to slaves without invitation or in the absence of the planters or managers and on baptizing them without the permission of the owners, and a requirement that missionaries reside on the island for a specified period of time before they could receive preaching licenses. Infractions of these measures were met with threats, banishments, and imprisonments.[59] In addition to legislative measures, the colonial authorities implemented measures to bolster the work of the Church of England and particularly to improve the condition of the clergy in its attempt to compete with the evident success of the Nonconformists. For example, Jamaica and Barbados accepted the appointment of commissaries (church officials representing the bishop of London) in 1800 after having rejected them earlier. To boost morale and to attract better prepared clergymen, they also granted salary increases in 1807 to those ministering in the Caribbean. Intimidation and violence were other elements in the arsenal of tactics aimed at repression of the Nonconformists, including, as we have seen, arrests and imprisonment of Baptist preachers, the execution of Christian slaves accused of fomenting rebellion, and the mob destruction of church property in Jamaica. The same kind of destruction of church property and harassment of missionaries prevailed in Bridgetown, as is evident in the treatment of William Shrewsbury, a Methodist minister whose chapel was violently destroyed and who had to hastily depart from the island because of danger to his life.[60]

Nonconformists refused to submit to the restrictions placed on them by the authorities in the colonies. They insisted on their rights as British citizens, often justifying their activities by appealing to the "Act of Toleration" passed by the British Parliament in 1689, which granted religious freedom to Nonconformists. They even appealed to the Crown against local legislation that infringed on their freedom. For example, when the Jamaican Assembly passed laws in 1800 and 1807 prohibiting preaching without proper licenses, the Crown invalidated these laws after appeals by the Nonconformists.[61] In response to the repressive measures taken against the Baptists after the "Baptist War," a delegation of Baptists went to England in 1833 to argue their case and succeeded in shaping public opinion against the planters and the institution of slavery.

While the Nonconformist missionaries were convinced of the humanity of the slaves, were willing to defy the Anglican establishment by preaching to them and sometimes teaching them to read and write, and were even advocates for more humane treatments, they in no way believed in slaves' equality or advocated their freedom. In fact, the missionaries all had orders not to disturb the social order by doing anything to incite uprising or stimulate agitation among the slaves. One argument they used to justify their activities among the slaves was that Christian slaves were more likely to be peaceful, submissive, and loyal than non-Christian ones. Even Thomas Coke of the antislavery Methodists famously attributed the ready participation of hundreds of blacks in staving off a French attack on Antigua in the 1790s to the Christian influence they had imbibed.[62]

Christianity and Emancipation

The changing social and intellectual mood in England in the late 1700s and early 1800s was disposed toward reforms affecting social conditions both at home and in the colonies. The reforms included enfranchisement of the middle class, philanthropic endeavors based on Christian and humanitarian convictions, changes in the legal system to ameliorate the conditions of those in poverty and the penal system, and evangelical activism aimed at bringing the gospel to the lower classes and reforming society on the basis of Christian ethics. Nonconformist evangelical groups and the rapidly forming missionary societies were particularly supportive of these reforms and were quick in extending their activities to foreign fields, especially British colonies in Asia and the Caribbean. Framing and informing the changing attitudes in England were the American Revolution (1776), the French Revolution (1789), particularly the Reign of Terror that followed, and the Haitian Revolution (1791), in which thousands of people, black and white, were killed and the world's most thriving sugar economy was devastated.

In response to agitation against the slave trade and slavery by evangelicals and humanitarians in England, the British government embarked on a policy of amelioration that it hoped would begin a gradual abolition of the slave trade and, eventually, slavery. In general, this policy called for improvements in the working conditions and treatment of the slaves and required the planters and the Church of England to provide for their religious instruction. A series of resolutions passed by the British Parliament instructed the colonists to care for their slaves in such a manner that they could multiply naturally, obviating the need for further imports (1797), called for cessation of the flogging of female slaves, and urged that slave drivers refrain from carrying whips.[63] In 1817, the British government mandated a compulsory census of all slaves in an attempt to establish a baseline against which it could judge whether the amelioration measures were ensuring better treatments of slaves, which could be adduced from natural population growth. Anticipating an eventual emancipation of the slaves, an amelioration proposal by the British government insisted that education was of paramount importance in preparing the slaves for freedom. The proposal urged colonies that lacked the resources for such an undertaking to apply for grants from the Crown to provide such education.[64]

The ecclesiastical authorities in England threw their weight behind the amelioration measures and charged the clergy in the colonies with beginning to prepare the slave population for eventual emancipation. The bishop of London urged the clergy in the Caribbean to institute a system of Sunday schools in which the slaves could be instructed. The traditional Sunday market in which slaves traded the produce from their provision grounds were to be moved to midweek to free up Sundays for religious instruction. Slave marriages were to be granted legal status; the use of chains and branding irons was to be discontinued; the sick were to be provided medical services; and slaves were to be allowed to give testimony in courts.[65]

Initially, while some colonies accepted and implemented the amelioration policies, the planter class in the colonies, the absentee owners in England, and their supporters (called the West Indian Interest) resisted the amelioration policies or surrounded their implementation with such restrictions that made them ineffective. The Leeward Islands, for example, adopted and implemented the measures passed by the British Parliament in 1797. Most Crown colonies, by virtue of their direct governance by the Crown had to go along with the measures. However, the older colonies, especially Jamaica and Barbados, were particularly resistant, using a variety of means to frustrate the amelioration policies. They moved to strengthen the clergy of the Church of England by providing increased stipends, better living conditions, and funds to hire curates (assistants theoretically responsible for slave instruction) so that they could counter the influence of the Nonconformist Churches that were more supportive of the amelioration measures. Colonies sometimes adopted measures but made no provision for their implementation or implemented them in a way that preserved the status quo. For example, the Jamaican legislature approved religious instruction for the slave in an 1815 act, but the curates provided for this task ended up assisting the rectors in their regular duties instead of attending to the education of the slaves. Furthermore, the planters and clergy of the Church of England made every effort to frustrate the ministry of the Nonconformists among the slave population, employing the various measures discussed earlier.[66]

Because of the failure of the Church of England to meet the challenges of amelioration and to improve its ministry, the Crown and the ecclesiastical authorities in England eventually organized two dioceses in the Caribbean in 1824: Barbados (Barbados, St. Vincent, Grenada, Trinidad, Tobago, and British Guiana), with William Hart Coleridge as bishop, and Jamaica (Jamaica, the Bahamas, and British Honduras,later known as Belize), with Christopher Lipscomb as bishop. The British treasury provided funds to support the bishops and their assistants. Under the leadership of these bishops, the ministry of the Church of England was greatly improved, and the number of clergymen in the colonies increased significantly. For example, in Jamaica the number quickly went from thirty to forty-five; in Barbardos, it rose from fifteen to twenty-seven. To counter the church's reputation for low morals, the bishops enforced a higher standard of conduct among clergy and laity alike. The bishops also embarked on an ambitious church building program. Curates, catechists, and schoolmasters taught slaves on numerous plantations. In an effort to enliven the vapid church services in order to broaden their appeal, the bishops introduced music, though the experiment was short-lived in Jamaica because of the bishop's distaste for music in worship services. To meet the growing demand for ministers, the bishops revived one of the objectives of the Codrington Trust and established Codrington College in 1830 to provide ministerial training for the locals and to advance general education. The first graduates were ordained to the ministry by Bishop Coleridge in 1834.[67]

Keith Hunte argues that entrenched opposition among the clergy and planters to the conversion and education of slaves, slave revolts, and the rapidity with which the emancipation agenda proceeded in England limited the success of the measures taken by the new bishops of the Church of England. By the time emancipation was proclaimed in 1833 and a period of apprenticeship initiated in 1834 (leading to full emancipation 1838), the authorities in England were convinced that the Church of England alone was not up to the task of preparing the slave population for freedom. Thus, when parliamentary legislation provided for the Negro Education Grant in 1835, Nonconformist churches operating in the British Caribbean were granted access to the funds as long as they met the required conditions. While the Baptists declined government funds because of their principle of independence, Moravians, Presbyterians, and Methodists joined the Church of England in establishing a network of schools to educate the black population. These schools became the foundation of public education in the Anglo Caribbean. These churches and charitable foundations later established teachers colleges to train local teachers for these schools.[68]

Emancipation and Disestablishment

Prior to emancipation, the colonial authorities and the planters feared that, once freed, the former slaves would resort to violence to exact revenge against those who had enslaved them. However, on the eve of emancipation, huge crowds flocked churches, and, in the early years of emancipation, the churches became the centers around which the newly liberated Africans rallied. The more intellectually gifted quickly emerged as leaders in their local churches, teachers in church-run schools, and even pastors and missionaries in their denominations. Emancipation was a particular boon for Nonconformists, who operated in an atmosphere of tolerance and experienced substantial growth. In areas where the Nonconformist churches were strong, they played a pivotal role in facilitating the transition of the former slaves from plantation life to the establishment of an independent peasantry. These churches bought large tracts of land, which they then subdivided and sold to their members, creating new, independent villages. The settlers used the land for raising staples for their own consumption and cash crops that they sold in local markets or to various vendors.[69]

Before long, the initial influx of the emancipated into the churches started to wane. Churches lost members as people moved away from the plantations to new areas within a colony or to another colony altogether. While some of these migrants facilitated the spread of their faith to new areas, others drifted away from church life. In independent villages under church sponsorship, religious life remained vibrant, and ecclesiastical control of education ensured that churches exerted considerable influence over the population in these communities. But even these churches felt the effects of people's moving to new areas in search of arable lands where they could eke out a living. The churches, especially the Nonconformist churches, also had to wrestle with another issue. Black converts to Christianity did not always make the clean break with their African past and folk traditions that the missionaries expected. Particularly noteworthy was their penchant for emotional and ecstatic displays and preoccupation with healing by spiritual means. With its establishment by an African American and its large black membership, the Baptist Church seems to have been most affected by concerns about syncretism. In Jamaica, the Presbyterians accused Baptists of allowing untrained local leaders to incorporate "heathenish practices" into their worship. An observer from the British Baptist Society accused African American immigrants in Trinidad of introducing "fanatical notions and practices," including jumping and shouting, into Baptist church services.[70]

The Church of England scrambled to maintain its dominance in the British Caribbean after emancipation, but, in the new era of tolerance that came with emancipation, it increasingly had to cede grounds to other denominations. This was particularly true in the colonies that came under British control in the late 1700s and early 1800s. Despite efforts to assert itself in such recently acquired territories as Grenada, St. Lucia, Dominica, and Trinidad, the Church of England remained a minority faith because the majority of the population was rooted in Catholicism.

Another issue with which the churches had to grapple in the post-emancipation era was the training of local clergy. Diminishing funds and fewer personnel from England and the growing size of the various denominations increasingly made it apparent that it would be necessary for the churches to train locals to be ministers if they were to sustain vibrant ministries in the Caribbean. As we have seen, the Church of England revived a plan outlined in the Codrington Trust and established Codrington College in 1830. Through an affiliation with Durham University in 1875, Codrington College started granting degrees in the arts as well as in theology. To train their own ministers, Baptists opened Calabar College in 1843 in Rio Bueno, Jamaica, but moved it to Kingston in 1868. The Presbyterians started an academy in Montego Bay, Jamaica, in 1845 that offered both secondary and theological education to ministerial prospects.[71] These ministerial colleges trained personnel not only for the indigenous ministry but also for missionary outreach. Locally trained ministers became missionaries to Africa and also extended their ministry to indentured Indian laborers (from India), who started arriving in the Caribbean after 1838. Most notable was the ministry of the Presbyterian Church to Indian indentures in Trinidad, Guiana, Grenada, and Jamaica.[72]

Events and conditions of the post-emancipation Caribbean conspired to bring about the disestablishment of the Church of England in the British Caribbean. These conditions were ecclesiastical, economic, and political. Despite its favored status and financial support in all Caribbean colonies (whether or not it was officially established), the Church of England was at a decidedly numerical disadvantage. In terms of memberships and number of congregations, it was a de facto minority institution except in Barbados, and it was gradually losing its dominance in the religious marketplace. In Jamaica, for example, only one-fourth of the religiously affiliated belonged to the Church of England, whose membership figure of 48,824 was rivaled by those of the Methodists, with 41,775 members, and the Baptists, with 31,640. In former French colonies like Trinidad, Grenada, and Dominica, the Church of England was even more of a minority faith when compared to the Catholic Church, which had far more adherents.[73] On the economic front, the downturn in the sugar industry, which was the mainstay of the economy in the British Caribbean, meant a fall in revenues at a time when there was growing demand for public services such as education, roads, and water. This put pressure on the ability of local governments to continue to fund the Church of England from the public treasury. Additionally, other denominations were increasingly expressing their objection to the use of their members' taxes to support the Church of England, while they had to raise their own financial resources to support their ministries. Catholics, in colonies where they dominated, complained increasingly about the favored status and financial support of the Church of England.[74] To complicate matters, the imperial grant of £20,000, initiated in 1824 to support the work of the two newly established dioceses, was eventually ended after much debate in the British Parliament. The cessation of this grant marked the end of direct British support to the Church of England in the Caribbean.

Politically, by the mid-1860s, the older British colonies, except Barbados, had joined the more recently acquired colonies in becoming Crown Colonies, which meant that the British Crown had more direct control over local policies than it had in the old form of representative assembly that prevailed in the older colonies. So, when the British government decided to pursue a policy of disestablishment for the colonies and signaled this by ending its annual £20,000 subsidy for the Church of England in the colonies, the local governments, except Barbados, did not have the strength in numbers, the economic resources, or the political clout to resist. Given their political situation, the constraints of revenues, and the growing strength of the Nonconformist denominations, most colonies opted for disestablishment of the Church of England and/or pursued some form of equal treatment for the major Christian denominations. Under such arrangements, these denominations were eligible to receive available subsidies or grants to support work (such as education) considered to be for the public good. The Jamaican colony under the instruction of Governor J. P. Grant passed a law in 1870 confirming disestablishment and authorizing the bishop to organize a synod (governing council) of its members to formulate plans to raise support for and administer the affairs of the Church. The Antiguan Assembly passed a disestablishment act that provided for the repair of church properties before they came under the administration of the Church hierarchy. In some colonies, disestablishment became a fact without legislative action. In others, Montserrat and Trinidad, for example, the local government simply extended support to the major denominations.[75] Clergymen whose appointment pre-dated disestablishment continued to receive financial support according to the terms of their appointment, but, as they became deceased, that money was lost to the rectors, and funds had to be raised locally to support new ministers.[76]

Barbados, which was a representative assembly and where the Church of England had up to seven times more parishioners than any other denomination, categorically rejected the policy of disestablishment. The Church of England was in fact the choice of up to 90 percent of the population, and the Nonconformist churches had not been as successful there as they had been elsewhere. Because of these strengths, the legislature voted to re-establish the Church of England in 1872, continuing its status as the official, state-supported Church of the colony. The law also provided for grants to the Methodists and the Moravians and granted £50 annually to the Catholic military chaplain on the island.[77]

While disestablishment did not amount to the separation of church and state—major denominations and civil authorities cooperated in providing public services, especially education—it instituted the principle of voluntarism (already practiced by the Baptists) by which churches and denominations were responsible for their own financial upkeep. Disestablishment also provided the environment for reorganization of the various denominations. The Church of England created the dioceses of Trinidad in 1872 and of British Honduras in 1883, in addition to the two established in 1824. New synods were created under the leadership of bishops, comprising representatives of the clergy and the laity with responsibility for administering the affairs of the diocese. A provincial synod emerged in 1893, and Enos Nutall, then bishop of Jamaica, was elected as the first archbishop.[78]

Prompted by its missionary society in London, the Methodist Church in the Caribbean debated the merits and demerits of forming an independent regional structure to govern its affairs at a conference in 1884. It eventually agreed on the formation of a General Council to serve as a final arbiter of issues facing the Church. It also organized its various districts and circuits into two annual conferences—one consisting of Jamaica and Haiti in the northwest Caribbean and the other consisting of Guiana and the islands of the eastern and southern Caribbean. This experiment did not seem to work smoothly, and in 1903 the Methodists reverted to a district structure. The Moravian mission board, wanting to transfer responsibility for the affairs of Church to a local body in the eastern Caribbean, initiated a process of transferring power to a provincial body in 1879 by creating a Provincial Elders

Conference. The sparseness of financial resources and the failure to train local ministers delayed the creation of an independent regional body until the twentieth century.[79]

A number of general problems affected the efforts to reorganize the churches in the Caribbean and to foster provincial independence. All groups suffered from a lack of adequate local financial resources. Foreign boards and foreign clergy ministering in the Caribbean harbored entrenched prejudices concerning the abilities of black and colored clergy to assume positions of leadership. In addition, lack of adequate training opportunities and facilities and foreign ministers' determination to hold onto power thwarted the opportunities and ambitions of indigenous clergy to assume leadership in the various denominations

Toward the end of the 1800s and at the beginning of the 1900, agitation for political power by the emerging middle class, many of whom had gained education through church schools and colleges, pushed the issue of indigenous church leadership into the foreground. In response, several denomination renewed efforts to train local clergy. To complement Codrington College in Barbados, the Church of England founded St. Peters College in Kingston, Jamaica, in 1893. The Presbyterians initiated a training program for Indo-Trinidadian clergy in 1898, which eventually became Andrew's Theological College of San Fernando, Trinidad. The Methodists opened Caenwood College in Jamaica to provide theological training to potential ministers in 1928. Beginning in 1937, various denominations increasingly came together to provide joint theological programs, culminating in the establishment of United Theological College of the West Indies in 1970.[80]

When the Protestant nations of Great Britain and the Netherlands established colonies in the Caribbean, they also brought with them their national churches. In this, they were operating with the prevailing conviction that church and state should work together in concert for the common good of the society. Given the official support that they enjoyed, the Church of England and the Dutch Reformed Church were certainly the dominant religious institutions during the colonial era. However, as we have seen, the evolving religious pluralism in Europe increasingly appeared in the colonies, as well. The economic and defense needs of the colonies led to the settlement of people from nonconforming religious groups. Furthermore, in islands previously administered by Catholic nations, such as Curaçao, Trinidad, and Grenada, the majority of the population remained Catholic. Africans imported as slaves to the islands brought their own sense of religiosity, and, even when

they embraced Christianity, they often retained elements of African traditions, leading to the development of Afro-Christian traditions, which are
discussed later. So, even in the pre-emancipation era, the Caribbean was well
established as a meeting place for disparate peoples and religious traditions.
This diversity of religious traditions was greatly enhanced throughout the
1900s with the arrival of waves of U.S. missionaries in the Caribbean, also
discussed later.

Creole African Traditions

Santería, Palo Monte, Abakuá,
Vodou, and Espiritismo

The late colonial era in the Caribbean was marked by an explosion of religious traditions that both drew from and challenged the normativity of Christianity. The importation of large numbers of Africans for slave labor on the plantations introduced numerous ethnic groups and their cultural heritages to the Caribbean. In an attempt to negotiate their own diversity and their contact with Europeans, Africans created religious traditions such as Santería, Palo Monte, Abakuá, and Vodou, with adherents that crossed ethnic lines. Among Spanish colonists, the religio-philosophical system of Espiritismo became an alternative for Catholics who were becoming increasingly alienated from the institutional Catholic Church.

Research on these religious traditions varies greatly, with Santería and Vodou sharing the greatest body of scholarship. A fundamental aspect of the development of these religious traditions is their African roots, which are central for understanding their transformation into creole traditions in the Americas.

Santería

The term "Santería," which is the most recognized designation for the religious practices of Yoruba descendants in Cuba, is problematic for many practitioners. Since it is translated as "way of the saints," this designation emphasizes the Roman Catholic elements of this religion, which are seen as symbolic layers surrounding what is understood to be at its core an African religion. The Afro-Cuban religious scholar Mercedes Cros Sandoval argues that Regla Lucumí (rule or way of Lucumí) is the most appropriate name for Santería, since practitioners use "Lucumí" to refer to themselves and their language.[1] For others, the most appropriate name for the religion is Regla de Ocha (rule of *ocha* or *orishas*), though this is not a term that has common currency with many practitioners. In spite of the disagreements among scholars and practitioners alike, we will employ the term Santería because it has currency in both scholarly and popular usage.

Cosmology and Ceremonies of Santería

Santería's cosmology, adopted from the Yoruba religion, is an integrated system of beliefs concerning the constituent elements of the world and their interlocking and dynamic relationship. In this belief system, Olodumare is the self-existent supreme being who created the world and who ultimately controls it workings. According to Joseph Murphy, one of America's foremost experts on Santería, Olodumare means "the owner of all destinies."[2] Emanating from Olodumare and residing in all created entities in greater or lesser intensity is *ashe,* the divine/cosmic energy that is the animating energy in the universe, whether operating in the spiritual sphere, the human sphere, or the physical/material sphere. It is the principle or force necessary for the accomplishment of anything positive. The purpose of Santería's religious rituals and practices is to intensify one's *ashe* or to make stronger *ashe* available for the accomplishment of certain tasks.

Olodumare is usually not the object of ritual or ceremonial activities either in Yoruba or in Santería. The *orishas,* intermediate beings created by Olodumare and endowed with *ashe* to act on his or her behalf, are the focus of ritual attention. As such, they function mainly as intermediaries between Olodumare and the created order, especially humans. Depending on the kind or quality of power with which an *orisha* is endowed, he or she is responsible for a realm of nature or for human quality or activity (e.g., thunder, sea, rivers, crossroads, hunting, healing, maternity, love). In Africa, hundreds of *orishas* were recognized, but relatively few received extensive ritual attention. Most of the *orishas* did not survive the transatlantic voyage of the slave trade, and so relatively few are widely recognized in Santería, with eight emerging as the principal actors in the ceremonies and lives of santeros: Obatalá, guardian of the intellect, purity and morality; Elegguá (Elegba, Eshu), messenger between humans and the rest of the *orishas* and guardian of doorways, crossroads, and opportunity; Oshun, *orisha* of sweet waters (rivers) and of female beauty, sexuality and fertility; Yemayá, custodian of the sea, maternity and motherhood; Changó (Shango), the prototype of male power and sexuality and *orisha* of lightning and thunder; Orunmila (Orunla, Ifá), custodian of wisdom, divination, and human destiny; Ogun (Ogoun), controller of the power of iron, war, and anything to do with technology; and Ochosi, patron of the forest, hunters, nature, and those seeking justice. Other *orishas* are recognized and revered in Cuba, notably Oya, *orisha* of death, and Babalu-Ayé, patron of sickness and healing.

In Yoruba/Santería cosmology, ancestral spirits are part of the invisible realm but are also present and active in the lives of their children. Ancestors are either blood or "religious" relatives who, after death, have become part of "Ara Arun," or the residents or people of heaven. However, they are still present among and are able to give counsel to and provide protection to their living relatives.

While Santería has a clearly defined cosmology, its religious life revolves around rites and ceremonies that are designed to align adherents with the mysteries of universe and particularly to provide them with the necessary knowledge and power (*ashe*) to negotiate the challenges of life. Three major categories or ceremonies are divination, initiation, and celebration. In Santería (and Yoruba), the highest divination system is called Ifá and is the prerogative of *babalawos*, the most esteemed functionaries in the religion. Casting the *opele*, a sacred chain of eight oval-shaped medallions,[3] *babalawos* are able to diagnose a person's case and prescribe a remedy. This ability come from the *babalawos'* knowledge of what human condition each pattern (*odu*) represents and how these relate to the archetypical legends (*patakis*) of Yoruba and Santería. Depending on the cause of the person's problem, the *babalawos* prescribe a course of action, ranging from a simple gift to an *orisha*, to a purification rite, to an animal sacrifice, all to counteract the negative influences or to ensure continued good fortune. On special occasions, *babalawos* utilize the *ikin*, or sixteen sacred palm nuts, to divine the destiny of important personalities. In Yorubaland, this ceremony was performed on the occasions of the crowning of kings and chiefs, but in Santería, it is performed to provide a blueprint for the vocation of individual *babalawos*.[4]

Since there are relatively few *babalawos*, consultations are done mostly frequently by santeros/santeras (priests and priestesses) utilizing the *diloggun*, which consists of sixteen cowrie shells. The casting and reading of the *diloggun* is done in a manner similar to that for the *opele* to determine the causes of people's problems and to determine a course of action to bring good luck or to ward off bad influences. Both *babalawos* and santeros/santeras also read the *obi* (four pieces of coconut rind) during ceremonies to determine if the *orishas* are pleased with the rituals. When cast, the four coconut rinds form one of five patterns indicating varying degrees of positive or negative answers with an attendant oracle or message.

The major initiations in Santería are the *fundamentos*, the *asiento* (*kariocha*), and *ifa*. The *fundamentos* mark the entrance of the individuals into a conscious, lifelong relationship with the *orishas* and involve investment with the *elekes* (necklaces) of five major *orishas* (Elegguá, Obatalá, Changó, Oshun, and Yemayá) and the symbols of *los guerreros*, or warrior *orishas* (Elegguá, Ogun, Ochossi). The necklaces are symbols and conveyors of the blessings and protection of the *orishas*, and the warriors are meant to protect the initiates against accidents and malicious attacks and to assist them in the acquisition of material possessions.[5]

The *asiento* or *kariocha* is the initiation ceremony that confers the status of santero/santera and qualifies one to become a priest of Santería. This ceremony signifies the "making" or "crowning" of the *orishas* on the head of the initiates. The *asiento* itself is a complex ceremony lasting at least eight days. The first five days are a period of isolation in the *ile* (house). This isolation signals both the symbolic death of the old self and a period of gestation leading to rebirth. During the last three days, the *iyawo* (as the initiate is called) undergoes various rituals, culminating with the determination of his or her destiny. Various purifications, shaving of the head to prepare it to receive the *orishas*, investitures with the various symbols and tools of Santería, and sacrifices to the *orishas* are all a part of these rituals.

The most elevated initiation in Santería is the making of Ifá, or the initiation into the mysteries of Orunla (Orunmilla), which is open to men only. Those receiving this initiation are called *babalawos* and are regarded as the high priests of Santería. Since Ifá represents the highest mysteries of Santería, the ritual procedure for the initiation of *babalawos* is treated with the greatest secrecy, and the specific procedures and aspects of these ceremonies are known only to the initiated, and they are forbidden to reveal the details.

A third category of Santería ceremonies is what is variously referred to as *bembes*, *tambors*, or *fiestas de Santos*. These are parties or feasts given to honor the *orishas* on their anniversaries, to celebrate an *asiento* or its anniversary, or to express gratitude to one or more *orishas* for their assistance with a personal problem. Ritual drumming, singing, and dancing, the essential features of these ceremonies, invite the *orishas* to come among their followers "by mounting their horses." Each *orisha* has his or her rhythms, songs, and dance steps by which it is invited to take possession of the heads of its initiates. The possessed then dance like and display the characteristics and idiosyncrasies associated with the possessing *orishas*. Since this is a feast, food and refreshments are provided, and at intervals (the drumming goes on for hours) the attendees are invited to partake of the fare. Special foods are prepared for the *orishas*, who are fed when they possess the dancers.

Two important aspects of most rites and ceremonies of Santería are *ewe* and *ebbo*. *Ewe* is the collective term for the herbs and herbal concoctions used pervasively in Santería in all ceremonies and medicinal "prescriptions."[6] *Ewe* are categorized as either sweet or bitter. Sweet attracts the good and the positive, and bitter dispels the bad or the negative. Santeros/santeras often prescribe herbal bath (*despojos*) and various herbal brews, teas, and ointment as therapy for various ailments. Herbal concoctions are also used in the rites of various ceremonies. In the broadest sense, *ebo* is any gift given to the *orishas* in solicitation of their assistance or in thanksgiving for their assistance. Only the more serious cures and important ceremonies call for blood sacrifices. The offerings, whether large or small, are based on the principle of reciprocation. The santeros/santeras strengthen the *ashe* of the *orishas* through offerings, and the *orishas* make their *ashe* available to the santeros/santeras to assist them with the demands of life.

Social History of Santería

Santería derives its cosmology and practices mainly from the Yoruba people of West Africa. Long before their enslavement by European colonizers, the Yoruba developed a complex culture consisting of independent city-states that were united into a single civilization with a common language and shared religious tradition. The sacred city of Ile-Ife emerged early as their religious and political center. The whole Yoruba culture was infused with religious traditions that shaped its artistic production, social relationships, and healing practices. The Oyo Kingdom, founded in 1350, became the most powerful political entity among the Yoruba people during the 1600s and 1700s, surpassing Ife in political influence, though Ife remained the religious center. Toward the end of the 1700s, the Oyo Empire experienced a dramatic decline due to internal and external conflicts. The *alafin* (political leader) was overthrown by lesser chiefs, plunging the empire into political instability and social chaos. Meanwhile, the Fulani, an Islamic kingdom to the north, embarked on an expansionist campaign that made incursions into the Yoruba territory. The weakened empire was eventually invaded by the slave-trading Fon Kingdom in Dahomey. The slave-raiding campaigns of the Dahomeans became a significant supply line for the Atlantic slave trade.

While the Oyo Empire was falling apart, developments were taking place in the Americas that occasioned the transportation of hundreds of thousands of Africans to Cuba. The British captured Havana in 1762, and, as part of the agreement under which they handed the island back to the Spanish, they negotiated the opening up of Cuba to British trade and British capital. A few decades later, the Haitian Revolution (1791–1804) destroyed the largest sugar-producing economy in the world. The destruction of the sugar plantations in St. Domingue (Haiti), combined with the inflow of British and U.S. capital into Cuba, quickly made that island the leading sugar producer in the world. The demand for large numbers of field and factory hands for the Cuba's huge sugar plantations led to a massive importation of African slaves into Cuba between 1774 and 1865. Estimates are that close to a million slaves were brought to Cuba; of these, 850,000, or 85 percent, were brought in the nineteenth century, in spite of the fact that Spain had signed an accord with England prohibiting the trafficking of slaves in 1820.[7]

Though transplanted into a different geographical and social space, the Africans in Cuba devised means of keeping their cultural memories and practices alive. To begin with, in pre-emancipation Cuba, Catholic and civil laws gave some measure of legal protection to the slaves. Among these was the right to procure their freedom and the requirement that they be Christianized. By 1850, a third of the black population—almost a sixth of the overall Cuban population—was free. The presence of numerous persons from the same ethnic or cultural group facilitated the Africans' adaptation to their island home. In urban areas, the Africans, particularly the Yoruba, soon developed strong communities with guilds, social halls, and fraternities. These communities, which were organized along ethnic lines, kept alive the cultural beliefs and practices of Africa.

Though the *cabildos* might not have been initially linked to Catholic Church, the Church embraced them as a means of organizing the African population according to *naciones* (ethnic groups) for the purpose of religious instruction. Additionally, fear of pan-African solidarity and revolt and the need to develop a means of controlling the African population seem to have played a roll in the institutionalization of the *cabildos*.[8] In addition to their role in catechizing the Africans, the *cabildos* provided support for the aged and infirm, assisted members with funerals for their deceased, and raised funds to purchase the freedom of members. As social clubs, the *cabildos* sponsored various forms of entertainment: dancing, drumming, carnivals, and fiestas on holidays. Particularly noteworthy were elaborate processions and festivities sponsored by the *cabildos* on religious holidays, especially Epiphany, "*Dia de los Reyes*," when much attention was paid to black Melchior, who, according to Christian tradition, was one of the wise men who visited the baby Jesus.

In the *cabildos,* Afro-Cuban religious beliefs, music, and dance were pre-served, adapted, and developed. Whereas the Catholic establishment meant to use the *cabildos* for evangelization and social control, the Africans used them to preserve their ethnic identity and their African worldview and to ease their acculturation to their new home. Here the practice of hiding one's African beliefs in the guise of Roman Catholic iconography began. In time, every *orisha* in the Santería pantheon was associated with a Roman Catholic saint or other figure. St. Barbara, for example, came to be associated with Changó, the *orisha* of war. While the *orishas* became associated with the saints, the *orishas,* not the saints, were always the focus of ritual attention.[9]

In the mid- to late 1800s, several priests of Yoruba religious traditions facil-itated the entrenchment of Santería in both Havana and Matanzas. Among them were three notable priestesses: Obá Tero (Ma Monserrate "Apóto" González), who arrived in Cuba in the mid-1800s and was in the Matan-zas region; Latuán (Timotea Albear), a priestess of Changó who arrived in Matanzas 1863 but whose influence extended to Havana; and Efunshé (Ñá Rosalía Abreú), who worked with Latuán in Havana and who was known as a knowledgeable and effective priestess. Along with Latuán, Lorenzo (o Ciriaco) Samá was pivotal in unifying Yoruba-derived religion under the heading of Regla de Ocha.[10]

During Cuba's struggle for independence and in the post-independence era, the *cabildos* came under strong pressure as a result of several changes in the society. Viewed as part of the colonial structure and considered a reactionary organization, the Catholic Church found its ability to shelter the *cabildos* attenuated. Furthermore, the abolition of slavery meant the loss of the constant reinforcement of African religious beliefs and practices for-merly provided by a steady stream of new arrivals from Africa. The end of new recruits caused by the end of slave trafficking and the rise of intermar-riage or mating between persons of different ethnic groups eventually led to the disappearance of the ethnic basis of membership in the *cabildos.* As ritual initiation became the basis of memberships, the Yoruba tradition, or *Lucumi,* became the most widespread and dominant force in Afro-Cuban spirituality.

Though Africans in general and the *cabildos* in particularly supported the wars of independence (1868–1878 and 1892–1898), the leaders of independent Cuba feared that the *cabildos* might foment rebellion among the black popu-lation. Between 1885 and 1900, a series of official measures was put in place to regulate, monitor, and restrict the activities of the *cabildos.* These included annual licensing, oversight of each *cabildo* by a government official, and prohibition against drumming and street processions during *Dia de los Reyes*. A 1888 act effectively outlawed the organization of old-style *cabildos* and placed newly organized *cabildos* on the same legal footing as any other social club, thus removing their religious underpinning. The attempt, led by William George Emmanuel, to unify the *cabildos* into a national, social, and political force in late 1800s and the early 1900s produced an even greater fear of black insurrection among white Cubans. In the early 1900s, this heightened suspicion of black organizations, combined with a wave of nationalism in which Cuban attempted to establish a European cultural identity, produced even greater denigration of African influences on Cuban society and culture and efforts to eliminate them. These efforts include persecution of *cabildos*, confiscation of religious articles, proscriptions against the use of drums, and studies to understand and eliminate sorcery and witchcraft.[11] Official repression of Afro-Cuban culture and organizations found its most egregious expression in 1912 in the massacre of thousands blacks after the formation of the Cuban Independent Party of Color, which agitated for social and political reforms.[12]

Once the *cabildos* were outlawed, African religious were essentially driven underground. In the early 1900s, observation of the practices of Santería transitioned from the public *cabildos* to the private setting of the home, with each house (*ile*) "composed of a single extended 'ritual family' (*familia de santo*) directed by a single priestly elder who practiced within a private domicile in more or less discreet and underground fashion."[13] The founders of the early houses became significant figures in the history of Santería. These founders "gave birth" to ritual families and *ramas* (branches) of Santería, thus becoming foundational in the genealogy of the religion. One scholar traces all of Cuba's *babalawos* to five *ramas* established in the early 1900s: Ño Carlos Adé Bí (Ojuani Boká), Ño Remigio Herrera Adechina (Obara Melli), Joaquin Cadiz Ifá-Omí (Ogunda Tetura), Olugueré Kó Kó (Oyekún Melli), and Francisco Villalonga Ifá Bí (Obe Ate). Another significant figure was Bernardo Rojas Torres, who between 1915 and 1959 brought together and trained *babalawos* from the five *ramas*.[14]

The 1920s and 1930s saw a reappraisal of the African contribution to Cuban culture in the movement dubbed Afro-Cubanism (*Afro-Cubanismo*). Rejecting modernism, with its valorization of empiricism, science, and technological progress, Afro-Cubanism adjudged the "purer, nobler primitivity" of Afro-Cuban culture to be more indicative of humanity and more reflective of a healthy approach to life.[15] Afro-Cubanism, though short-lived as a movement, helped to remove the stigma from Afro-Cuban culture and facilitated the embrace of Afro-Cuban religion among whites and people of mixed race. Of course, prior to the 1930s, some whites and mixed-race persons had been involved in Santería either as initiates or as clients of the santeros.

While the Cuban Revolution elevated the status of blacks in several ways, its adoption of Marxist historical materialism, which saw religious beliefs as false consciousness, marked Afro-Cuban religious beliefs as obstacles to be eliminated in the pursuit of a Communist society. While the revolution had to work out an accommodative relationship with the Catholic Church, no such accommodation was granted to Afro-Cuban religion. Santería and other African-based religious traditions were effectively driven underground. Any public practice of these traditions was relegated to folkloric performances. Since the late 1980s, however, there has been a greater toleration and encouragement of Afro-Cuban culture and religion, though the government tends to package both as aspects of exotic Cuban culture.

Since 1950, Santería has become an increasing presence in the United States. The famed *babalawo* Poncho Mora (whose ritual name is Ifá Morate) migrated to the United States in 1946. Along with another migrant priest, he founded an *ile* (literally meaning house but also designating a Santería community or "family") in New York.[16] Mora and other priests took a number of persons back to Cuba for initiations. During the 1950s, several Cuban artists (especially drummers) living or performing in New York contributed to the strengthening of the Santería community by playing at ceremonies and by taking the music of Santería to the public in various performances.[17] The rush of exiles after the Cuban Revolution in 1959 and the Mariel boatlift of 1980 brought about 900,000 Cubans to the United States after 1960.[18] Though Cubans have adapted to their new home, they have maintained their Cuban identity and have preserved many aspects of their traditions (e.g., language, food, music). Among the elements of their culture that have been transplanted in the United States are the traditions and practices of Santería.[19] Santería itself has had to make adjustment to its new environment and to the conditions in its old home. One adjustment has been a move to initiate priests in the United States instead of taking them to Cuba. The first initiations were done in New York in 1961.[20]

At about the same time that Mora and other priests were introducing Santería in New York, the search for cultural roots led some African Americans to embrace Santería. The most famous adherent was Nana Oseijeman Adefunmi (Walter Eugene King), who was initiated as a priest of Obatalá in Mantanzas, Cuba, in 1959. In 1960, he founded the Yoruba Temple in Harlem, which introduced many African Americans to Santería and the Orisha tradition of the Yoruba in Nigeria. Adefunmi referred many African Americans to Cuban priests for initiation. His embrace of Vodou, probably through his association with Katherine Dunn, produced a kind of *Orisha*-Vodou hybrid in his temple.[21]

Since African Americans saw Santería as a means of affirming their African cultural and racial identity, the prominence of white Cuban priests and the use of pictures of white Catholic saints were very problematic to them. Furthermore, they could not appreciate the Cubans' commitment to the secrecy that surrounded religious ceremonies and practices, and the opening of a public temple by Adefunmi did not sit well with the Cuban priests. These tensions led many African Americans to look directly to Nigeria, instead of to Cuba, as the source of their practice of the Orisha tradition. The tensions continue today, as is evident in the refusal of some Cuban priests to acknowledge initiations done in Nigeria or by Nigerian priests, since they are construed as attempts to bypass their authority.[22]

Today, the largest communities of Santería practitioners in the United States are in Miami and in the New York-New Jersey area. However, most large cities in the United States have at least small numbers of practitioners. Estimates of the actual number of people committed to Santería in the United States varies from 250,000 to five million.[23] Cuban exiles, African Americans, Puerto Ricans, and Dominicans (from the Dominican Republic) make up most of the adherents, but persons of various other ethnicities are among the practitioners. Cuban exiles have also taken Santería to Puerto Rico, the Dominican Republic, and Central and South American countries.

Palo Monte

La Regla de Palo Monte, whose origins are Bantú (sub-Saharan African), is also known as Regla Congo. The name "Palo" comes from practitioners' use of branches and trees. While the various religions described as Reglas de Congo have their origins in the Congo region, in Cuba they have been decidedly influenced by the Yoruba religion. Unlike the Yoruba, whose mass arrival in Cuba occurred in the nineteenth century, the importation of Bantu speakers to Cuba spanned the entire period of the slave trade. The same sugar boom between 1835 and 1862 that resulted in the mass importation of Yoruban slaves to Cuba also led to the arrival of significant number of people from the lower Congo region. They were transported primarily to Cienfuegos, which was the heart of the Cuban sugar industry. Palo is considered the most syncretized of the Afro-Cuban religions and is often referred to as a *religion cruzada*, that is, a crossed or mixed religion.[24] Palo Monte thrived in the areas of Matanzas and Las Villas, where the *cabildos* practiced Congolese religions clandestinely. Palo Monte, the most well-known of the Congolese religions, must be situated within the other Congolese Reglas that have survived in Cuba. No scholarly consensus exists on the distinctiveness of each of the branches of Congolese religion, but their existence as discrete Congolese traditions is certain. Briyumba is popular in Havana and Matanzas and is very similar to Mayombe. Kimbisa, the most organized and hierarchical of the Congolese religions, is older and draws more heavily on Spiritism (belief in communication with the dead via mediums) and Catholicism. Kimbisa was founded by Andrés Facundo Cristo de los Dolores Petit, who lived in a Franciscan monastery and was a secular monk who practiced Catholicism and various Afro-Cuban religions. Regla Kimbisa combines Palo, Spiritism, Catholicism, and Regla de Ocha. The primary ritual object is a hollowed-out crucifix that contains the spirit of a dead person. The religion also has distinct musical instruments. Kimbisa temples include Christian iconography, including an altar to the religion's patron saint, San Luis Beltrán.

Of the three, Mayombe is the most widespread in Cuba (the name also refers to a religious tradition in present-day Angola). Congolese religion in Cuba cannot trace its heritage to the Congo in the same manner as Yoruba religion. We do not have a distinct lineage to parallel that which contemporary scholars have discovered for Yoruba. There is also significant diversity within Congolese religion in Cuba, and, while it has adopted elements of Yoruba religion in its mythology, its Bantu core remains intact. The first nine *nkisi* (or branches of Palo) were established in nineteenth-century Cuba in honor of the nine sacred clans of the Manikongo region of Bantu; two *nkisis* were founded in Pinar de Río, one in Havana, two in Santa Clara, one in Matanzas, one in Camagüey, and the last two in Oriente.[25] From them, the religion grew and spread to become Palo Monte as we know it today.

The transplantation of Bantu religion to Cuba and the creation of what we call Palo Monte is the result of three processes: "deculturation," or abandonment of certain cultural elements; "acculturation," or accommodation to European culture; and "neoculturation," or creation of other cultural elements. The anthropologists Jesús Fuentes Guerra and Grisel Gómez Gómez outline various elements of Bantu religion that remain in Palo. These include the cauldron at the center of Palo ritual (*prendaor nganga*), ritual initiation, anniversary rituals, the use of ritual drink (*chamba*), drumming and dances at funeral rites and to contact the dead and spirits, the use of animal sacrifice, offerings of food and beverages to the gods and spirits, use of herbal healing and cursing, baptism, presence of ritual assistants, magical actions based on different body parts (to do good and evil to oneself and to others), call of the spirits to authenticate initiation, use of sacred instruments, and lack of central organization. It is also a house religion, one in which religious ceremonies take place in the houses of adherents. Fuentes Guerra and Gómez Gómez also outline various elements of Palo that are foreign to African Bantu religion: in Cuba, the roles of healer and witch doctor are collapsed into one, a phenomenon that would never occur in Bantu, where they are distinct; Palo puts more emphasis on the *nganga* (ritual cauldron) itself than on the cult of the ancestors; Yoruba elements, especially of initiation and divination, have been incorporated into the tradition; and Catholic symbols, some Muslim terminology, and elements of other religious traditions have been adopted. Several elements of Bantu religion have been lost in Palo, most notably the practice of communal and familial rituals.[26] In Cuba, Palo Monte is often marginalized and castigated as a religion that performs witchcraft.

Palo Monte is a hierarchical religion with distinct roles for its ritual leaders. The *palanquero*, one who plays a singing role in ceremonies, is at the base of the Palo hierarchy. A *mansanero* gathers the items for rituals, serving as the *taata* (father) of a Palo family. The *yayi* is a *curandera* (spiritual or faith healer). The *bakunfula* is the apprentice to the *taata*. A family head who is a priest is called a *taata nkisi*. A *taata nganga* "is a priest who has initiated others who are now in their turn initiating a new generation of priests."[27]

The Palero's (practitioner of Palo Monte) transcendent God is Sambia, who is abstract and unreachable. Palo is an animistic religion that holds the number seven to be sacred. In addition, Paleros believe that there is a universal spirit named Nzambi, and this spirit has three aspects in Cuba: Mayombe, Brillumba, and Kimbisa. The universal spirit can manifest itself in human, animal, plant, and mineral forms. Everything, therefore, has a magical or spiritual element to it, because everything is a manifestation of Nzambi. After Sambia comes a pantheon of deities such as Tierra Tiembla, owner of the earth, and Lucero Mundo, Khuyu, who opens and closes pathways as Elegguá does in Santería. There are also the spirits of the ancestors, the dead, and the nature spirits that dwell in trees, plants, and rocks.

In their excellent introduction to Palo Monte, the anthropologists Jesús Fuentes Guerra and Armin Schwengler list seven components of the religion: (1) presence of a magical receptacle, called a *(n)ganga, enganga, prenda, (en) kisi, fundamento, caldero,* or *cazuela,* that contains different magical elements (vegetable, mineral, animal, human bones); (2) belief in spiritual entities that are associated with these receptacles (cult of the dead); (3) use of initiation rituals and rituals that mark rites of passage; (4) use of drums, songs, and dances; (5) use of animal sacrifice related to animistic beliefs; (6) use of food and beverage offerings to the spirits; (7) organization as a house religion with godparents (*tata nganga* and *ngudi nganga*).[28] As this last component indicates, Palo Monte is primarily a house religion (a religion whose worship spaces are in private homes), where the *Munanso,* or temple house, serves as the center of communal ritual life. A typical Palo society is headed by a shaman, a Congo Father or *tata nganga.* As was the case with Santería, after the suppression of the *cabildos,* temple houses emerged "in which the different lines or tendencies of the amalgamated Congo traditions merged and became even more complex and imprecise."[29] Along with this process came intermarriage between different tribal groups. This resulted in a Cuban Congolese ritual language that draws on various ethnic groups and also incorporates elements of the Spanish language.

Palo Monte Rituals and Practices

Palo Monte ritual centers around the *nganga.* In the Bantu religion, *nganga* refers to priests or ritual leaders; however, in Cuba it came to refer to the ritual cauldron used in Palo Monte ritual practices. This cauldron carries relics, most often a skull, of a deceased person with whom a priest has entered a ritual contract. For devotees of Palo Monte, "the *nganga* is said to represent 'the world in microcosm' over which the priest can exert control. To this end, a variety of sacrifices are offered the *nganga,* which is ideally kept in contact with the earth, either under a tree outdoors or in a shed."[30] The *nganga* also refers to the magical spirit that can be either good or evil and that is kept in the cauldron. In a sense, practitioners enter into a sacred relationship with their spirit. The older the spirit one possesses, the better. The *nganga* represents the liturgical core of Palo: "Without the *nganga* there is no Regla de Palo, no Mayombe; 'there is nothing.' Within it are contained all the *mpungus,* the saints or supernatural beings."[31]

Though *prendas* at times are referred to as *ngangas,* they are more appropriately seen as secondary to *ngangas. Prendas* are more like a talisman, though a *nganga* can be seen as a large or more powerful *prenda.* These cauldrons (*ngangas*) often contain human remains, trees, stones, shells, and iron objects. They *also* contain the spirit of the dead. Palo practitioners believe that human remains, as well as other material objects, have magical powers. When they are gathered in the cauldron, they gain a strong ritual power. Paleros are said to be able to perform magic through their control of their spirits.

A practitioner may have more than one *nganga*, and most Paleros have two or three. In order to make a *nganga*, one has to follow a complex ritual with various elements, many from the natural world, and enter into a pact with one's spirit. The cauldron is then buried for a period of time.[32] The *nganga* is said to contain three powers: its natural elemental power, the spiritual power of the human remains within it, and the divine power residing in the deity to which it is consecrated. The *mayombero* or Palero works with plants, animals, rocks, sticks—anything natural can be used in Palo rituals.[33] In this very animistic religion the Palero is the servant of nature.

To summon the spirit of a cauldron, one must write his or her *firma* (signature). The *firma* is written in white if it is to do good work (known as *trabajo cristiano*) and in coal if it is to do evil (*trabajo judío*). Not only does each supernatural being have a *firma;* so does each priest. Signatures are drawn on walls, on the ground, on cauldrons, on cloths, and on headbands worn by Paleros. As the art historian Robert Farris Thompson asserts, "The cosmogram of Kongo emerged in the Americas precisely as *signing and drawing points of contact between worlds*."[34] Also, some Paleros were known to make figures to attack enemies, such as their slave masters. This is perhaps the origin of the contemporary mythology behind the pop-culture voodoo doll.

Paleros also emphasize healing and the use of talismans. Unlike in Santería, where the *orishas* cannot be controlled by humans, in Palo spirits are manipulated by Paleros. Indeed, the manipulation of the spiritual realm is central to Palo Monte. This probably started in Africa, where the Kongolese did not have an understanding of good and evil as in Christianity, but instead believed in a power that is neutral and that can be manipulated for one's own self-interest (negative) or to the benefit of others (positive). Before the practice of driving nails was prominent, banging or striking a *nkisi* was the common way to induce a reaction. Young points out that the practice of nailing began at the turn of the eighteenth century and was a result of contact with the crucifix. For many Kongolese, Young argues, Christ was the most powerful *nkisi*, and they connected with his nailing on the cross. Young further contends that "both [crucifix and *nkisi*] were objects of power that were aroused/resurrected after being nailed and evidence suggests that many Kongolese understood the crucifix as yet another powerful *nkisi*."[35] The *nkisi* emerged in the Americas renamed *prenda* in Cuba, where it denoted the ritual cauldrons used in Palo.

Abakuá

La Sociedad Secreta Abakuá (Abakuá Secret Society) is one of the most mysterious and least studied of the Afro-Cuban religions. Its African origins may be traced to the Cross River region in the southern part of present-day Nigeria, to the Ejagham and Efik peoples. The word "Abakuá" itself "is apparently a Cuban creolized rendering of the Efik or Ejagham term Abakpa, reported to be an Ekoi (Ejagham) subgroup of the Cross River Area of West Africa."[36] The word "Abakuá" refers to the first or original residents. Members of the society are often called *ñáñigos*. The word *ñáñigo* comes from *nyan-nyan*, used to describe the dancing of some Abakuás. This society is made up of various lodges that exist outside the home. Its members are initiated with an oath to protect the sacred Voice of Ekue, a manifestation of God. Ekue is believed to be embodied in sacred drums.

Historically, Abakuá societies have been concentrated in the Havana and Matanzas provinces in Cuba, in the cities of Havana, Regla, Guanabacoa, Matanzas, and Cardenas, where they have been associated with dockworkers and unions in Cuba's ports. The following statement underscores the status of these societies in Cuban society: "In Cuba as in Africa, the system of lodges and the high cost of initiation gave Abakuá a character that was as much political and economic as religious. . . . They were highly hierarchical and disciplined in their internal procedures. The aura of secret mystical knowledge that surrounded members conferred further prestige and authority, and the lodges also accumulated significant earnings and financial resources."[37] This association of Abakuá societies with financial gain gave rise to the widespread belief that the societies control the docks, and some have likened them to the mafia. Despite, or perhaps because of, the political and economic clout of members of these societies, they have historically been a persecuted group since their emergence in the 1830s.

The Afro-Cuban ethnographer Lydia Cabrera traces the origins of the Sociedad Secreta Abakuá to Carabalí *cabildos* in Cuba. The members of the *cabildos* supported each other in the various social struggles they faced as a community. They also supported each other in maintaining their religious traditions, protecting the cult of Ekue and its secret rituals. The first society was founded in 1836 in Regla, the port just outside Havana. This first official society was named Efik Butón (meaning "divine voice of Efik"). At first, only Africans of pure race could enter the society, but eventually it was opened to those of "mixed blood."

Andres Petit, a mulatto, was key in these reforms; he founded the first Abakuá brotherhood of whites in 1857, which was officially sanctioned in 1863. He is remembered by some as a traitor for revealing the secrets of Abakuá to whites.

From their inception in Cuba, Abakuá lodges (known as *juegos*) raised the suspicion of Spanish officials. By 1882, there were, by police estimates, 83 *juegos* in Havana, some with white members, and overall membership was more than a thousand. They became associated with crime, gangster life, and *brujería* (witchcraft). In the late nineteenth century, during the wars of independence, the Spanish began a wave of deportations in an effort to suppress Afro-Cuban culture and traditions. Among those caught up were the *ñáñigos*, who were deported without trial to prisons in Africa as part of an effort to remove what the Spanish saw as witches from the island. The societies were also associated with pro-independence movements, and "[p]ro-Spanish *guerrilleros* often referred to Afro-Cuban insurgents as *ñáñigos*, an indication that they perceived them as criminals empowered with secret African magic rather than as separatists."[38] Abakuá was officially outlawed in 1876.

All Abakuá rituals are performed in secret, and outsiders are excluded as participants and observers. One can identify an Abakuá member by the ritual markings placed on the body at the time of initiation. These marks link the members of the *cabildo* throughout life and beyond it, connecting them in the afterlife to spirits and ancestors. Each group has thirteen to twenty members in leadership positions and an unlimited number of initiates, named *Abasekesongos*. Women are excluded from the society. The Abakuá's depiction of Ekue is that of a hypermasculinized warrior who detests anything feminine. In the words of Cabrera, "Ekue is a masculine figure, extremely strong, brave—earthly—that hates women and effeminate men, and only concedes his service to strong and brave men."[39] Some scholars link the exclusion of women to purity laws having to do with menstruation, though this has not been firmly established.[40]

Because of their high level of secrecy, very little is known about the ritual life of the Abakuá. Each *potencia* (the term literally means "powers" but refers to an Abakua group) celebrates rituals once a year. The purpose of this celebration is to pay homage to Ekue, feed him, and maintain his strength. Initiation and funeral rites, acknowledgment of leadership in the group, and the establishment of new organizations may also occur during the celebration. Abakuá ceremonies are always done in a temple. The temple is divided into two spaces, the *fambá*, where rituals are performed and only initiates can enter, and the *isaroko*, the patio where noninitiates can participate in some rituals. In the *fambá*, there is a small room called the *iriongo* where the sacred drum or *ékue* is kept. There are five principal types of Abakuá rituals (called *plantes*): initiation, elections (usually after someone has died), *refrescar una potencia*, funerals, and a rite to mark the birth of a new *potencia*. *Refrescar una potencia* refers to a problem or tension among members that must be addressed through religious ceremonies. It is said that in Africa the Abakuás practiced human sacrifice, but that never occurred in Cuba. Abakuá societies are widely known for their public dances.[41] These public dances are one of the few time when the public can witness Abakuá rituals, which include elaborate costumes and drumming. The Abakuá tradition has a form of ritual writing called *anaforuana* that is composed of sacred signs and tracings. These *firmas* (signatures) mark ritual space. There are four levels of ritual functionaries in Abakuá religion: *Isué* is the high priest; *Iyamba* is in charge of initiation and drumming; *Mokongo* oversees rituals in the outer temple area; and the *Isunekue* is the guardian of the sacred drum.[42]

Vodou and the Struggle for Survival

Vodou posits a dynamic and organic view of reality, in which all events and conditions, whether natural, spiritual, or social, are believed to be animated by spiritual forces. While recognizing a Supreme God called *Grand Mèt* or *Bon Dieu* (also *Bondyè*), Vodou centers on the *lwa*[43] or spirits that are the active agents *Grand Mèt* has placed in charge of the ongoing operation of the world. Collectively, they are the repository of the invisible power or energy that animates the world. All natural, social, and human phenomena, conditions, qualities, and activities are in some way expressions of their power and character.

A *lwa* should really be considered a family of spirits or a collectivity of various emanations or aspects of the same spirit. The *Gedes* (headed by *Bawon Samdi*), for example, is a family of spirits associated with the dead. The family of *Ezili* represents various aspects of womanhood, sexuality, or femininity: *Ezili Dantò* manifests the persona of protective mother; *Ezili Freda* embodies a flirtatious female sexuality; *Ezili Je-Rouge* exemplifies female anger or rage; *Grann Ezili* takes on the persona of an elderly woman; and *Ti-Jean Dantò* is an aspect of *Ezili Dantò* associated with trickery. *Legba*, the spirit of transition, who guards and opens gates, doors, and crossroads, as well as the path between the human and the spirit worlds, appears as *Papa Legba*, *Atibon Legba*, and *Mèt Kalfou*. The *Ogou* family is associated with the exercise of power; thus war, iron, and technology come under its control. The peasant *lwa*, *Azaka* (*Kouzin Zaka*, *Papa Zaka*) is lord of subsistence agriculture and a symbol of family. These and many other *lwa* are at the center of the Vodou cult. Furthermore, the integrative impulse of Vodou has led also to a fusion of the personalities of the *lwa* with their counterparts in Catholic hagiography, creating additional personae for the *lwa*.

Ceremonies and rituals are probably the most vital aspects of Vodou through which humans align themselves with the *lwa* whose power and energy are responsible for the events and activities of our world. This alignment takes place most forcefully through initiations ceremonies, ceremonies honoring the *lwa*, and healing ceremonies.

Initiation ceremonies cement and develop the individual relationship with the Vodou community and with the *lwa*. Vodouisants (adherents of Vodou) undergo a series of initiatory rites that progressively deepen their relationship with the *lwa* and provide them with the knowledge (*konesans*) of the working of the world of the spirits. Initiation ceremonies usually involve a ritual cleansing of the head (*lav tèt*) to strengthen and prepare it to receive the spirit of the *lwa*, a period of ritual and physical isolation (*kuche*) during which the initiate undergoes ceremonial death and rebirth, and investment or seating of one's governing *lwa* (*met tèt*) in one's head. Through these ceremonies, vodouisants assume the responsibility to honor and serve the *lwa* and secure the privilege of calling upon the *lwa* to assist them with life's challenges.

Vodouisants hold a numbers of ceremonies, collectively called services, in which they honor and feed the *lwa* and draw on their power to strengthen the community and its members to deal with their life circumstances. These services are convened on various occasions: on feast days of Catholic saints identified with corresponding *lwa*; when demanded by individual *lwa* during possessions or in dreams; according to family traditions of honoring and feeding its *lwa* and ancestors at certain times; and as expressions of gratitude to a *lwa* for their assistance in providing healing or some other good fortune. The services are convened in the sacred space of the *ounfo* (temple) called the *peristil*. At the center of the *peristil* is the *poto-mitan*, the center post, which is the symbolic nexus of sky, earth, and the underworld and the conduit through which the *lwa* enter the *peristil* to the take possession or "ride their horses." The high points of services are the *manjè-lwa* and the *dansè-lwa*. The *manjè-lwa* refers to the sacrificing of animals and the offering of the blood and portion of their carcasses, as well as other foods, as gifts to the *lwa*. During *dansè-lwa*, vodouisants dance to the drums' rhythms and sing songs of each *lwa* honored in the *ounfò*. During the playing of their rhythms, the *lwa* usually arrive to mount one or more of their "horses" (usually persons in whose head they have been seated during initiation). The possessing *lwa* temporarily displace the personality and consciousness of the persons who serve as their horses and use their bodies to communicate with the community. The possessed exhibit the mannerisms associated with the possessing *lwa*, speaking in their characteristic manner and dancing with their characteristic movements. Because of the volatile temperament of many *lwa*, the *oungan* or *manbo* (priest or priestess) controls and regulates their coming and going with the *ason*, the ritual rattle that is the symbol of the priest's or priestess's power.

The various healing rites of Vodou address physical and psychological maladies, problems with human relationships, issues of economic hardships, and all kinds of misfortune. Healing takes place in the context of individual consultation with Vodou priests (*ougans* or *manbos*) known for their ability to channel the power of the *lwa* to solve human problems. Healing rituals include diagnostic readings (usually using playing cards), ritual baths, various offerings to the *lwa*, the preparation and ingestion of various herbal concoctions, and the preparation of charms and protective packets (called *wangas* and *gardes*). The underside of Vodou is also populated with rituals, in which practitioners of sorcery known as *bokos* deploy supernatural forces to harm or heal.

Though its basic cosmology and orientations of Vodou are West African at its core, Vodou has woven a tapestry that includes Taino, Catholic, Masonic, and other elements. While Africans from numerous ethnic groups were represented among the enslaved in Haiti, religious elements from the Fon/Dahomey, the Yoruba, and the Kongolese came to dominate in Vodou. Most of the major spirits or *lwa*, a number of rituals and rituals implements (e.g., *govi*, *ason*, drums), and much of Vodou's vocabulary, including the word "vodou" (meaning spirit, invisible force, mystery) have their origin in the Fon/Yoruba religious system. The Kongolese (and the Angolans) also contributed a number of *lwa*, mostly of the *petwo* ("hot" or "fiery") variety, ancestor veneration, the cult of the dead, various charms or *gardes*, and the practice of sorcery to the Vodou ethos. Though the Tainos did not survive colonialism as a distinct ethnic group, traces of their culture survive in world of Vodou.[44] For example, scholars have traced *Azaka*, the beloved peasant *lwa* of agriculture, the *vèvès* as symbolic representations of the *lwa*, the use of sacred stones as repositories of the power of the *lwa*,the use of the *ason* as the sacred symbol of the priest's power, and the belief in *zombies* or the living dead to Taino origins.[45] The Catholic influence on Vodou is extensive, but the most readily observable elements are the identification of Vodou spirits with Catholic saints. For example, the Virgin Mary is regarded as a manifestation of *Ezili*, St. Jacques as *Ogou*, and St. Patrick as Dambala. On Vodou altars pictures and figures of Catholic saints often represent the *lwa*. In addition, Vodou services honoring the various *lwa* generally follow the Catholic ritual calendar, and Vodou ceremonies have adopted the lighting of candles, the use of holy water, the singing of hymns, the use of Latin words in the ritual language, and the recitation of Christian prayers and litany of the saints.[46] Another significant influence on the formation of Vodou is the Freemason secret society. Vodu appropriated the masonic title *"Gran Mèt"* or "Grand Master" to refer to the Supreme Being and the masonic handshakes and secret passwords as a form of ritual greetings. The most dramatic appropriation of masonic symbols is probably the black outfit and top hat associated with the persona of the *lwa* of the cemetery, *Bawon Samdi*.[47]

Vodou may thus be regarded as a form of cultural bricolage constructed from the broken pieces of Haitian history and society. For the masses of Haitians, it has become the only coherent system that provides them with a sense of themselves in the world. But this is not a static system that has remained frozen since its construction. It is remade and modified according the exigencies of the times. That is why Donald Cosentino, editor of *Sacred Arts of Haitian Vodou*, ascribes to Vodou an aesthetic that, like jazz, is "improvisational, never 'finished.'"[48] This "improv" has continued throughout a history of repression and resistance.

The first Africans began arriving in Hispaniola (as the Spanish called the whole island) in the early 1500s. Since the Spanish did not developed large-scale plantations on the island, their numbers remained relatively few until the western third of the island was ceded to France in 1697. During the next century, France made St. Domingue (Haiti) the most profitable sugar producer in the world. In the process, it secured the services of approximately 864,000 African slaves.[49] The harsh realities of plantation life are abundantly demonstrated by the fact that slaves lived an average of seven to ten years under the rigors of the system.[50] Though the French brought more than 860,000 Africans to the colony in the hundred years they ruled it, at the time of the Haitian Revolution, fewer than 500,000 were in the colony, an estimated two-thirds of whom were African born.[51] These statistics reveal that colonial Haiti was a virtual death camp for its huge African population.

Equally damaging to the African population were assaults on its cultural identity. Africans were subjected to concerted attempts to rid them of any vestige of their Africanness and to remake them into docile, compliant cogs in the wheel of the colonial machinery. To this end, the *code noir* (black code), which boasted a humane face allegedly for the protection of slaves' rights, demanded that all slaves be converted to and instructed in Catholicism. It further prohibited all religious practices except Catholicism. When African culture, especially religion, managed to rear its head, it was relentlessly suppressed and denigrated as full of superstitions, idolatry, and sorcery. Constant fear of slave uprisings led to the outlawing of slave gatherings, drumming, and dancing, and infractions led to arrests, fines, and corporal punishment.

Despite the repressive nature of the plantation society, Africans nurtured the desire for both physical and cultural freedom. To this end, they employed whatever means were available to them to preserve and perpetuate their sense of self. Ignoring the interdiction and condemnation of their religious practices, they sneaked into the woods in the middle of the night to perform their rituals and dances. These gatherings not only preserved African religious traditions and cultural identity but also served to establish a communal bond among people with diverse backgrounds. Even when they were inducted into Catholicism through forced baptism and indoctrinated in segregated parishes, the slaves soon learned to pursue their African religious practice within the ambit of Catholicism, especially through the association of the Catholic saints with *lwa* and the invoking of their powers according to their African religious outlook. As Cosentino suggests, the real conversion was not of the Africans to Catholicism but of elements of Catholicism to buttress African religiosity.[52]

Another means of resistance was to abscond and join with others to form maroon communities in the interior of the island, which was mostly inaccessible to the European authorities. Maroon communities were a constant threat to the stability of colonial government and the plantation system. These communities often served as bases and provided the leadership for rebellions and other forms of resistance against slavery. In the second half of the 1700s, the most famed maroon leader, François MacKandal, generated great fear among the slave masters and the colonial authorities, because of his reputation as a sorcerer who concocted potent magic potion and his ability as a charismatic leader who inspired rebellion among the slaves.[53]

Both maroon communities and Vodou were pivotal in the outbreak of the Haitian Revolution. Dutty Boukman, the initial leader of the revolution, was both a maroon leader and a Vodou priest. He and Cecile Fatiman, an elderly priestess, presided at the *petwo* ceremony at "Bois-Caiman" that served as a catalyst for the revolution in August 1791. According to tradition, the elder priestess, possessed by *Ezili Kawoulo, lwa* of lightning and thunder, sacrificed a pig and presented the blood to all those assembled while Boukman enjoined them to pledge to resist slavery to the point of death.[54] The spirit of resistance that Vodou embodied burst forth in a wave of violent activities that produced the most successful slave rebellion in the historical records of humankind.

In spite of Vodou's pivotal contribution to the revolution, it found itself subjected to repression and suppression by the political leadership that emerged from the revolution. Motivated by a desire to rid Haiti of its reputation for primitiveness and superstition and by the fear of the "revolutionary potential of the Vodou ceremonies,"[55] which could not be controlled institutionally, Toussaint L'Ouverture, Jean Jacques Dessalines, Alexandre Pétion, and Henri Christophe, who were leaders in Haitian Revolution and who served as the first five heads of state of independent Haiti, all embraced Catholicism as the national religion and sought to suppress Vodou in order to gain international recognition and respectability. While President Jean-Pierre Boyer (1818–1843) paid little attention to Vodou in the early years of his rule, his penal code, enacted in 1835, named Vodou among the superstitions that were illegal.[56] Vodou, however, was too deeply entrenched to be uprooted.

The Vatican's refusal to acknowledge Haitian independence and to send priests to fill the parishes left vacant by priests who died in the revolution or who fled the country reduced the influence of the Catholic Church to an all-time low.[57] In this atmosphere, Vodou thrived among the Haitian populace, though most people openly professed to be Catholic. Ironically, the policies of Haitian political leaders in the early 1800s contributed to the entrenchment of Vodou in the rural areas. Dessalines's "militarized agriculture," forced labor aimed at reviving the devastated agricultural economy; Petion's land grants to soldiers; and Boyer's 1826 rural code, which restored to mulattoes lands lost during the revolution drove many into deep rural areas, where they eked out a marginal subsistence from the land but were relatively free to engage in and develop their practice of Vodou.

During the presidency of Faustin Soulouque (1847–1860), a Vodou devotee, Vodou enjoyed a reprieve from official repression. After the overthrow of Soulouque, in 1860, the new president, Fabre Nicolas Geffrard, and the Vatican were able to resolve the conflicts between the state and the Church, thus opening the way to a renewal of the influence of the Catholic Church on the life of the nation. In tandem, the Church and the state carried out repeated campaigns aimed at stamping out the religious superstitions and political threats of Vodou. Concerted campaigns were carried out in 1864, 1896, and 1912. During the U.S. occupation from 1915 to 1935and shortly thereafter (1940–1941), Vodou was again the object of repressive measures. In response to the *corvée*, a forced-labor system employed by the U.S. Marines for a public infrastructure building program, the peasantry, under the leadership of Charlemagne Péralte, rose up in a revolt inspired by the spirit of resistance in Vodou. Since the Marines associated the rebels with Vodou, their campaign against the uprising was in a sense a campaign against the practice of Vodou. In the aftermath of the U.S. occupation, the Haitian social, religious, and political elite joined together in yet another effort to dislodge Vodou from Haitian peasant life.[58]

Beginning in the 1920s, some Haitian intellectuals of the *noirist* (black consciousness) movement began to advocate a reappraisal of Vodou, contending that it represented the authentic culture of the masses and should be made the basis of Haitian nationalism. Eventually, in 1946, a *noirist*, Dumarsais Estimé, became president of Haiti, succeeding Élie Lescot, who was the architect of the 1940 to 1941 campaign against Vodou. Under Estimé, Vodou was no longer subject to political suppression and was celebrated as the culture of the Haitian people. However, staged Vodou ceremonies with chants and dances for the entertainment of tourists and the urban elite tended to "folklorize" the religion.

François Duvalier, a member of the *noirist* movement, was elected president of Haiti in 1957, and after changing the Haitian constitution to make himself president for life, his dictatorial rule lasted until his death in 1971, after which he was succeeded by his son, Jean Claude Duvalier. While Duvalier was an advocate of Haitian nationalism based on the culture of the black masses, he seemed most interested in coopting and controlling Vodou as he did the army and the Catholic Church. He portrayed himself as the embodiment of Vodou powers to instill fear in the peasant class and enlisted numerous Vodou priests into his vast network of secret police organization, called the *Tonton Macoutes*, who used terror to quell the smallest inkling of opposition to the Duvalier regime.[59] When Jean-Claude Duvalier was exiled in 1986, a wave of terror was unleashed against Vodou in general and Vodou priests in particular. As part of the *dechoukaj* (uprooting), the attempt to rid Haiti of all those believed to be complicit in the horrors of the dictatorship of the Duvaliers, mobs murdered numerous Vodou priests and destroyed Vodou temples, sacred implements, and symbols.[60]

Surviving the *dechoukaj*, Vodou has once again gained recognition as an essential component of Haitian culture. Freedom of religion enshrined in the new Haitian constitution of 1987 and the support of Father Jean-Bertrand

Aristide, elected president in 1990, have ensured the right of vodouisants to practice their religion without political and religious reprisal. Haitian politics remains volatile, as exemplified by the political career of Aristide, who was overthrown and exiled in 1991, returned to power between 1994 and 1996,was re-elected in 2001, and served till 2004, when he was forced into exile again. However, Vodou continues to enjoy official religious freedom and some Vodou priests have been granted the rights to perform marriage ceremonies and the privilege to officiate at civic and state ceremonies. Vodou has thus traveled the long road from the clandestine, nocturnal meetings of African slaves on the plantations and from the cloistered meetings of their maroon counterparts in their interior hideouts, through waves of suppressions, campaigns of terror, and ideological assaults, to a more accepted, if insecure, existence in Haitian society. Though the continued fragility of Haitian political, economic, and social life makes the return of terror a constant threat, for the moment Vodou is not only accorded the right of religious freedom but is celebrated for its contribution to Haitian culture, particularly in music and the visual arts.

Espiritismo

Though not exactly a religion per se, Espiritismo is one of the most distinctive dimensions of Caribbean religion. Espiritismo is best described as a religious metaphysics or worldview. The story of Espiritismo and its arrival in the Americas is a fascinating tale of the belief systems of an elite, educated in Europe, that transformed the religious landscape of the population as a whole. Espiritistas believe that there is a spirit world that interacts with the material world. Spirits exist in a hierarchy: the lower spirits remain attached to the material world, are ignorant, and try to do harm to human beings; the highest level of spirits, called *espíritus de luz* (spirits of light), protect humanity through their higher state of spiritual perfection. Espiritismo embraces a dualistic model of humanity in which people consist of a body and spirit, though one's essence is located in one's spirit. After death, one moves on to another plane, yet one's spirits still have the ability to develop both morally and spiritually. Espiritistas also believe in reincarnation and the notion that actions in one's past lives shape one's present one. Spirits also have the ability to control human beings, sometimes in a very negative fashion.[61] The material world in which humans live has a direct relationship with the spiritual plane. Spirits interact, communicate, and influence people. Caribbean Espiritismo has its roots in France, where the writings of a French educator, Hippolyte Léon Denizard Rivail, became a critical alternative for Latin Americans who were studying in Europe and who were disenchanted with the Roman Catholic Church.

Rivail (1804–1869), popularly known as Allan Kardec, was a well-known scholar of pedagogy when he began to study spirit mediumship. These studies cemented his beliefs in reincarnation, the astral body (a spiritual body in addition to a physical one), and communication with spirits through mediums. Reincarnation is linked to Kardec's notion of the moral progression of the soul through the many lives we live. Kardec believed that the soul became increasingly elevated or evolved morally as it became incarnated in its different lives. The central text within Kardecan Spiritism is his *Book of the Spirits*, which is structured as a collection of questions posed by the author to the spirits. Among the many spirits that Kardec claimed helped him to write this book are Augustine, Plato, John the Baptist, and Ben Franklin.

Within Kardecan Spiritism, mediums serve the purpose of mediating the spirit and material worlds and everyone has the ability to become a medium. For Kardec, there was a visible and an invisible world, one with incarnated spirits, the other with disembodied ones. Spirits go through a process of incarnation until they advance to a nirvana-like state. The nonincarnated and embodied spirits are linked, sometimes due to past lives. We all have spiritual guides that serve as our teachers and guardian spirits. We can also fall under the influence of lowly spirits, *enviaciones*, which can cause us to do wrong.

Rooted in rationalism and romanticism, Kardec's Spiritism offers a synthesis of nineteenth-century European thought. He drew from a variety of religious, philosophical, and intellectual traditions: esoteric tradition, Indic philosophy, Protestant theology, Catholicism, social reformism, and science.[62] Kardec rejected the Christian notions of the Trinity, Christ's divinity, and the physicality of heaven and hell. In spite of his rejection of several key Christian beliefs, Espiritismo became, for Latin Americans, a manner of being Catholic without remaining connected to the institutional Church.

Román dates the diffusion of Spiritism in Cuba to the 1860s when the elite Cuban classes got access to Kardec's writings. The first international congress of Spiritists in 1898 in Barcelona had three Cuban representatives.[63] The first Cuban Espiritista society (Sociedad Espíritista de Cuba) was founded in 1915, and a national federation of Espiritistas was established in 1936. Despite this level of organization, there is a great amount of diversity within the practices labeled as Espiritista, often determined by the social class of the practitioners and the religious traditions they fold into Espiritista beliefs.

The expression of Kardecan Spiritism in Cuba is often described as *Cordoneros*, which began in the colonial era. "*Cordonero* describes the manner in which people are joined by a spiritual chain that helps enhance communication with the spirit world. . . . *Cordoneros* reach into the world of the spirits mentally and make contact with the spirits so that mediums at the earthly level can speak for these spirits."[64] The name *Espiritismo de cordon* comes from the ritual of standing in a circle holding hands, walking counterclockwise and chanting and praying as practitioners beat their feet and swing their arms until they fall into a trance. Water plays a significant role in their practices. It is used to ritually purify and is said to give clarity. As a result, in pictures, the deceased, Mary, and the saints often have glasses of water placed in front of them. *Cordoneros* do not have a structured set of beliefs or practices, and initiation is not required.

Román categorizes Espiritismo in Cuba into two branches: the elite academic branch associated with cities and the more "superstitious" type associated with the countryside.[65] However, such distinctions are usually made by the elites themselves. Róman points out that Espiritismo arrived in Cuba as a hybrid of practices. The historian Christine Aroyinde, conversely, describes three types of Espiritismo in Cuba: the urban, elitist, philosophical branch that emphasizes mediums and is closely aligned with Kardec's teachings; the rural, lower-class *Espiritismo de cordon,* which includes séances, ritual cleansings, and healing; and *Espiritismo cruzado,* which is mixed with Afro-Cuban traditions.[66] *Espiritismo cruzado* is most clearly found in the incorporation of Espiritismo into Santería rituals. The boundaries between the various Espiritista practices are much more fluid, and the philosophy of the elite has influenced the folk practices of rural Espiritistas.

The roots of Espiritismo in Puerto Rico are in the nineteenth century, when middle-class boys were sent to Europe for their education and came under the influence of Allan Kardec. Espiritismo was embraced by liberals who saw it as an attractive alternative to colonial Catholicism. The first Espiritista groups in Puerto Rico met clandestinely and were thought to be organizing revolutionary activities. The first Espiritista center, *Luz del Progreso* (Light of Progress), was founded in 1888 in Mayagüez. Groups also began to publish magazines and become involved in educational reform. Though Espiritismo began in Puerto Rico as a middle-class intellectual movement that emphasized its philosophical and social framework, among the lower classes the healing dimension of Espiritismo was its greatest appeal. This Espiritismo was a mixture of Catholicism, Kardecan Espiritismo, faith healing, and herbal medicine.[67] Folk healing predates the arrival of Kardec's Espiritismo, seen for example in the practice of *Santiguos* (healing hand massages). This emphasis on healing is in sharp contrast to traditional Kardecan Spiritism; Kardec was wary of any reference to healing as any sort of miracle.

The transmission of Spiritism in Puerto Rico came through books and pamphlets brought by students studying in European universities. Spiritists were associated with masons and liberals and were very anticlerical. A distinction was made between *Espiritistas* (true Spiritists) and *Espiriteros* (spirit mongers). The former were seen as scientific and rational, the latter as superstitious. The center of Espiritista ritual life is the meeting, where a medium contacts spirits and tries to help the participants. This occurs at a table covered with a tablecloth on which are placed water, images of saints, flowers, cigars, and other ritual objects. Often an excerpt from Allan Kardec's *The Gospel According to Spiritism* is read at the beginning. Mediums try to determine whether someone is trying to harm a person and if the person is ill; they also attempt to determine whether the cause is spiritual or physical. In addition to these more formal Espiritista gatherings, Espiritismo has become part of the texture of everyday Caribbean religion.

The encounter of African diaspora religions with Christianity marked the eighteenth and nineteenth centuries in Caribbean religious development. The mass importation of slaves to Cuba, the freedoms of a newly independent Haiti, and the introduction of Espiritismo created a textured religious landscape that led to the mingling of religious symbols, ideas, and rituals. It was in this era that the distinctions among African religions, Catholicism, and Espiritismo began to blur. While this era was marked by the emergence of distinctive religious traditions in the Caribbean, these distinctive traditions drew from and cross-fertilized other traditions. In the case of African diaspora religions, it was only in the twentieth century that their adherents would truly expand beyond black populations. As we explore in chapter 9 of this book, in the twentieth century questions of race, identity, institutionalization, and authenticity would come to plague these religions.

Afro-Christian Faiths

Revival Zion and Spiritual Baptists

The historical trajectories of Revival Zion in Jamaica and Spiritual Baptists in Trinidad (and other eastern Caribbean islands) provide salient examples of cultural convergence, adaptation, and agency at the Caribbean crossroads. These faiths arose from the meeting of various religious traditions from Africa and Europe in the Caribbean arena. They also emerged from the need of Africans under slavery to fashion a cohesive worldview and a cultural identity that reflected their African heritage and the realities of their lives on the plantations. Once formed, these traditions never became static cultural artifacts but were dynamic, evolving traditions that responded to new influences and adapted to the changing realities in the region.

Revival Zion and Spiritual Baptists may be considered as Afro-Christian (or African-Christian) because, while the adherents of these traditions unambiguously identify themselves as Christians, they retain African orientations and aesthetics in the way in which they understand and deploy their faith to deal with the exigencies of life. Unlike Creole African religions such as Vodou and Santería that retain African pantheons of a Supreme God and a host of lesser deities that govern the various natural and social forces, Afro-Christian traditions such as Revival Zion and Spiritual Baptists abandoned these, affirming belief only in the Christian God of Father, Son, and Holy Spirit. However, Revival Zion and Spiritual Baptists tend to understand and relate to these entities in a manner reminiscent of African religions. The Father, while acknowledged as the creator and all-powerful sovereign of the universe, is not the central focus of ritual attention. He is somewhat transcendent and removed from the milieu of everyday life. Jesus and the Holy Spirit are the vital presences that are believed to empower and sustain the lives of adherents as they struggle to sustain themselves spiritually, socially, and materially in this world. In addition, a host benevolent and malevolent spirits, including the spirits of dead, inhabit the world of Revival Zion and

Spiritual Baptists. Furthermore, unlike their more "orthodox" Christian counterparts in the Caribbean, Revival Zion and Spiritual Baptists do not emphasize a rational-ethical orientation to their Christianity that stresses correct belief and correct behavior but are more oriented to having experiences of the divine in the body and marshalling spiritual resources to deal with aspects of everyday existence such as health issues, material resources, and social relationships.

Revival Zion

Revival Zion is a folk religion—that is, it emerged from and among the common people—that was forged by Jamaica's black population as it imbibed various African and European influences between 1655 and the 1860s. The roots of this folk religion go back to the twin conjuring and healing traditions of Obeah and Myal, the Native Baptist movement that merged Christian and African religious elements, the spirit possession cult of Kumina brought to Jamaica by African indentured workers after emancipation, and evangelical revivals in Jamaica in the 1860s. Since its emergence, Revival Zion has been further shaped by the ministry of the charismatic Alexander Bedward and the proliferation of evangelical and Pentecostal sects in Jamaica in the 1900s.

Obeah and Myal

The religious ethos of the slaves by the mid-1700s consisted of a juxtaposition of an aggressive magical tradition called Obeah and a more palliative healing tradition called Myal. Most scholars have traced the etymology of the word "obeah" to *obayifo* or *bayi,* meaning witch or wizard, from the Twi language of West Africa. Others point to the Efik word *ubia,* which refers to elements of a charm intended to inflict harm, as the derivation of the word. At least one scholar, the sociologist Orlando Patterson, points to another Twi word, *obeye,* as the root of the Jamaica word "obeah."[1] Some scholars have identified the etymological root of Myal with *maye,* a Hausa word referring to sorcery or intoxication, presumably also connoting the ecstatic or trance-like state of spirit possession. However, Dianne Stewart, an expert on African elements in Jamaican folk religions, makes a strong argument for a Central African Kikongo origin of the word "myal." She traces the root of Myal to *mayâla,* meaning "one who leads/rules," and/or *mwela,* meaning "breath" or "breathing power." She goes on to argue that *mwela* is the cosmic energy that a leader is able to activate to address a community's problems.[2] We have no conclusive answer about the exact origins of these words and the ideas and practices they denote. In fact, given the tendency to adopt and adapt various influences in the religious ethos of these slaves in the mid-1700s, we should probably postulate a theory of multiple origins. The beliefs and practices of both Obeah and Myal reflect traditions and practices that were and are widespread in West and Central Africa.

The historical sources of the 1700s and the early 1800s often conflate Obeah and Myal, either describing them as the same or making Myal a subcategory of Obeah. This has led Stewart to propose that Obeah was a generic term referring to the African religiosity of the slaves in general. She goes on to argue, on the basis of written reports from the late 1700s and early 1800s, that the assumed antagonism between Obeah and Myal was not necessarily true in the religious ethos of Jamaica's black population prior to the Myalist anti-Obeah campaigns of the 1840s and 1850s.[3] Admittedly, these sources conflate Obeah and Myal. However, they are not the kind of sources that can support so fine a theoretical point. The conflation is more likely a result of the ignorance of European writers who did not understand the intricate workings of the religious ethos of the slaves. As late as the 1840s, the Baptist missionary James Phillippo admitted that the Myalists did not disclose all their secrets to those outside their religious community.[4] Furthermore, most early reports given by Europeans are marked by the ethnocentric assumption that African traditions are primitive, superstitious, and uncivilized, and hence to be lumped together as sinful. Even more important, the antagonism between Obeah and Myal is most likely a carryover of the African distinction between the malicious and socially destructive activities of witches and wizards and the healing or palliative activities of African medicine men and women. If the antagonism is not somewhat endemic, then it is difficult to explain the Myalists' campaigns against Obeah in the 1840s and 1850s. Even though these efforts may have been fueled by Christian rejection of sorcery and by the economic afflictions of the period, they only acerbated the embedded antipathy of Myalists toward the practitioners of Obeah, who were seen as inimical to the community and as responsible for the afflictions many were facing, including a spate of deaths.[5] Interestingly, the Myal "outbreaks" were equally aimed at the planters, missionaries, and other community members deemed responsible for or complicit in the hardships that the newly emancipated were facing.[6]

Obeah and Myal can be considered to have existed in the same complex of religious ideas and practices that came to inform and reflect the Afro-Jamaican view of the world. Obeah, as an aggressive form of magic or witchcraft, relied on the knowledge and skills of an expert to manipulate spiritual powers and the secrets of herbs and other substances to fulfill the wishes and desires of consulting clients. These wishes and desires could call for the deployment of forces to inflict harm or even death on an enemy or on someone toward whom the consulting client felt some form of malice or envy. They might also involve seeking success in relationships or gaining wealth through one's occupation, business, or gambling. Illnesses, especially those of a chronic nature, also brought people to experts in Obeah in search of therapeutic relief. An expert in the practice of Obeah was thus consulted by someone "wishing to effect some change in his or her life: reach a specific goal, awaken someone's affection, seek revenge for an evil done, obtain protection from a 'fix' by another Obeahman, or change his [or her] luck."[7] Therapeutic or protective treatment might involve some combination of taking herbal baths; ingesting herbal concoctions; and wearing charms made of herbs, animal bones or blood, and human matter such as hair or bodily fluids. Aggressive Obeah, intended to inflict harm, could involve the burying of substances in the yards or the paths of the victims or catching and imprisoning their shadows, believed to be the doubles of their souls or personalities.

In the Jamaican context, therefore, those versed in the art of Obeah came to be recognized as experts for hire, and as such their activities were believed to be guided more by desire for personal gain than by concern for the welfare and well-being of the community. They were and are both respected and feared because of the mysterious powers they possessed and their ability to release destructive forces in the community. Fear sometimes turned to loathing, especially when the practitioners of Obeah were believed to be engaged in extraordinarily egregious acts.

Unlike Obeah, with its individual practitioners sought out by individual clients, Myal involves a community of worshippers relating to the spirit world through ritual means. While subsuming Myal under Obeah, sources from the both the 1700s and 1800s recognized the corporate nature of Myal by describing it as "a kind of society" and "a secret fraternity."[8] They also reveal that the typical ceremony of the Myalists was the "Myal dance," a high-energy dance accompanied by drumming and singing. The goal of the dance was to induce a trance state or possession by supernatural agents. Observers of this dance attributed the inducement of the trance state to the use of certain powders, "narcotic potions," potent liquor, and "excessive dancing and uses of poisonous drugs." Describing those in the trance state as "dead" or deprived of "sensibilities," these observers tell how the "dead" were brought back to "life" when they were fed or anointed with certain herbs.[9]

The purpose of the Myal dance was to connect the participants to sources of spiritual or cosmic energy. This energy from the deities and the spirits of the dead (ancestors) was regarded as the source of healing of physical maladies, interpersonal strife, and economic distress. These conditions were often believed to be the results of malicious sorcery (Obeah) or the malevolent spirits. Even the state of enslavement was attributed to the strong sorcery of white men. Thus, Myal was not a religious tradition that sought to prepare people for a better life in the hereafter but a religious practice aimed at equipping its members to deal with everyday personal and community problems and with the greatest evil of all, their enslavement and exploitation on colonial plantations. In addition to the Myal dance, Myalists sought healing, protection, and empowerment through individual consultation with ritual experts. Like Obeahmen, the Myalmen, as these experts were called, were knowledgeable about the pharmacopeia of herbs and skilled in establishing contacts with the supernatural realm. However, their services were available only for curative and protective purposes, not for malicious or injurious ones. Since the Obeahman and the Myalman operated in the same sphere of spiritual and herbal knowledge, the distinction was not always clear, and the lure of personal reputation and financial gain may have enticed some Myalist experts into the practice of aggressive and malicious magic. In this case, they operated like the *boker*, the Vodou religious expert who practices with "both hands," doing both good and evil.

During the slave era, both Myal and Obeah were in themselves expressions of cultural resistance. Drawing upon African heritage, they constituted a religious ethos with beliefs and practices that countered the Christian ethos of the dominant class. Though conquered physically, exploited economically, and dominated politically, the slaves exercised the freedom of their minds and drew upon the memory of their past to fashion beliefs and practices that enabled them to understand and endure their current afflictions. In plotting and executing revolts against the slave system, rebels often drew upon the resources of Myal and Obeah. Speaking of the emergence of a pan-African religious ethos in the mid-1700s, the historian Monica Schuler asserts that "believing these evils to be caused by sorcery, this religious tradition claims to have the weapons with which to eradicate them." She continues, "This tradition has been a powerful catalyst for Afro-Jamaican resistance to European values and control. It also explains why sociopolitical protest has usually been expressed in religious terms in Jamaica."[10] The Tacky Rebellion of 1760, the most significant slave uprising of the 1700s in Jamaica, clearly demonstrated how the evolving religious ethos provided inspiration and resources for resistance to British domination. Tacky, the chief fomenter and leader of this revolt, prepared his fighters by administering a sacred oath and providing them with a potion that should make them invulnerable to European weaponry. In responding to this uprising, the colonial authorities passed laws outlawing Obeah, citing its complicity in rebellion that engulfed much of the island. Of course, no distinction was made between Obeah and Myal, making any African-inspired religious practice susceptible to prosecution. The most notable uprising of the 1800s, the "Baptist War" of 1831–1832, was masterminded and orchestrated by leaders in the Myal tradition, most notably Daddy Sharpe (Sam Sharpe).

Myal and the Native Baptist Movement

Beginning in the late 1700s, elements of Christianity were increasingly grafted onto Myal and, to a lesser extent, Obeah. Incorporation of Christianity into Myal came about through the influence of George Liele and Moses Baker, the African American Baptists who brought the Baptist faith to the Jamaica's black population, slave and free. Though Liele and Baker were Christians, their preaching and worship had the flavor of African aesthetic sensibilities that became characteristic of black Christianity in the American South. This included lively call-and-response singing, vehement and demonstrative preaching, and ecstatic emotional displays. What is more, Liele seems to have cultivated an African-centered identity or a kind of Ethiopianism for himself and his group, often commencing his sermons with "Arise ye sons of Ethiopia" and citing biblical references to Africa and Ethiopia. In fact, before migrating to Jamaica, Liele had been partly responsible for establishing the "First African Baptist Church" in Savannah, Georgia.

Among the black population in Jamaica, both the free and the enslaved, the response to the preaching of Liele and Baker was enthusiastic, and many embraced Christianity. However, it was soon apparent that the new converts were interpreting and practicing their newfound faith through the lens of Myal. While they adopted the Christian cosmology and revered the biblical personalities, they were still oriented to experience God or the Holy Spirit in the body during worship services, and this was demonstrated in ecstatic emotional displays. Furthermore, instead of focusing on receiving some kind of abstract forgiveness for sin and cultivating moral lives in the European mode, new converts deployed their Christianity for the healing of personal and community ills. Even Myalists and Obeahmen who did not convert to Christianity began to adopt and employ elements of Christianity in their rituals. For example, the rite of baptism by immersion was adopted by Myal as a rite of initiation. The Bible itself became a kind of magic object, and certain passages could be invoked in healing or magical incantation.

A combination of the rapid growth of the Baptist faith they introduced, the difficulties involved in ministering to the slave population under the restrictions imposed by colonial authorities and individual planters, and their inability to impose and maintain discipline among their converts led Liele and Baker to appeal to the Baptist Missionary Society in London for assistance. Responding to this request, the London Baptists started sending missionaries to Jamaica, beginning with John Rowe in 1813.[11] Along with expanding the evangelization and religious instruction of the black population, the missionaries were charged with countering the "excess" of Africanisms and the "unruliness" on the part of the rapidly growing congregations of Baptists in the island. The missionaries' attempt at reining in what they considered fanaticism and superstition was only partly successful. Many who were members of the Baptist church controlled by the missionaries were often also active in the Myalist cult. The most salient example of this was Sam Sharpe, who spearheaded the 1831–1832 slave rebellion known as the "Baptist War" or the "Native Baptist War." Sharpe was both a deacon in the Baptist Church and a "daddy" or leader of a Myalist group. He used the networks he had established in both to plan and execute a massive slave revolt that is believed to have hastened the abolition of slavery in the British Caribbean. In addition, a number of converts who had become leaders of congregations under the supervision of Liele or Baker refused to submit to the authority of the missionaries and maintained their own networks of congregations, known the Native Baptists, that retained the emotionality and expressiveness characteristic of Myal religious services.

The immediate post-emancipation era was marked by the "Myal outbreaks" of 1840s and 1850s. This was a resurgence of Myalism aimed at the eradication of the hardships and afflictions that Afro-Jamaicans faced in the wake of the failed promises of emancipation. As Schuler points out, in Myal understanding of cause and effect, these hardships and afflictions were attributed to the malice of humans and spirits.[12] Thus, as we have seen, one aspect of this Myal resurgence was a series of campaigns to rid communities of Obeah in 1841 and 1842 and again in the 1850s. The first of these ritual cleansings of communities occurred in St. James, on the northwest coast of Jamaica. In a community close to Montego Bay, the death rate among young males seems to have been on the rise for about ten years. Concerned about the inexplicable rise in the number of deaths, community members decided that evil was at work and invited Myalists from nearby to rid the community of the Obeah that was responsible. Soon, other communities were commissioning their own cleansings. Before long, the anti-Obeah campaign spread to sugar estates in St. James and Trelawny and popped up in such faraway places as St. Thomas in the east and Westmoreland in the west. Cleansing a community of Obeah involved ingesting an herbal concoction, singing and dancing until the onset of spirit possession, and then, at the direction of the spirit, proceeding to discover and unearth the objects that had been deployed by Obeahmen to cause harm. In some such cleansings, offending individuals were also identified and required to confess and to disavow any future involvement with Obeah.[13]

Schuler argues that these outbreaks were not only or primarily about ridding these communities of individuals who practiced malicious sorcery. She demonstrates that they were in fact responses to the failure of emancipation to improve the life conditions of Afro-Jamaicans. The combination of low-paying work on the sugar estates, the difficulty of eking out a living on marginal lands, and inauspicious droughts activated the Myalist sense of afflictions as resulting from malicious activities of humans and/or malevolent spirits. This also activated their sense that countervailing action was needed. Couching their discourse in "prophetic and Millennial terms," these Myalists saw themselves as doing "the work of the Lord" and "clearing the land for Jesus." The implication is that they were preparing Jamaica for the appearance of Jesus to bring about the economic and social liberation promised but not delivered by emancipation.[14]

What is more, the Myal activities were an implicit if not a direct challenge to both planters and missionaries. Citing the fact that while doing the "Lord's work" the Myalists were unavailable for work on the plantations and that they were repeatedly accused of "disturbing the peace," Schuler suggests that the Myal outbreak in 1841–1842 amounted to "industrial action." Perceiving the activities as such, the planters called in the police to squelch Myal ceremonies. Furthermore, when the missionaries resorted to the condemnation of the Myalist activities, characterizing them as a display of madness, the Myalists stood their ground, arguing that God had spoken to them as he had to the prophets in the Bible and accusing Christian ministers of not performing baptism properly. In some cases, Myalists even attempted to gain control of Christian meeting houses on sugar estates and succeeded in at least one case.[15]

The repeated outbreaks of Myalist activities in the 1840s and 1850s were met with repressive measures by colonial authorities. The repression eventually drove Myal underground. Interestingly, while these outbreaks and repressions were taking place, new Africans were arriving in Jamaica with their own religious traditions that would reinforce and adopt elements of religious ethos of Myal.

Kumina and the Myal Ethos

After the emancipation of slaves in the British Caribbean, in 1838, the plantations faced a looming labor problem. Many former slaves abandoned the estates to settle in villages where they survived mainly through subsistence farming. Even though many continued to work on estates, they were now a free labor force that could negotiate wages according to supply and demand. To address this problem, the planters turned to indentured laborers from Africa, Asia, and even Europe. Most of the African indentures brought to Jamaica were of Kongolese origin and were taken from Spanish and Portuguese slave trading vessels that were interdicted by British navy ships trying to enforce the abolition of the slave trade. The "recaptives," as these Africans seized from slave trading ships were called, were taken to Sierra Leone and St. Helena (a South Atlantic island) pending their eventual disposal. With the growing demand for labor in the British Caribbean, some of them were encouraged to migrate there voluntarily as indentures. As the demand for labor grew and the number of recaptives rapidly increased, the pressure for them to migrate to the Caribbean was ratcheted up until they were virtually forced to concede. They were given the options of joining the British West India Regiments (militarily units consisting of former slaves from the Caribbean, North America, and West Africa), emigrating to the British Caribbean, or fending for themselves in Sierra Leone and St. Helena.[16] This was the historical context in which more than eight thousand Africans were brought to Jamaica as indentured laborers during the period 1841–1865.[17]

Most of the Kongolese indentures taken to Jamaica were settled in St. Thomas, east of Kingston, but smaller numbers were settled in pockets in St. Mary, Portland, and St. Catherine.[18] These Africans brought their Central African religious traditions with them and adopted elements of the existing Afro-Jamaican religious ethos to create their own possession and healing rites, which they have maintained to the present time. More specifically, Central African religious outlooks and practices converged with the existing healing rites of Myal, Obeah, and the Maroons' *Kromanti play* (a possession rite).[19] The result is what is known as Kumina, a religious ceremony that is essentially a spirit possession rite.

Drawing on their cultural memory, Kumina practitioners initially invoked a host of African spirits. Over the years, the names and functions of many of these spirits have faded into the background, and Kumina rituals have become focused mostly on ancestors, including the departed spirits of ritual experts who have distinguished themselves in the knowledge and practice of Kumina in St. Thomas, Jamaica. However, the practitioners of Kumina acknowledge the existence of a Supreme God, whom they call Nzaambi Mpungu or King Zaambi. As Supreme God, Nzaambi Mpungu does not interact directly with the living; instead, the power of Nzaambi Mpungu is mediated through the ancestors, or *nkuyu*, whom he energizes and enables to assist humans with their problems.[20]

Kumina ritual experts may convene ceremonies for various reasons and at different occasions. These ceremonies frequently mark transitional stages in life such as births, marriages, and deaths. They may celebrate significant days on Jamaica's national calendar or events more closely linked to the history of the people who are practitioners of Kumina. Persons wishing to express their gratitude to their ancestors for their assistance with particular problems may confer with the ritual experts to perform a ceremony of thanksgiving. Most ceremonies, however, are convened to access the vital energy of the ancestors to heal the physical body or the mind, relieve economic hardship, and/or help with social relationships.[21] On these occasions, Kumina practitioners use a combination of sacrifices, libations, music, movements, prayers, and singing to honor and invite the ancestors to appear in ceremonies by possessing the participants. Goats seem to be the standard sacrificial animal. After its ritual slaughter, the goat's blood is mixed with other ingredients and presented to the ancestors. A portion of the meat is also cooked and fed to the ancestors, along with other foods and beverages. This meal is usually placed before the drums, which are the agents that call the spirits.[22] A two-drum set provides the music for Kumina ceremonies. This consists of large bass drum called the *kimbanda* and a smaller, higher-pitched drum called the *playing kyas*. These drums, accompanied by other percussive instruments, provide the rhythms that invite the ancestral spirits to make their appearance. The drumming is accompanied by singing and movements by the participants. Once the ancestors take possession of the living, they dance to the special rhythms that are played for them. Herbs and herbal preparations, called *nkisi*, figure prominently in most ceremonies. Known for their healing properties, herbs are especially essential when ceremonies are convened for healing particular individuals.

In areas where the Kumina phenomenon made its appearance after 1841, it provided a much needed reinvigoration for Myal, which was undergoing a form of cultural repression after the Myal outbreaks of the period. In fact, while Myal as an independent tradition has all but disappeared from the folk religious ethos in Jamaica, its healing and spirit possession rites continue as essential elements of Kumina. Kenneth Bilby, an anthropologist who researches folk traditions of the Caribbean, argues that elements of Myal persist today in the *Kromanti Play* of the Maroons, in a drumming ceremony called *Gumbay* practiced in a few scattered communities in Jamaica, and in *Jonkonnu*, a masquerading dance performed on the streets during Christmas time.[23] The broader legacy of Myal is to be found in the Revival Zion that emerged in the wake of a wave of Christian revivalism that swept Jamaica in the early 1860s.

The Great Revival and Revival Zion

The "Great Revival" of 1860–1861 was a spillover of the religious excitement that was sweeping England and Ireland at that time. The British revival was itself influenced by the evangelical revival in the United States during the first half of the 1800s, with its emphasis on personal faith, transformational conversion, and a morally upright lifestyle. At its inception, the revival was a welcome phenomenon for the Christian denominations operating in Jamaica, especially the Presbyterians, Baptists, Moravians, and Methodists. During this Great Revival, Afro-Jamaicans flocked to churches that were brimming with excitement. Contemporary observers reported earnest prayers, gripping conviction, fervent confession, and dramatic transformation of the lives of many who were notorious for their sinful and immoral lifestyles. Revival services were themselves emotionally charged events, with people moaning, groaning, shouting, and even falling into trance. Those converted in these services, especially the young, were immediately possessed by an evangelistic zeal and went about imploring others to experience their newfound joy.[24]

But the initial joy of the missionaries was soon replaced by chagrin, as excitement degenerated into excess as far as they were concerned. Accusing the converts of mixing Myalist and Native Baptist superstitions and practices with Christianity, the missionaries made charges of "wild extravagance and almost blasphemous fanaticism." Such charges arose from practices that came to characterize much of the Great Revival: "oral confessions, trances and dreams, 'prophesying,' spirit-seizure, wild dancing, flagellation, and mysterious sexual doings."[25] The historian William James Gardner describes this insertion of Myal and Native Baptist elements into the Great Revival as similar to the corruption of a mountain stream, "clear and transparent as it springs from the rock, but which becomes foul and repulsive as impurities are mingled with it in its onward course."[26] Unwelcomed in the traditional Christian churches, the exuberance and expressive elements of the Great Revival took roots elsewhere and spawned a folk religious tradition that layered elements of Christianity on top of the Myal and Native Baptist ethos long established among Afro-Jamaicans.

Scholars have indentified two distinct groups as emerging from the Great Revival: Revival Zion and Pukumina, also derisively called Pocomania (meaning "little madness"). The distinction between the two is usually made by pointing out that, while Revival Zion invokes the persons of the Christian trinity, angels, and biblical personalities, Pukumina often invokes or appeases malevolent spirits such at Satan, fallen angels, and ghosts.[27] Bible reading and preaching are likely to be more prominently featured in Revival Zion services, while Pukumina is more likely to focus on ritual singing and dancing. Also, Pukumina is likely to employ witchcraft and more "African" techniques in healing.[28] Historically, the difference between these two groups has been hard to maintain because there is evidently much overlap in practices as well as in adherents. Groups indentified as Pukumina have never embraced that label, preferring to be called Revivalists or Baptists. Even the analytic distinction between the two does not seem to remain valid today, as Pukumina seems to have faded into the background, leaving the folk religious stage to Revival Zion.

The traditional Revival Zion that emerged from the Great Revival was decentralized, consisting of independent bands, as the various units are called. Each band was led by a shepherd or shepherdess, who often used the honorific familial title of "Daddy" or "Mother" before his or her name, as in "Daddy Sharpe" or "Mother Brown." The assumption of this office has traditionally been dependent on the individual's personal gifts and/or a call received through dreams, visions, or trance experiences. Most leaders could point to one or more of these experiences in which they received the revelation that leading a band and/or engaging in the healing "ministry" should be their life's vocation. Many also attributed their ritual and herbal knowledge to the teaching of the Holy Spirit or their spirit messengers, often communicated through visions or trances. In some cases, potential leaders apprenticed with established leaders and eventually succeeded them or branched out on their own. Depending on their gifts, some leaders functioned as shepherds of a band as well as folk healers. The premises of healers was known as a balm yard, because, in addition to leading the services in the ritual center, healers held consultations with clients seeking healing and other services.

Famous healers often drew clients from all over the island and from abroad, and many believers traveled long distances so that these healers could tackle their difficult and intractable cases.

While these independent bands still exist and leadership still often depends on a sense of personal call and spiritual endowment, many bands have merged with various Christian denominations emanating from the United States. For example, many Revival Zion congregations have merged with either the African Methodist Episcopal Church or the Christian Methodist Episcopal Church. Other groups have been become affiliated with various Pentecostal or Evangelical denominations since the mid-1900s. They therefore fall under the sway of progressive layers of hierarchy all the way up to the U.S. bishops. In addition to personal call and charismatic endowment, leaders, increasingly referred to as pastors or reverends, have to undergo ministerial and theological training and ordination by the authorized clergy or conference.

Those who forged Revival Zion in the second half of the 1800s replaced the African deities with the Father, Son, and Holy Ghost (Spirit) of the Christian trinity and the angels and famous characters of the Bible. For the most part, the Father was treated in an African manner, as creator and Supreme God, but was somewhat distant and hardly the object of ritual attention. Jesus and the Holy Spirit were the ones invoked, with the Holy Spirit being the primary possessing agent. Angels and biblical characters could also possess the individual, but they served primarily as spirit guides (as in "guardian angels"). Other spiritual agents, especially the spirits of the dead and demons, were recognized but received ritual attention only in burial and mourning rites and in healing rites where they were believed to be the agents of afflictions.

From its inception, Revival Zion utilized a number of symbols to attract and mediate the presence of the spirits. A center pole in Revival Zion meeting places was believed to be the route by which the spirits descend from the sky into the earth and then into the worshippers through their feet. Candles, crucifixes, wooden swords, plaques with scripture passages, and picture of Jesus or departed leaders were all part of the symbolic repertoire one encountered in these meeting places. Most Revival sites were identified by a pole in the yard atop of which flew the flag of the band. In proximity to the pole was a pedestal with a container of water, and around the base of the pole various herbs and flowers were planted. All these symbolic elements were designed to attract the beneficent spirits and to repel malevolent ones.[29] Many of these symbols are disappearing from Revival Zion, and, where they remain, their meanings are either lost or obscured. Recent study of Revival Zion in two congregations in a rural community in Jamaica shows that both the yard pole and the center pole have disappeared, and, while some symbols, such as containers of water, flowers, and bottles of beverages, are found in the worship center of one of these congregations, they have totally disappeared from the other. Respondents point out that these and other congregations that are affiliated with the African Methodist Episcopal Zion Church and the Christian Methodist Episcopal Church have come under great pressures from the U.S. leadership to eliminate many traditional symbols and practices deemed unbiblical or extrabiblical.

Throughout its history, Revival Zion has been known for a number of ceremonial and ritual events. Up to the 1950s and 1960s, it was typical for Revival bands to hold street meetings in many village squares as part of their effort to attract more people to the bands. Today these meetings have all but disappeared. Baptisms have always been a kind of spectacle for Revival Zion. Amidst much excitement, singing, and music, candidates for baptism are usually fully immersed in a river or sometimes in the sea when there is no river nearby. The "divine service" is the most typical worship experience of Revival Zion. "Divine service" refers mostly to the traditional Sunday worship but may also refer to services held at night. Revival bands also hold a special ceremony called "table," with a specially decorated table with various foods and symbols of the band as the focal point of the ritual activities. Tables may be celebratory events marking anniversaries or memorable events, thanksgivings for special divine assistance or the yearly harvest, occasions for the performance of special healing or cleansing rituals, or special fundraising efforts.[30] Band leaders who are adept at healing may convene special healing services. Those whose services are in high demand may hold healing services on week days or may conduct regular consultations with clients at their places of residence. Weekly prayer meetings are held by most bands, and fasting is undertaken regularly or periodically by member of most bands.

The traditional Revival services are characterized by much fluidity and improvisation. However, several elements are more or less constant. Choruses, accompanied by drumming, are often sung as a kind of warm-up to the services and at various points during the service, especially during testimony time and before the ritual dance that leads to possession. The opening invocation that officially begins the service is customarily followed by the singing of evangelical Christian hymns in a slow, mournful, a capella style. Responsive Bible readings, usually an Old Testament and a New Testament lesson, testimonies recounting experiences of salvation, healing, or revelatory dream or visions, various exhortations dispensing spiritual or moral advice, and a sermon are frequent elements of a service. Possession by the Holy Spirit or by angelic or biblical personalities is usually the objective and highlight of a revival service. While this can happen spontaneously at any time during the service, it usually occurs in the context of a concentrated period of dancing that transitions into "trumping," during which participants move in clockwise manner while stomping on the ground, breathing in a hyperventilating manner, and letting out grunting or shouting sounds. Once possessed, participants may dance around the church and on the outside, may deliver messages to individuals and the congregation, or may warn of impending danger.

Alexander Bedward, Pentecostalism, and Revivalism in the 1900s

After the public furor over the excessive display of emotionalism and "superstition" of Afro-Jamaicans during the Great Revival, Revival Zion emerged as a religious tradition created by and for the underclass in Jamaican society. For the most part, this religious tradition operated among the rural and urban poor on the periphery of the Jamaican mainstream and only occasionally inserted itself into the greater public arena. The most significant thrust of Revival Zion into public consciousness came in last decade of the 1800s and the first two decades of the 1900s. This was occasioned by a charismatic preacher name Alexander Bedward, whose ministry was centered in August Town, on the outskirts of Kingston. Bedward created a stir in 1891 when he started performing baptism in the Mona River and prescribing its "mineral" waters to those desirous of healing. At first, it seemed that people were skeptical, with only seven of the two hundred gathered agreeing to drink the waters. When these seven reported immediate healing, the fame of Bedward quickly spread, and people converged on August Town in search of healing. Such was the concern generated by Bedward's activities that the government reportedly tested the water in the Mona River and found that it was rich in minerals. At one of his gatherings at the Mona River, Bedward started railing against the British colonial government of Jamaica and called upon his listeners to "rise up and crush the white people." For such instigation, the government charged him with sedition, and, though he was found not guilty, he was placed in the custody of an insane asylum.[31]

On his release from prison, Bedward continued his healing and prophetic ministries until the early 1920s, when he started prophesying the end of the world and identifying himself as Christ. In anticipation of the end of the world, he set the date of December 31, 1920, as the day of his ascension to heaven. Many of his followers, wanting to observe the spectacle or perhaps wishing to ascend with him, descended on the premises where his church was located. When the day passed uneventfully, the colonial government recommitted him to the mental asylum, where he died about a decade later.[32]

In the early years of the 2000s, Jamaica's folk religion as manifested in Revival Zion once again finds itself at the crossroads of change. This time the changes are facilitated by religious forces that started to plant themselves in Jamaican society in the early 1900s and by the contemporary forces of social mobility and communication media. The emergence of a new type of Christian spirituality was led by local evangelists but quickly converged with a new missionary thrust into the Caribbean, mostly from U.S. churches that came out of the Holiness movement of the late 1800s and the Pentecostal movement of the early 1900s. Raglan Phillips, an expatriate English bookkeeper turned preacher, was the harbinger of this new type of Christianity. He became a phenomenal evangelist, healer, and church planter in the first three decades of the 1900s. He held emotionally charged revival meetings, especially in Clarendon and Kingston, and drew much public attention when he started selling anointed handkerchiefs that purportedly had the power to heal. Joining forces with a local woman from St. Ann, Mary Coore, Phillips preached around the island. Eventually, in 1924, they established the City Mission Church in Kingston, which has since been a leading Pentecostal church in Jamaica.

In the early 1900s, a number of Jamaicans invited Holiness and Pentecostal churches in the United States to send missionaries to Jamaica. In response to a request from a Jamaican Christian whose name was Isaac Delevante, the Church of God, Anderson (Indiana), sent two missionaries, George and Nellie Olson, who pioneered the Church of God in Jamaica and Grand Cayman.[33] In 1912, Ella Ruddock, a Jamaican woman who had studied at Taylor University in Indiana, started a church in Friendship, Westmoreland, under the auspices of Missionary Bands of the World, a Holiness organization with which she had become acquainted while studying in the United States. In 1915, Ruddock was joined by Susan Schlatter, a missionary from the United States.[34] This was the inception of what eventually became the Wesleyan Holiness Church in Jamaica. A local preacher, J. Wilson Bell, wrote to the Pentecostal denomination Church of God, Cleveland (Tennessee), in 1917, seeking affiliation. In response, the Church of God sent James M. Parkinson and Nina Stapleton, his sister, as missionaries to Jamaica. Their ministry and that of their early converts spawned the Church of God of Prophecy and the New

Testament Church of God, leading Pentecostal denominations in Jamaica.[35] By the mid-1920s, a number of Pentecostal groups were operating in Jamaica. These included the Apostolic Church of God, under the leadership of an Elder Harper from the United States; the Church of God in Christ, founded by Charles H. Mason, an African American Pentecostal pioneer; and Pentecostal Assemblies of the World, a "oneness" or unitarian Pentecostal group founded in Portland, Oregon, in 1912.[36] Throughout the 1900s, various schisms led to a proliferation of Pentecostal churches in Jamaica, some affiliated with denominations in the United States and many existing as independent churches.

The religious ferment of the early 1900s emphasized the experience of a personal conversion and healing through the power of the Holy Spirit. Participatory, expressive worship and joyful, emotional response to the Holy Spirit were characteristic of church services. Reflecting the ethical moralism of Holiness and Pentecostal churches, evangelists and ministers enjoined moral rectitude, especially in advocating marital monogamy and inveighing against sexual promiscuity. The established churches in Jamaica derogatively referred to the churches emerging from this new ferment as "clap-hand churches." The established churches regarded the emotional charged services and preoccupation with healing as a form of fanaticism and hence dismissed the Holiness and Pentecostal churches as denuded forms of Christianity imported from the United States. However, these churches found many converts among the same lower-class Jamaicans who had embraced the Revival ethos. What is more, many from the lower middle class gravitated to these new churches, which afforded them opportunities for lay and ministerial leadership. Soon Holiness and Pentecostal Christians began to counter the discourse of the established churches that painted them as inferior Christians. They defended their lively services and healing ministries as biblical and described the services of the established churches as cold and lifeless and their members as nominal—Christian in name only.

While many Revival Zion churches have continued in their independent ways until today, some have embraced the emerging Pentecostal ethos because it enabled them to be Christian while still maintaining their African and Jamaican folk preoccupation that privileges ritual encounter with the divine through baptism of the Holy Spirit. Speaking in tongues and healing of physical and other maladies are also seen as characteric of the Holy Spirit's operation in the lifes of Pentecostal believers. As noted, some Revival Zion congregations have become affiliated with Christian denomination from the United States and have come under increasing pressures to abandon many traditional symbols and practices. Furthermore, younger leaders and younger, socially upwardly mobile members have come of age being exposed to popular Christianity on television and radio and have imbibed the lively Pentecostal or evangelical style that is the stable fare of these media. Former Revival Zion churches are transforming themselves in the image of Pentecostalism. The trappings of Revivalism—yard poles, center poles in the worship center, container of waters, the presence of herbs and fruits, traditional white dresses, and head-wraps—are fast disappearing from some churches. The traditional two-drum set, comprising a bass and a "rattler" or "kettle" (kete), have disappeared in some places and have been replaced by keyboards, guitars, and modern drum sets. Younger, more educated leaders have also embraced the Evangelical and Pentecostal theological emphasis on biblical authority. They find many traditional practices to be unchristian or extrabiblical and hence unacceptable and have led the charge to remove them from their churches.[37] As the cultural anthropologist Barry Chevannes observes, Revivalism is now in the process of shedding its Myalist "garb and is now wearing Pentecostal clothes."[38]

Afro-Trinidadian Religions

The religious history of the twin island republic of Trinidad and Tobago provides a particularly good example of the meeting of multiple religious traditions at the Caribbean crossroads. Becoming a Spanish colony after it was claimed for Spain by Columbus during his third journey to the Caribbean in1498, Trinidad remained sparsely settled and poorly developed until the last decades of the 1700s, when Francophone immigrants and their slaves from Martinique, Haiti, Domenica, and Grenada[39] boosted the Trinidadian population from less than three thousand in 1782 to almost eighteen thousand by 1797,[40] when the British took control of the island.[41] The black population of Trinidad and Tobago was significantly enhanced between 1838 and 1870, when Africans captured by the British from slave trading vessels were brought to work on the sugar plantations as indentured laborers. Most of these were of Yoruba ethnicity and were to put their stamp on Afro-Trinidadian religious traditions. With the abandoning of the plantations by former slaves, the new African arrivals were not nearly numerous enough to meet the needs of the plantation economy. The importation of 144,000 indentured laborers from India between 1845 and 1917 was the major solution to the problem. In addition, Portuguese, Venezuelans, Chinese, Middle Easterners, and African Americans have all contributed to the mix of what is now Trinibagonian (Trinidad and Tobago) culture.

Afro-Trinidadian religious traditions emerged in the context of this cultural mix, absorbing influences not only from African sources but also from the indigenous (Carib and Arawak), European, and Indian traditions. While our main focus here is on the Afro-Trinidadian tradition called Spiritual Baptists, its close relationship to the Orisha tradition,[42] also called Shango, necessitates that we look at both traditions in some detail. Spiritual Baptists and followers of the Orisha tradition have historically operated within the same folk ethos and come from the same social stratum (poor blacks) of Trinibagonian society. Though these traditions maintain separate identities, they are often lumped together under the Rubric of "Shango Baptists" in popular perception. The anthropologist Stephen D. Glazier, who has conducted extensive research on Spiritual Baptists, points out that the "heterodoxy and heteropraxy" of both traditions give rise to much variation and overlapping, including in adherents and leaders.[43] As a consequence, Spiritual Baptist churches often share compounds with Orisha shrines, and Orisha feasts (major ceremonies) are often held in Spiritual Baptist churches. Initiates in the Orisha traditions are often urged to undergo baptism in the Spiritual Baptist tradition, as well.[44]

The Orisha Tradition of Trinidad

Most slaves of the pre-emancipation era were creoles—that is, they were born in the Caribbean—or had their roots in West and West-Central Africa. The majority of African-born slaves were Igbo, Moco, or Kongolese. The importation of almost 6,500 Africans, mostly Yoruba, from an area that is currently a region of Nigeria, between 1838 and 1870 brought another layer of African culture to the island. Though remnants of a Fon/Dahomey religious tradition, called Vodunu, which has the same provenance as Haitian Vodou, have survived in Trinidad,[45] it was the Yoruba who stamped their imprint on and came to dominate the African-derived religious tradition that developed in the island. The Orisha tradition that has developed maintains the essential Yoruba cosmology of a High God, a pantheon of *orishas* (spirit forces) that control nature and human affairs, and ancestors as significant actors in the affairs of the living. It also accepts the Yoruba ritual structure as the most effective means of cultivating relationship with the *orishas* and securing their assistance.

Exhibiting an African disposition for absorbing elements of other religions, Trinidad's Orisha tradition adopted elements of Catholicism, most notably the recognition of Catholic saints as aspects or manifestations of the *orishas*, the use of chromolithographs of saints to represent the *orishas*, and the adoption of Catholic liturgical elements such as the Lord's Prayer, the Hail Mary, and the litany of the saints. Kabbalah is another tradition often exists alongside and informs Orisha. Though it has its origin in Judaism, the Kabbalah that was brought to Trinidad was an amalgam of various European esoteric mystical, religious, magical, and even occultist practices, and, in the hands of Orisha practitioners, it has become a conjuring or magical practice. Often regarded as evil, Kabbalah tends not to be intertwined with Orisha practices the way Catholicism is but is juxtaposed with them.[46] Since the mid-1900s, elements of Hinduism have become incorporated in the Orisha tradition, as well. This does not seem to be thoroughgoing, but some Hindu deities are being associated with *orishas*; some Orisha compounds have shrines to Indian deities, and Hindu flags and ritual implements are making their appearance at Orisha shrines and altars.[47]

For most of its history, the Orisha tradition was subjected to derision and denigration in public discourse and to official repressive measures by government authorities in Trinidad. A 1869 law against the practice of Obeah was also aimed at the beating of drums, singing, and dancing during all-night Orisha feasts. Laws passed in the 1880s outlawing drums in carnivals extended to a general banning of drums, thus affecting Orisha worship.[48] Though the Shouter Prohibition Ordinance of 1917 was aimed specifically at the Spiritual Baptists, proscribing many of their practices, it effectively drove Orisha practices underground along with those of the Spiritual Baptists until the ordinance was repealed, in 1951. Since then, Orisha religion has been accorded public recognition through the official incorporation of two Orisha organizations (in 1981 and 1990) that give collective voice to Orisha practitioners; an official state visit by the recognized leader of the Yoruba religion (which is based on the veneration of the *orishas*) in Nigeria, the Ooni of Ife; attendance of political and civil leaders at Orisha public ceremonies; and the attendance of Orisha representatives at political and civil functions. Additionally, the government of Trinidad and Tobago has set aside March 30 as a public holiday for Orisha and Spiritual Baptist celebrations, has given land to groups belonging to these religious traditions, and has enacted a law (in 1999) permitting Orisha priests to perform marriages.[49] This public recognition has been accompanied by a move toward the Yorubanization of Orisha, especially among younger and more educated members who, in their quest for what they consider an authentic African identity, seek to purge non-African elements from the religion and to make it conform more to Yoruba religion as practiced among the Yoruba in Nigeria, since this is regarded as the African root of Trinidad's Orisha tradition.

Having its foundation in the Yoruba tradition brought to Trinidad by indentured Africans imported in the mid-1800s, Orisha religion recognizes Olodumare as the creator and supreme power in the universe. However, ritual attention is directed mostly at the *orishas*, whom Olodumare has charged with governing the elemental forces of nature such as wind, lightning and thunder, water, and the forest, as well as human qualities and activities such as love, war, and maternity. These *orishas* are believed to be very powerful and are disposed to use their powers to assist humans with the exigencies of life, especially health issues, material success, and relationship problems. However, if they are disrespected or not venerated properly, they are likely to become angry and inflict harm on the offending individuals. The symbols and ceremonies of the Orisha tradition are intended to invoke the *orishas* to make their presence and power felt in the lives of the devotes. *Orishas* make their appearance in possession rituals, where they displace the personalities of the individuals they possess and use those believers' bodies to dance and to deliver messages to those assembled. They often communicate through dreams and visions and divination rituals performed by priests reading obi seeds (Kola nuts) or gazing in water.

As many as thirty *orishas* are recognized in Trinidad. The major ones include Shango (also the name used for the Orisha tradition until recent times), the powerful *orisha* of fire, lightning, and thunder; Eshu, the guardian of doorways and mediator between humans and the other *orishas*; Ogun, the warrior and ruler of metal tools; Shakpana, the healer and master of ceremonies; Osain, the master of the forest, who is associated with herbs and herbal healing; Mama Lata, mother earth; Obatalá, associated with the brain, intelligence, and reason; Oshun, a female water deity who governs love and sensuality; and Emanje (Yemanje), another water deity who rules all thing maternal. The names of some Catholic saints, such as Peter, Anthony, and Raphael, often appear as *orishas*. The significance of ancestors has always been recognized, but until recently the Orisha traditions have dealt with them only in mourning and memorial rites. With the recent attempt to re-Africanize Trinidad's Orisha traditions, ancestors are being given a more prominent place.

In Orisha religion, the most important functionary is the priest, called a *mongba* or *baba* if he is a man or an *iya* if she is a woman (widely recognized priests may be accorded the title *babalorisha* or *iyalorisha*). Men and women usually attain this status through a sense of calling, spiritual endowment, and/ or an apprenticeship with notable and knowledgeable priests that can last for years. Expansive knowledge of the tradition and effectiveness in conducting ceremonies are required of these functionaries. Next to priests are rituals assistants, who perform various functions in ceremonies, and drummers whose services are pivotal in bringing down the orishas to possess the worshippers ("ride their horses"). *Mongba* and *iya* usually own their own Orisha compounds (sometimes a couple consisting of a *mongba* and *iya* jointly heads an Orisha group) with various sacred spaces of the religion: a *chapelle*, a rather small building (about ten feet by ten feet) that houses altars of principal *orishas*, implements and symbols of the religion, chromolithographs of Catholic saints identified as *orishas*; a *palais*, a large structure (that can vary in size) with a roof, a wall about waist-high, and an earthen floor, where "feasts" or large gatherings are held; and *peroguns* (also called "tombs" or "stools"), small enclosures made of concrete or tin or just earthen mounds that serve as shrines of the *orishas*. The *peroguns* are believed to be the passages through which the *orishas* descent to participate in ceremonies or assist in healings. Thus, their implements and the flags bearing their colors are usually planted in these shrines. Some Orisha compounds also contain Spiritual Baptist churches, shrines to and flags of Hindu deities, and Kabbalah shrines.[50]

Like most African diaspora religious traditions, Orisha religion traditionally has no centralized organization and no prescribed liturgy or creed. Each group operates autonomously, without administrative oversight from any religious hierarchy. However, some groups maintain fraternal relationships with one another, and some distinguished elder priests may exercise paternal oversight of groups or compounds established by their fictive children. Papa Neezer (Ebenezer Elliot), for example, maintained a network of as many as twelve of his "children" who had established Orisha compounds, and he frequently presided at their "feasts" in the 1950s and 1960s. In fact, Pa Neezer developed such a reputation as a knowledgeable priest and powerful healer that he became recognized as the indisputable, if unofficial, head of Orisha religion in Trinidad. Isaac "Sheppy" Lindsay occupied a similar status in 1970s and 1980s.[51]

As noted earlier, since the 1970s, calls for and movement toward some form of centralization and collective identity have been made. This is manifested in the formation and incorporation of two organizations, Egbe Orisha Ile Wa, under the leadership of Iyalorisha Melvina Rodney, and Opa Shanga (or Opa Orisha), under the leadership of Molly Ahye.[52] Egbe Orisha seems to have been the dominant group representing the traditional practitioners from the Afro-Trinidadian working class, whereas Opa Shango tended to attract followers from middle-class practitioners who were newer to the religion. Ahye and other leaders sought to develop relationship with other practitioners of Orisha traditions in Brazil, Cuba, and the United States. For some time, much conflict existed between the two groups, but they came together in 2000 to form one organization under the joint leadership of Iyalorisha Melvina Rodney and Babalorisha Clarence Ford.[53] Since 1988, a National Council of Orisha Elders has existed in one form or another. Said to have been formed initially at the direction of the visiting Ooni of Ife, the council serves to guard and lobby for the public interest of Orisha religion and to formulate principles and strategies to guide and develop the religions.[54] Despite the efforts toward centralization, heterodoxy and heterodoxy prevail in Orisha religion. Frances Henry, an anthropologist who has studied it since the 1950s, argues that the kinds of extensive networks that once obtained in Orisha religion are now being replaced by greater atomization in which priests tend to focus on their group, discourage their members from attending the feasts of others, and frequently "bad-mouth" others as engaging in evil practices or not practicing the traditions correctly. Thus, Orisha religion is still marked by variations and innovations depending on the talents, dispositions, and sometimes whims of the individual priests.

The main Orisha ceremony is annual the "feast," or *ebo*, in honor of the *orishas* that are recognized and venerated in a particular compound. A feast generally lasts from Tuesday evening to Saturday morning (some last from Sunday to Saturday morning). People gather in the *palais* at the compound at about eight or nine in the evening. After the congregants have spent time socializing, the ceremony gets under way when the priest or priestess enters the *palais* and starts a series of Catholic invocations, including the Lord's Prayers, the Hail Mary, and the Litany of the Saints. The end of these lengthy invocations may be signaled by the signing of a hymn, after which a ritual assistant places a candle in the middle of the *palais* and a container of water and a container of ashes on either side of the candle. A libation of olive oil is poured, making a circular pattern on the ground. The drummers, playing a set of three drums and accompanied by other percussion instruments, strike up a rhythm to Eshu, the mischievous guardians of doorways and mediator between humans and the other *orishas*. This begins a series of up to seven songs to Eshu, during which some worshippers gather and dance in a circle around the items in the middle of the floor. This segment of the ceremonies is seen as giving Eshu his due, since he is the guardian of the "doorway" to the *orishas*. The invocation of Eshu ends when the items on the ground of the *palais* are gathered and deposited at the *peroguns*, or "tombs" of the *orishas*.

After ritual assistants place candles at the four corners of the *palais*, the drumming and singing continue for the rest of the night as the worshippers invoke as many as a dozen *orishas* in turn, beginning with Ogun, the warrior. During the playing of the rhythms and songs of each *orisha*, he or she may arrive to "ride" or take possession of some worshippers. During these possessions, the "horses" assume the personality of the *orishas* and may distribute oil for the participants to drink or rub on their faces; call for their implements and act out the activities associated with them; and visit the *chapelle* or their *peroguns*. Possessing *orishas* may make predictions or perform healing for those with maladies.

At daylight, the animals to be sacrificed are ritually cleansed; the priest performs a divination rite with the obi seeds (Kola nuts) to determine if they are acceptable to the *orishas*. The animals are then killed in the *chapelle* and their blood sprinkled over the *peroguns* of the *orishas*. With this, the first night of the feast is officially over. Some people find a place to sleep; others go off to their homes or workplaces; yet others remain to prepare and cook the meat from the sacrificial animals. Some of the meat is prepared without salt and "fed" to the *orishas*. The rest is consumed by the attendees of the feast. This pattern is repeated every night till Saturday morning.[55]

Initiation ceremonies are also central to the practice of Orisha religion. In the strict sense, adherents of this tradition do not proselytize. People become devotees through family connections to the traditions, visitations from the *orishas* via dreams, or the experience of possession. Others come into the tradition after bouts of chronic illnesses or other persistent difficulties (economic or relationship woes), the resolution of which came through the services of a *mongba* or *iya*. These visitations and persistent maladies or hardships are regarded as signs that the *orishas* desire those visited to enter into a committed relationship with them. In some instances, initiates are first required to undergo baptism in the Spiritual Baptist church (see discussion of this in the next section). The Orisha portion of the initiation is presided over by an Orisha priest. It involves a period of three to nine days spent in ritual isolation in a *chapelle*, during which initiates undertake a fast, receiving mostly liquids and minimal nourishment and receiving instructions concerning the traditions of Orisha. The experience constitutes ritual death and rebirth. The initiation culminates with the preparation of the head to receive the guiding *orisha*. This involves sacrificing an animal over the head of each initiate, washing of the initiate's head, making an incision on his head and forehead, and anointing the incisions with herbs and oils to prepare it for the reception of the *orishas*. The initiates are now ready to be receptacles or "horses" of the *orishas*. The manifestation of one's guiding *orisha* in the head (possession) or through a visionary experience, though not required, is a desired occurrence during this rite of initiation.[56]

In addition to the annual "feasts" and initiatory ceremonies, healing is a crucial element of the Orisha ethos. As indicated earlier, *orishas* may conduct healing while they are manifesting themselves in the bodies of their devotees. However, most healing rites take place through individual consultations with priests who are so gifted. Priests either read obi seeds or gaze into ponds of water as diagnostic tools for determining the causes and remedies for people's problems. Various ritual and herbal cures are often prescribed (offerings to the *orishas*, herbal baths, ingestion of concoctions of herbs and other substances). As a rule, Orisha healers deal only with the power of the *orishas* and are vested only in curing maladies, creating auspicious circumstances for believers' success, and providing protection against malevolent forces. But, as was mentioned earlier, Kabbalistic practices are often juxtaposed with Orisha, and some priests involve themselves with the manipulation of the evil forces believed to be at the center of these practices. Other Orisha adherents and priests frown at and often inveigh against such involvement with Kabbalah.

Spiritual Baptists of Trinidad

As indicated earlier, Spiritual Baptists operate in the same social milieu as the Orisha tradition, often sharing ritual spaces and overlapping adherents. While the Spiritual Baptist faith is mostly associated with Trinidad, through inter-island migration it has spread to islands in the southeastern Caribbean such as St. Vincent (often associated with its origin), Grenada, and Barbados, and is found even as far north as St. Croix in the U. S. Virgin Islands. Through Caribbean migration to North America and England, the faith has also been transplanted to such places as Toronto, London, Brooklyn, Miami, and New Orleans.[57] Because the religion of the Spiritual Baptists was part of an oral culture for most of its existence, documentation of its history prior to the 1950s is very sparse, and evidence for its origins in Trinidad is inconclusive.

In his book *Spirit, Blood and Drums: The Orisha Religion in Trinidad*, the anthropologist James T. Houk isolates at least four claims for the historical roots of Spiritual Baptists: Africa, the United States, St. Vincent, and Grenada.[58] The claim for an African origin points to three separate traditions and ethnic groups. The first traces the roots of the Spiritual Baptist faith to a Dahomean who changed his name to Robert Antoine and who founded a Rada center near Port of Spain in 1855. His practice of African religious traditions supposedly became popular among Afro-Trinidadians and inspired others to commence their own African-style religious activities. The Spiritual Baptist traditions began here but incorporated elements of Christianity.

Another claim points to a Kongolese provenance for the "shouting" (making of sounds by hyperventilating) and ritual chalk drawings that are trademarks of Spiritual Baptist ceremonies. The Kongolese who brought these practices to Trinidad may have been exposed or even converted to Christianity before their arrival in Trinidad. Others, including Eudora Thomas, who is a Spiritual Baptist elder and the author of a Spiritual Baptist history, contend that Spiritual Baptist faith is an offshoot of Yoruba/Orisha practices. Some contemporary adherents of the Spiritual Baptist faith still maintain that it cannot be fully separated from Orisha and maintain a presence in both traditions.[59]

The origin of the Spiritual Baptist faith is often traced to the arrival of African American immigrants in the islands. These were African Americans who fought on the side of the British against the Americans during the Revolutionary War and the War of 1812. In return, they were granted freedom and settled in British territories, including Trinidad, between 1815 and 1827. They brought with them the Baptist faith they had adopted and the black church aesthetic they had developed in the United States. Their beliefs and practices have become the basis of the Spiritual Baptist faith in Trinidad.[60]

A third theory suggests that the Spiritual Baptist faith in Trinidad began with immigrants from St. Vincent. The immigrants are believed to have been members of an indigenous Afro-Christian tradition called Shakers that developed from British Methodism. The outlawing of Shakers' practices in 1913 coincided with the discovery of oil and the development of Trinidad's petroleum industry in the early 1900s. Fleeing persecution and seeking employment, many Shakers flocked to Trinidad in the 1910s and 1920s and propagated their faith there. The result was the development of the Spiritual Baptist faith. This position is strengthened by the fact that, as late as the 1970s, a significant number of the Spiritual Baptists studied by Stephen D. Glazier claimed to have migrated to Trinidad in the 1910s and 1920s.

A fourth postulation locates the origin of Spiritual Baptists in Grenada and suggests that the originators were really Trinidadians of Yoruban ethnicity who, after they converted to Protestantism, came under extreme pressures from both their Yoruban neighbors and the Catholic Church. To escape harassment, they migrated to St. Vincent, where they experienced a similar fate. So they migrated again, this time to Grenada. With the discovery of oil in Trinidad in 1910 and the opportunities for employment that its exploitation generated, these self-exiles returned to Trinidad and settled in the southwest, where they implanted the faith they developed while in Grenada. As they migrated to the more developed areas in the northeast, their faith quickly spread there as well.[61]

Both Stephen D. Glazier and James T. Houk suggest that the multiple claims cannot all be right. They tend to favor the Vincentian theory because it has more tangible historical and ethnographical support. However, the multiple claims may be indicative of the multiple streams that have flowed into what is now the Spiritual Baptist faith. Unfortunately, we do not have the historical documentation to demonstrate this conclusively, but we do have oral traditions that must not be dismissed lightly. Spiritual Baptists may have evolved along the same trajectory as Revival Zion, imbibing various influences and mutating along the way. The multiple claims regarding its origin are thus perhaps best regarded as fragmentary memories of the various sources of this tradition, kept alive and passed on in an oral culture. The historical and contemporary manifestations of the Spiritual Baptist faith indeed show traits that are easily identified as reflecting European, African, West Indian, and African American influences. Theologically, the Spiritual Baptist faith is essentially Christian, accepting the Christian Trinitarian belief in God as Father, Son, and Holy Spirit and the Bible as the authoritative source of its beliefs and practices. Liturgical practices, such as shouting and mourning (fasting in isolation leading to vision experiences) are decidedly African and/or African American in form and function. Probably influenced by Orisha possession rites, altered states of consciousness attributed to the Holy Spirit, joyous celebrations, physical and psychological healing, and ecstatic emotional displays are all regarded as authentic and genuine expressions of encounters with the divine. We also know that African Americans brought their Baptist faith to the island in the early 1800s and that they sought to maintain their distinctiveness in the face of the efforts of British Baptist missionaries to tone down their expressive worship style. The Spiritual Baptist "trumpet songs" (short refrains sung during hyperventilating and shouting) may have had their roots in Negro spirituals brought to the islands by African American immigrants.[62] In light of the developmental trajectory of other African diasporic religious traditions, where we observe multiple influences on their origin and evolution, we are disposed to view the multiple claims of origin for the Spiritual Baptist faith as evidence of the various currents that flowed in the tradition as it developed historically.

By the 1910s, the Spiritual Baptist faith had come into full historical view. Alleging that the noisy, late-night singing, shouting, and bell-ringing ceremonies were disturbing the peace and refusing to accept the Spiritual Baptist faith as a legitimate religion, the British colonial government of Trinidad and Tobago in 1917 enacted the Shouter Prohibition Ordinance. This was followed by additional legislation in the 1920s that enacted injunctions against Obeah (conjuring), certain forms of healing, and the playing of drums and dancing between 10 p.m. and 6 a.m.[63] Between 1917 and 1951, the Spiritual Baptists were subjected to a campaign of suppression by the state. Police broke up services, beat and arrested worshippers, and hauled them into court to answer charges under the Shouter Prohibition Ordinance. Witnesses against the Spiritual Baptists gave evidence of their "binding of the head with a white cloth, ringing a bell at intervals during meetings, holding lighted candles in the hand, violent shaking of the body and limbs, shouting and grunting, holding flowers, and putting white chalk marks on the floor."[64] Though the campaign drove some adherents and some practices underground, Spiritual Baptists devised means of performing their ceremonies, often posting watchmen to alert worshippers when strangers were approaching.[65] Some, both women and men, were more defiant in the practice of their religion and were repeatedly hauled into court to face charges and imprisoned, fined, or put on probation when found guilty. Some Spiritual Baptist adherents, such as Jeremiah Tobias and Clementina Ford, fought back by filing successful suits against policemen for injuries and damages incurred during police action to break up services and arrest worshippers.[66] The Trinidadian novelist Earl Lovelace immortalized the struggle of the Spiritual Baptists against official repression in his book *The Wine of Astonishment*.[67]

By the 1940s, opposition to the Shouter Prohibition Ordinance was growing in political circles, and devotees started an organized campaign aimed at securing a repeal of the prohibition. An important figure in effort was Uriah Butler, an Afro-Trinidadian politician and labor leader with close ties to the Spiritual Baptists. Another local politician, Albert Gomes, took up the call for repeal of the Shouters Prohibition Ordinance. His call for the Legislative Council to form a committee to investigate the issue led to the eventual repeal of the law.[68] The Spiritual Baptists themselves were actively engaged in the campaign to have the prohibition repealed. The leading role in this campaign was undertaken by Elton George Griffiths, a Pentecostal minister from Grenada, who had a vision that called on him to go to Trinidad to liberate the Spiritual Baptists from this oppressive law. Once in Trinidad, he joined the Spiritual Baptist faith, formed the West Indian Evangelical Spiritual Baptist Faith as an umbrella organization for Spiritual Baptists, and started petitioning and lobbying the Legislative Council of Trinidad and Tobago to repeal the prohibition. Though still a colony of Great Britain, Trinidad and Tobago had gained self-rule by this time and thus could take certain legislative actions on its own. After debating the issue, the Legislative Council repealed the Shouter Prohibition Ordinance on March 30, 1951. Elton George

Griffiths and his supporters, who attended the legislative session that day, held a Baptist thanksgiving celebration in Woodford Square outside the council building.[69]

The Baptists dubbed March 30 "Liberation Day" and commenced annual celebrations on that date to commemorate this victory in the legislature. After much parliamentary and public debate, March 30 was officially designated Spiritual Baptist Liberation Day and a public holiday declared in February 1996 by act of Parliament. The same day doubles as Indian Arrival Day, commemorating the coming of the first Indians to Trinidad in 1845.[70] Other developments have also contributed to the legitimation of the Spiritual Baptist faith. Spiritual Baptist ministers were given the right to perform marriages and conduct funerals and are invited to officiate at state and civic functions; government officials and civic leaders attend Spiritual Baptist functions. In addition, public land has been granted to the Spiritual Baptists for the establishment of a school and the creation of a venue for public celebrations. Furthermore, leaders of the Spiritual Baptist faith have sought to enhance the status and advance the interests of the faith by establishing and incorporating national (and international) organizations to promote unity and provide a united front for the movement. However, multiple organizations have vied for supremacy among the faithful. This competition is manifested in the holding of rival Liberation Day celebrations each year.[71] For the most part, these organizations are associational, without much power to ensure orthodoxy and produce unity. Individual churches remain mostly self-governing; some have membership in more than one national organization, and a large percentage remains independent of these organizations.

Though the leaders of national Spiritual Baptist bodies bear powerful-sounding titles such as bishop or archbishop, they exercise very little power over the individual churches, which are left to formulate beliefs and practice rituals according to their own convictions. At the congregational level, however, a traditional hierarchy exists, with the greatest spiritual and administrative power vested in the leader ("paramount leader") or pastor. Despite much debate about whether women should be allowed to be leaders, many congregations have been and continue to be led by women. A leader, sometimes called Father or Mother, oversees all the activities of the church and usually takes the leading role in directing ceremonies. However, a female leader is not supposed to perform baptisms, and therefore they often invite a male counterpart to conduct the actual immersion. The leader is assisted by a host of functionaries in the performance of the various activities and rituals of the church. Researchers have identified as many as twenty-two such functionaries and ranked them according to status and importance. The most important of these seem to be teachers, who instruct candidates for baptism and who can interpret dreams and visions; provers, who test the claims and sincerity of others; preachers, who are interpreters of the Bible; pointers, who give spiritual direction to those undertaking "mourning"; nurses, who care for the spiritual needs of those who are "mourning" or those needing assistance during services; shepherds or shepherdesses, who watch over children during worship; and captains, who have the responsibility of caring for the physical structure and maintaining order (such as timely beginning and ending of services). Adherents are elevated to these positions on the basis of the revelation they receive during the mourning process.[72]

According the Houk, different groups of Spiritual Baptists fall on a spectrum from orthodox to unorthodox. The orthodox tend to be more thoroughly Protestant in their theology, accepting the doctrine of the Trinity and the authority of the Bible and repudiating any association with the Orisha tradition, which they tend to view as preoccupied with evil spirits. Other Spiritual Baptist churches tend to be more eclectic, absorbing an array of influences from other religious traditions. For example, the Reverend Eudora Thomas, a prominent Spiritual Baptist leader, argues that the Spiritual Baptist faith is based on the genuine core of Yoruban spirituality, which focuses on "the God of light and life." She further asserts that biblical revelations have confirmed the ancient truths already present in African religions.[73] These churches often exist alongside Orisha shrines, practices, and symbols on the same compound; have many members who share dual membership in the Orisha faith; and display in their church buildings objects and symbols from varied traditions including Orisha, Catholicism, Hinduism, and even Kabballah.[74]

Baptism and "mourning" are two essential rituals that serve as rites of passage into greater involvement and higher status in the Spiritual Baptist community. While people may be exposed to the Spiritual Baptist faith through attending services or through personal contacts with adherents, decisions to join a Spiritual Baptist fellowship are most often precipitated by dreams or visions (sometimes used interchangeably and sometimes considered to be different), which are interpreted as calls to join the church by undertaking the rite of baptism.

The baptism ceremony is preceded by an all-night vigil by the members of the church. The vigil begins with the "banding" of the heads of the candidates in a manner that effectively blindfolds them; this is to block all distractions so that they can concentrate on the spiritual "journey" they are undertaking.

They are each presented with holy objects such as the Bible, a hand bell, a lighted candle, and a bouquet of flowers in a bowl or glass. The Bible represents God the Father; the ringing of the bell dispels or wards off evil spirits; the candle is symbolic of the Holy Spirit; and the flowers represent Jesus, who prayed in a garden the night of his betrayal. Throughout the night, the candidates engage in singing, dancing, and praying and are spun around to make them susceptible to manifestations of the Spirit. In the early morning, the candidates may be allowed to sleep or rest for a short time before they are aroused between 4:00 and 5:00 for more singing and praying. They then proceed to the baptismal site by the sea, a river, or a pond. The officiating minister fully immerses each candidate three times, repeating some variation of "in the name of the Father, in name of Son, and the name of the Holy Spirit." Some emerge from the water rejoicing in the power of the Spirit. Sometimes the attendees and the candidates partake of light refreshment at the baptismal site before returning to the church to give thanks. This mostly consists of marching the newly baptized into the church to circumambulate the center pole and to salute the four corners of the structure. In the evening, the members of the church congregate to observe the anointing of the new members with olive oil and accept them into the church "by extending to them the right hand of fellowship."[75] Some Baptists later undergo further immersions called "emerging," which is considered a form of rededication.[76]

The Spiritual Baptist "mourning" rite is the most arduous activity undertaken by adherents. It is a period of ritual isolation and fasting that lasts anywhere from three to twenty-one days, during which the mourner alternates between lying on the floor and kneeling in prayers in the isolation chamber. Since the ritual requires a fast, the mourner's consumption of food is minimal, consisting mostly of teas and fruit juices. While some groups now relax this practice, usually the mourner is "banded" with a head wrap that covers the eyes throughout this ordeal. Mourning is the process through which believers determine what role or function they will perform in the church. During this time, they take visionary journeys during which they "travel" and engage in activities that are symbolic of what their engagement in their fellowship will be. The mourning traditionally ends on a Sunday, when mourners recount their journeys or "tracts" before the congregation. The mourners are elevated to certain statuses with attendant responsibilities on the basis of the interpretation of these tracts. For example, a mourner whose journeys involve reading the Bible or preaching may become a preacher; a mourner who has to deal with children during her journeys may be elevated to the status of a shepherdess. Adherents undertake additional mournings, called "building," as they seek to advance to higher statuses or qualify for other functions in the religion.

Several other activities are part of Spiritual Baptist traditions. Pilgrimages involve traveling to other temples to participate their activities, particularly special celebration services. Thanksgiving services show gratitude to God for his blessings and are annual affairs in some temples. Healing rites are performed by some Spiritual Baptists (not necessarily leaders of congregations). These usually occur outside the regular worship service (before or after) and during personal consultations. Anointing and "doption" (hyperventilated shouting) are believed to be the most effective means of ridding the body of the intrusive spirits deemed responsible for producing sickness. Some healers may prescribe herbal remedies in some cases.[77] Animal sacrifices, mostly of chickens, are performed by some leaders. This does not occur in the temple during worship services but is performed outside afterward or at some other place during the week.

The most regular ceremony for Spiritual Baptists is the regular Sunday service and the weekly prayer meetings. These are held in a church or temple, which is a fairly large rectangular building whose dimensions depend on the size of the congregation and its economic resources. Against the back wall of the temple is a platform with a pulpit (usually to the right facing the platform) from which readings and preaching are done; an altar, above which there is a crucifix and on which are vases of flowers and a candle; a "mourner's" bench for those undergoing baptism or mourning; seats for church leaders; and perhaps a flag representing the church. Temples general have a raised altar in each corner on which sit a container of flowers and a lighted candle. Another altar rises around the center pole that is characteristic of each temple. On this altar sits a bell in addition to the flowers and candle. Spiritual Baptist temples are decorated with symbolic ritual drawings made with chalk. For example, each cardinal point around the center pole is represented by the drawing of a cross. Spiritual drawings may also appear in the doorways and on the head wraps that are parts of the characteristic outfits of worshippers, especially women. Benches arranged on either side of the center pole provide seating for the worshippers.[78]

The regular services of Spiritual Baptists begin with the ringing of bells and the pouring of water before the altars to purify the sanctuary of evil spirits. The service itself tends to alternate between being "cool" and being "hot." The "cool" periods are characterized by the singing of traditional hymns (Sankeys) in slow, mournful, or contemplative tones. Glazier believes that this portion of the service is directed at God the Father and is associated with the quiet pursuit of wisdom. The "hot" periods are centered on the Holy Spirit and try to induce his manifestation through such means as lively singing, clapping, and "doption" or adoption, a type of shouting.[79] Worshippers in whom the Holy Spirit is manifested are given to dancing, shouting, and speaking in tongues. In addition to the singing and manifestation of the Holy Spirit, scripture readings, various exhortations, and a sermon are all elements of a regular service. All these activities extend the length of the service to three or four hours.

As Glazier observes, music and singing suffuse Spiritual Baptist services. They are used "to dispel unwanted spirits, set a mood, and mark ritual phases."[80] Almost all activities are introduced, "interrupted," and concluded by songs; singing is participatory, and any worshipper may "raise" a song (even if he or she is tone deaf), often giving rise to competition regarding which song will be sung at any given moment. Interestingly, musical instruments are banned from Spiritual Baptist worship services, but songs are accompanied by hand-chapping, rhythmic striking of shepherd's staves on the floor, and simulated drumming on benches. Glazier's observation is quite apt: "Spiritual Baptist music features the body itself as the ultimate musical instrument." He continues, "Baptists assign a privileged position to the body as the primary negotiator between the subjective experience and sociocultural context by which 'the body receives the spirit and through it the spirit flows into the world.'"[81]

Even today, the Spiritual Baptist faith is a relatively small religion in Trinidad and Tobago, numbering an estimated ten thousand members. However, government and public recognition have conferred much legitimacy on it beginning in the second half of the 1900s. Once considered the religion of ignorant, superstitious Afro-Trinidadians, it has made converts among more affluent blacks, some Indo-Trinidadians, and even some whites and Chinese. Since the 1950s, the faith has also spread to other locations abroad. It was introduced to Barbados in 1957 by Granville Williams and has gone on to receive government and public recognition like that enjoyed in Trinidad and Tobago.[82] Caribbean immigrants to the United States and to Canada have established large Spiritual Baptist congregations in Brooklyn and a Toronto suburb, respectively.

Revival Zion and Spiritual Baptist, as well as the Orisha religion, have emerged from the shadows of European religion in the twenty-first century. They are generally and widely regarded as the genuine quests of ordinary folks for spiritual fulfillment and spiritual resources to help them negotiate the exigencies of life. However, these faiths seem to have arrived at another crossroad in the twenty-first century. Revival Zion seems to be heading down the Pentecostal path, which enables it to maintain its expressive worship and to focus on healing while becoming a more mainstream Christian tradition. Spiritual Baptists seem to be divided between those who understand themselves in orthodox Christian terms and those who treasure connections to their African past. The Orisha tradition is experiencing a strong pull toward re-Africanization, with some pushback from those who treasure the distinct Afro-Trinidadian traditions that have evolved over the years.

Mainline and Sideline

Post-Independence Mainline
Protestantism and Pentecostalism

The 1900s were marked by the departure of Europe from the Caribbean as colonies struggled for their independence. However, as European powers faded into the background, the United States emerged as a dominating presence. The new U.S. hegemony was fueled by the Monroe Doctrine, in which the United States declared its intention to be the gatekeeper of Latin America and the Caribbean and vowed to oppose the expansion of European influence. This stance was to affect the political, economic, and religious landscapes of the region.

The 1900s were also marked by two interconnected radical transformations of the Christian landscape that defined the century. The first was the arrival of Protestant missionaries in formerly Spanish Roman Catholic colonies. The second was the explosion of Pentecostalism and Evangelical Christianity across Latin America and the Caribbean. The latter was part of a worldwide surge in such groups, particular within the global South (Latin America, Africa, and parts of Asia).

A Catholic Prelude to Protestantism

The post-independence Catholic Caribbean had an ambiguous relationship with the Roman Catholic Church, which simultaneously was a symbol of colonial rule and yet was deeply entrenched in the culture and everyday life of the island nations. While the 1900s were marked by the surge of Protestantism in the Catholic Caribbean, one cannot ignore certain Roman Catholic surges in the midst of this Protestant rise. One such development was the rise of Our Lady of Charity as a national devotion and her becoming the patron saint of Cuba, as well as the manner in which her popularity united Catholic beliefs, Afro-Cuban culture, and Yoruba religion. The late

1800s and early 1900s were pivotal for the elaboration of a Cuban national identity. It was during this time period that Cuba gained independence from Spain and Cubans began the struggle to define themselves. Race and religion functioned significantly in this process. Perhaps the clearest demonstration of this is found in the figure of the patroness of Cuba, La Caridad del Cobre (Our Lady of Charity of Cobre). La Caridad del Cobre, or Cachita, as Cubans have affectionately nicknamed her, is a vital symbol of Cuban religious and national identity. She is, even for those without religious beliefs, a symbol of what it means to be Cuban: "What Cuban has not heard at least once about La Virgen de la Caridad del Cobre? You don't even need to have religious beliefs in order to interpret her as a symbol of Cuba. The origin and evolution of her popular devotion is an unavoidable aspect of any study on the formation of our national conscience."[1] La Caridad began as a local devotion within a community of slaves in the seventeenth century and grew over the years to become the national patroness of the island.[2] Perhaps for this reason alone, she represents not only Cuba but also the Afro-Cuban roots of Cuban identity and religiosity, for in devotion to La Caridad we have an example of an Afro-Cuban practice that came to represent what it means to be Cuban regardless of one's race.

The earliest account of La Caridad is a 1687 interview with Juan Moreno, a royal slave in Cobre.[3] He recounted that, while he was searching for salt in the Bay of Nipe with the indigenous brothers Rodrigo and Juan de Hoyos, they came across a statue of Mary with the words "Yo soy la Virgen de la Caridad" ("I am the Virgin of Charity") attached to it. The statue was turned over to Spanish authorities, a shrine was built in her honor, and devotion spread among the slave community in Cobre. Her popularity and prominence grew as Cuban nationalist sentiments spread across the island. Local tales relate that after the first victorious battle of the Ten Years' War for independence from Spain (1868–1878), General Manuel de Cespedes gave La Caridad his sword in gratitude for Cuba's victory. Seventeen years after a truce between the Cuban rebels and the Spanish Crown, the Cuban War of Independence began (1895–1898). During that war, Cuban soldiers began to appeal to La Caridad and to wear images of her on their uniforms. A mass was said at her shrine in Cobre to celebrate Cuba's final victory, in 1898. On May 10, 1916, she was named patroness of the island, and a new shrine was constructed for her, thus formally elevating what was originally a local devotion of a slave community in eastern Cuba. Throughout Cuban history, her significance and her very appearance have shifted to meet the needs of the Cuban community, whose devotion to her has grown from a local to the national level.

With her growing prominence as a representative of what it means to be Cuban, La Caridad's imagery and narrative were transformed to suit the needs of the dominant population. Essentially, a "whitening" of her image occurred. Her skin was lightened in artistic representations, and the racial identity of the three men to whom she originally appeared as the statue was transformed. The two indigenous men and one African man were replaced by an African, a white, and a racially mixed man. The construction of Cuban *criollo* (island-born Cubans of Spanish ancestry) identity was projected onto the image of La Caridad. As the religious scholar Joseph Murphy highlights, "La Caridad del Cobre has been invested with expressing something of the racial and class dynamics of Cuban society. She is at once a figure in the struggle for racial and social identity among African Cubans as well as a symbol of the inalterable mixture of identities in a Creole society. She is herself a Creole, born out of the stormy waters of the Atlantic."[4] The transformation of La Caridad's story, which parallels her growth to national prominence on the island, is symbolic of the manner in which Cubans have attempted to whiten their identity and their history: the Afro-Cuban roots of her devotion are lost, and the figures surrounding her apparition are lightened. For many, the fact that the roots of La Caridad's devotion were in a slave community is forgotten.

La Caridad's association with Afro-Cuban devotion did not end once her story and iconography were lightened. As Afro-Cuban religious practices evolved into more formalized religions, they began to influence the broader Cuban culture. This was seen in the growing association of La Caridad del Cobre with the *orisha* Oshún. As we have seen, this Afro-Cuban practice of associating or hiding an African deity behind a Catholic image dates to the *cabildo* era. Most Cubans and Cuban-Americans, despite their religious affiliation, are well aware of the relationship between Oshun and La Caridad, demonstrating the extent to which this Afro-Cuban devotion has saturated the Cuban ethos. As Murphy argues, "La Caridad del Cobre is a 'way' that Òsun is present to Cubans who come from an array of social, economic, and racial groups. A mask reveals as much as it conceals, and it is this dynamic simultaneity of inner and outer, African and Catholic, black and white, that informs my interpretation of Òsun's reflection as La Caridad del Cobre."[5] La Caridad's prominence in contemporary Cuba and among the Cuban diaspora demonstrates the lasting imprint of Roman Catholicism on the island. At the same time, the Afro-Cuban population has resisted the elimination of its heritage from Cuban culture and identity making.

Similarly, the patron saint of Haiti, Notre Dame du Perpétuel Secours, is a Marian devotion that first became prominent in the 1900s. Her devotion cuts across economic classes in Haiti, and she is interwoven into the everyday faith of Haitians. In the second half of the 1800s, this Marian icon began to be associated with healing and other miracles. Monsignor François-Marie Kersuzan, bishop of Cap-Haïtian (Haiti), saw her as a public face of Catholicism and a tool that would combat Vodou. Unfortunately, nothing could be further from the case. Instead, for many Haitians, "Mary had already long been identified with Ezili, the Vodou spirit of love, and the introduction of another Marian icon only provided new avenues for Marian syncretism with Ezili."[6] Her history is one of a struggle between a fervent popular devotion among the masses that at times associated her with Ezili and the institutional Church that sought to solidify and control her as an exclusively Catholic icon. While there are various Marian devotions in Haiti, Notre Dame du Perpétuel Secours is by far the most prominent, valued for her undying care for the nation during various natural disasters and health epidemics at the end of the nineteenth century. She was elevated to the status of patroness of Haiti in 1942. Like La Caridad, she demonstrates the prominence of Marian Catholic devotion and its intersection with African diaspora religion in spite of the overwhelming growth of Protestantism in the Caribbean during the twentieth century.

The Arrival of Protestants in the Spanish Catholic Caribbean

In his excellent overview of Protestantism in Latin America, the Latin Americanist Christian Lalive d'Epinday highlights five types of Protestant churches: immigrant or diaspora churches, which often arrived in conjunction with a business venture; ethnic (often German or Anglican) churches; mainline Protestant denominations; Holiness churches (i.e., Nazarene); and indigenous Latin American Protestant churches.[7] While each Caribbean nation has its own distinctive history, there are some broad trends that characterize the spread of Protestantism in the region. These trends include the arrival of North American cultural values with evangelization, an alienation from Spanish colonial Catholicism, and the incorporation of indigenous leadership into the evangelization process.

Puerto Rico

The distinctiveness of the Puerto Rican religious context is characterized by the new religious movements on the island, the explosion of Protestantism and in particular Pentecostalism, and the strong presence of Espiritismo. Historically, what distinguishes Puerto Rico from the other Caribbean countries is the strong European presence on the island and the smaller slave population. Puerto Rico also had the largest number of European immigrants in the nineteenth century Caribbean in proportion to its population. This may be why many Puerto Ricans do not see themselves as typical Caribbean islanders. As the anthropologist Samiri Hernández-Hiraldo thoughtfully points out, "To many Puerto Ricans, Caribbean and Latin American identities share a lower position compared to Puerto Rican identity. Furthermore, many Puerto Ricans consider the island to be physically in the Caribbean, but historically and culturally related to Latin America."[8] Many Puerto Ricans connect their worldview to that of Latin America and disassociate themselves from nations such as Haiti, Jamaica, and Trinidad. In addition, Puerto Rico has the dubious honor of remaining a colony of the United States, a status it has held since the turn of the twentieth century.

Protestantism arrived in Puerto Rico with the Lutherans' introduction, in the late 1500s, of Bibles on the island. However, it was not until the late 1800s that Protestant missionaries began to arrive from the United States in significant numbers. Soon Puerto Rico had the fastest-growing Protestant population among all the former Spanish Catholic colonies in the Caribbean. Though Puerto Rico has been historically and traditionally Catholic, "the number of Protestants there has almost quadrupled since the 1960s, making it the country with the highest growth rate of Protestantism in Latin America and the Spanish-speaking Caribbean." According to one estimate, of the four million Puerto Ricans, two million are Catholic and one million are Protestant (mostly Pentecostals). [9]

The first Protestants in Cuba and Puerto Rico immigrated from North America in the 1800s. Many Protestants worshipped in secret and even conducted their public lives as Catholics; homes and hotel rooms became the sites of Protestant worship. The first established Protestant congregations in Puerto Rico were Anglican and were located in Ponce and Vieques.[10] The first Protestant service was held on November 28, 1869, in Ponce, where the first Protestant church building, the Anglican Church of the Ever Blessed Holy Trinity, led by John C. DuBois, was completed in 1873. The first congregants were primarily wealthy foreigners who provided financial support to early missionary efforts. Because these congregations consisted mainly of immigrants, they did not become heavily involved in the island's political struggles; the Ponce community, however, had various foreign consuls among its leadership, which allowed them to have a fairly public role under the Spanish Catholic colonial government. While an 1869 law approved religious tolerance on the island, these first Protestants were careful not to appear to be attempting to convert locals. It was not until 1880 that a Protestant community was organized in Vieques, a small island off the coast of Puerto Rico, organized by Joseph N. Bean, a lay Anglican from Bermuda. He and the majority of the church's parishioners were black, and there was a clear distinction between the manner in which the Antiguan bishop treated this community and the treatment accorded the white, affluent one in Ponce. Unable to find a permanent rector, Bean traveled to the United States to study at St. Augustine College and was ordained a deacon in 1890. In 1893, he was ordained presbyter. At the turn of the twentieth century, there existed only two Protestant congregations in Puerto Rico. It is important to remember that Cuba and Puerto Rico remained colonies of Spain for a good eighty years after the colonies on the mainland of Latin America became independent and that Protestantism therefore became established much later in their history, after the Spanish had departed.

After the United States acquired the island, the missionary field was divided among nine Protestant denominations: Lutheran, Presbyterian, Methodist, Baptist, United Brethren, Congregationalist, Christian Church, Disciples of Christ, and Christian Missionary Alliance. Each agreed to acquire a particular geographic territory.[11] In 1899, American Baptists and Presbyterian missionaries arrived in Puerto Rico. They were followed by the Methodists in 1900, the Disciples of Christ in 1901, and the Congregationalists and Episcopalians during the following two years. The assimilation of Puerto Ricans into North American culture was an aim of this missionary endeavor, seen in the emphasis on the English language and in the structure of the churches. In addition, these churches were funded by U.S. dollars, giving "the appearance of propagating religious colonialism."[12] Protestantism was seen by its followers as coming hand in hand with democracy on the island. Critics of the United States presence on the island, in contrast, viewed the arrival of Protestants warily and saw it as a symbol of the annexation of Puerto Rico by the United States. At the end of ten years of missionary work on the island, the number of Protestant pastors on the island numbered 260 (57 foreign born and 203 native Puerto Ricans), with five hundred congregations and 13,255 converts.[13] Protestant missionaries enjoyed the full support of the U.S. government, which saw a clear connection between the conversion of islanders and the Americanization of the island. Thus, "[t]he full resources of the government—education, government agencies, social services— cooperated with protestant ministers and their wives, who descended on the island as missionaries and school teachers and who were among the few to speak the official language of Puerto Rico, which was decreed English in 1991."[14] In response, the Roman Catholic Church ensured that all bishops on the island until 1960 were North American, a move that was intended to bolster the pro-U.S. image of the Roman Catholic Church on the island; in addition, the overwhelming majority of priests and women religious (members of religious orders) were North American. The Church attempted to shake off its Spanish past and to participate in the future of the island as a U.S. territory. In spite of the Roman Catholic Church's efforts to "Americanize," with the arrival of Pentecostalism on the island, the Catholic face of Puerto Rico would be forever changed. The Roman Catholic Church met a similar fate in the Dominican Republic.

Dominican Republic

Protestantism arrived in the Dominican Republic via African American immigrants from the United States. As in Puerto Rico, the first pastors arrived in order to attend to these immigrant groups rather than to the established Dominican population. In 1824, when the Dominican Republic was under Haitian rule, Haitian president Jean-Pierre Boyer (1818–1843) permitted the arrival of 2,400 missionaries who resided in the Dominican Republic, and, shortly thereafter, the first Methodist Wesleyan Society was established in Puerto Plata. The Free Methodist Church was founded in 1889 under the leadership of the Ohioan Samuel E. Mills, but it experienced very little growth among the island's natives. The Episcopal, Evangelical, and Moravian churches centered their missionary efforts among the English-speaking communities on the island.[15] This was true of the majority of mainline Protestant churches on the island, which evangelized in English, focused on immigrant groups, and generally ignored the Dominican citizens. With the U.S. occupation of the island, more missionaries arrived, sent by the Board for Christian Work, an organization that consisted of Methodists, Presbyterians, and United Brethren.[16] In 1919, the Reverend Samuel Guy Inman, secretary of the Protestant Committee for Cooperation in Latin America, arrived in Hispaniola in order to pave the way for Protestant missionary work. In 1920, the Board for Christian Work in Santo Domingo was founded, and in 1921, a group headed by a superintendent from the United States and Puerto Rican pastors began its missionary work under the name of the Dominican Evangelical Church, which gained autonomy from the United States in 1955.[17]

Protestant missionaries met much resistance among native Dominicans because the local populations associated Protestant churches with the U.S. occupation of their country in the years 1916–1924. The Episcopal Church fared relatively well because it did much of its missionary work among foreigners who already lived on the island. Overall, however, early Protestant missionary efforts met with little success. When the United States withdrew, in 1924, Protestant missionaries were subjected to hostility and persecution from the Roman Catholic Church, which felt threatened by the well-funded U.S.-backed missionary efforts.

When Rafael Trujillo seized the presidency, in 1930, the Roman Catholic Church faced other obstacles as a weakened institution functioning under a dictator. Trujillo attempted to use his control over the nation to manipulate the Church and its leadership. Given the historic shortage of clergy in the Dominican Republic, many Roman Catholics had been marginally evangelized. However, once the Church came under Trujillo's sway, it was rewarded in many ways: it constructed new buildings, received financing, and saw its religious leaders given personal rewards. In the final years of Trujillo's dictatorship, however, the Catholic Church had a change of heart and began openly denouncing the president. This led to an era of persecution of Roman Catholic priests that ended only in 1961, with Trujillo's assassination. As in Puerto Rico, Protestantism did not have a profound effect on the religious landscape of the Dominican Republic—a situation that would change radically with the arrival of Pentecostalism.

Haiti

The first Protestants to arrive in Haiti were the Methodists, in 1807. Their mission was not overwhelmingly successful, for they focused their ministry on the English-speaking population. Nine years later, the Quakers followed, though they did not establish a sustained ministry. The Baptists established themselves in 1823 with the arrival of the Massachusetts Baptist Missionary Society and the work of Thomas Paul. While they were not extremely successful, one hundred years later the American Baptists Home Missions Society arrived and had an extremely active ministry. Eventually, the Baptist ministry "gathered strength to such a point that it is possible to speak of a mass conversion, and is one of the most interesting phenomena of Haitian Protestantism."[18] African Americans seeking a better life in Haiti brought the Episcopalian Church to the island in 1861. The Church flourished there, and by 1964 its membership had reached fourteen thousand.[19]

Cuba

The spread of Protestantism in Cuba dates to the late 1800s. The Monroe Doctrine and the spirit of Manifest Destiny (the belief that the United States was divinely destined to spread across the continent of North America to the Pacific Ocean) played a role in this expansion. Protestantism was equated with the spread of U.S. values, and Cuba's Spanish Catholic past was maligned. Paraphrasing the writings of Columbia University professor Dr. Samuel G. Inman, writing in the early 1930s, the Caribbean Church historian Adolfo Ham Reyes notes, "Protestantism is a modern and progressive form of Christianity which represents freedom, whereas Catholicism ("Romanism" for them) represents retrograde and reactionary mediaeval Christianity; the Protestant churches in the USA have received from God the mandate to be the vanguard of Protestantism and to be the saviours of the world."[20] Some Protestant missionaries understood their role in the Catholic Caribbean as spreading not only the authentic Christian message but also U.S. values and social norms. Not all missionaries, however, agreed with this position. The Southern Baptist Convention, for example, had a different perspective, arguing that "The USA flag is not the Bible."[21] Interestingly, the first North American missionaries to arrive to Cuba understood their presence on the island as an expansion of their national work. "Symptomatically these missionary labours remained under the jurisdiction of the *national* mission boards, precisely as in Puerto Rico, which shows that Cuba was regarded as USA territory."[22]

The first Protestant missionaries in Cuba were from the United States. In 1871, Episcopal bishop Henry B. Whipple arrived on the island and was shocked at the deteriorated state of affairs among Protestants. Edward Kenney, a recently ordained deacon, was appointed to the Episcopalian church in Cuba that same year. At first, he held services on a U.S. warship and then later moved them to the U.S. consulate; eventually, the Spanish government allowed him to rent a space in the Hotel San Carlos. His mission remained thoroughly dependent on funding from the United States. The situation in Cuba was quite different from that in Puerto Rico. Because of the Ten Years' War for independence from Spain (1868–1878), Cuban Catholics, who associated the Roman Catholic Church with Spanish colonial rule, were often distanced from the institutional Catholic faith. At the end of the war, Kenney found many of the restrictions about ministering publicly loosened, though it was much more acceptable to minister to the black population or the fifty thousand Chinese on the island (brought as contract laborers between 1847 and 1873) than to Spanish Catholics, who became a central focus of Kenney's ministry. After ten years of working on the island, Kenney returned to the United States because of deteriorating health.

The end of the Ten Years' War opened up new missionary opportunities on the island, most notably with Cuban exiles who had left the island during the war and who now returned from the United States as Protestants. Methodists arrived in 1879, and, sponsored by funding from the United States, Alberto J. Díaz, himself a Methodist, established a nondenominational reformed mission in 1883. Díaz, along with the missionary Pedro Duarte y Domínguez, was able to establish a strong ministry centered on the distribution of Bibles. In 1884, John F. Young, an Episcopal bishop from the United States, began active ministry in Cuba, working with Díaz and Duarte.

As mentioned earlier, Protestantism found fertile ground in Cuba. For the many Cubans who were extremely anti-Spain and consequently anti-Catholic, "Protestantism symbolized modernity, popular participation, and liberalism."[23] Because the majority of Protestants on the island were working class, Protestant missions depended heavily on funding from the United States. In the 1880s, there was a backlash against Protestants on the island, and many were harassed. Bishop Young died in 1885, and the Episcopalians experienced problems with funding. At the same time, the Southern Baptist Convention was doing aggressive missionary work, and Díaz's church affiliated with the Baptists. Overall, the Episcopalian mission experienced considerable setbacks as the Baptists experienced significant success.

Protestant missionaries in Cuba were unique in the history of missionary activity; most were Cuban born, yet their missions and ministries were guided and funded by the United States. Nonetheless, U.S.-born missionaries were also essential to the establishment of the Cuban Protestant ethos. Dr. M. McCall is known as the Baptist apostle of Cuba for his successful missionary activity on the island and his establishment of churches. He arrived in Cuba in 1905 and passed away on the island in 1947. The Reverend Stirling Augustus Neble was a Methodist pastor who became the president of the Cuban Council of Evangelical Churches in 1942 and four years later founded the Evangelical Seminary in Matanzas. The seminary began as a collaboration between Methodists and Presbyterians and was later joined by Episcopalians. Despite these Cuban initiatives, the intimate relationships between the Protestant denominations and their U.S. churches became increasingly problematic after the Communist revolution in 1959, which eventually declared Cuba to be an atheist state. The same anti-Spanish, pro-U.S. stance that made Protestantism appealing at the turn of the 1900s would become a hindrance to Protestantism in Castro's Cuba.

At the time of the Cuban revolution, the majority of Protestant churches in Cuba were mainline denominations with intimate ties to the United States. For the most part, "Protestants in Cuba depended on the United States for money, equipment, training, literature, and much of their identity. There were only a handful of congregations that could stand on their own financially, and even those largely depended on the United States for certain major expenses, like construction."[24] Most Cuban churches were entirely dependent on their northern neighbors for their livelihood. As in other former Catholic colonies, U.S. Protestant missionary efforts in Cuba were seen as an effort to modernize and Americanize the island. At the time of the Cuban revolution, while the majority of Cubans identified as Catholic, very few were linked to the institutional church. Protestants who arrived on the island after the Spanish-American War associated Catholicism with the colonial Spanish past of the island. At the time of the revolution, close to fifty Protestant groups existed on the island, some having established themselves as late as the 1950s. Most of these denominations were overwhelmingly staffed by missionaries from the United States; when pastors were Cuban, they had often trained in institutions in the United States. Protestant churches and ministers outnumbered their Catholic counterparts in the 1950s; Roman Catholic priests were overwhelmingly Spanish, while the majority of Protestant leaders were Cuban.[25]

Both Catholics and Protestants initially greeted the revolution with a certain openness. However, for the Catholic Church, this optimism was short-lived as the increasingly leftist nature of the revolution was revealed. The Catholic Church's relationship with Castro's government soured almost instantly over bishops' public critiques of the connections between the revolutionary government and the communist Union of Soviet Socialist Republics (USSR). In contrast, Protestant leaders initially denied that there was any connection between the revolutionary government and communism. Many U.S. missionaries defended the new government's policies in Cuba, which were at times in conflict with U.S. interests. Even among Protestant missionaries who "had equated their goals for Cuba with those of the U.S. government and U.S. businesses, in the first two years of the revolution, a significant number instead identified their interests with the revolutionaries, and many were eager to defend them."[26] Missionaries spoke out against U.S. policy because they believed that the revolution was not in any way contrary to that country's values. Protestants blamed Catholics for all the bad press and even went so far as to support the execution of war criminals and to demonize the Catholic hierarchy.

However, the Protestant response was not monolithic. Some groups, such as the Quakers, and more recent denominations like the Brethren in Christ, Conservative Baptists, and Mennonites were more critical of the revolution and of their Protestant colleagues. By late 1961, however, the communist nature of the new government was clear, and Protestants began to wonder about their role in a Marxist government. Also, the Bay of Pigs invasion, backed by the U.S. Central Intelligence Agency, in April of that year, in which Cubans living in exile in the United States tried to overthrow Castro's regime, was a major turning point for all Christians, because it led the Cuban government to tighten its control over the island's religious institutions. Most U.S. missionaries began to leave in 1961 at the encouragement of the U.S. government. In 1964, the World Council of Churches initiated the Cuba Project to fund Protestant churches on the island and to foster ecumenism in Cuba. It was also a way to maintain funding to Protestant churches on the island in light of U.S. policy.[27] At the same time, the government of Cuba began harassing Christians on the island and closed churches. The Cuban context is quite distinctive in this sense. Unlike the situations in Puerto Rico and the Dominican Republic, Protestant and Catholic churches in Cuba faced direct discrimination and persecution by the government. The government would also monitor the growth of Pentecostalism in Cuba, which emerged in a distinct manner.

Pentecostal and Evangelical Churches

In discussing Pentecostalism and Evangelical Christianity, it is important to clarify their distinctiveness among Protestant denominations. As the political scientist Edward Cleary notes, "One of the marks of confusion about Pentecostal churches is calling them 'evangelical.' The long-standing Latin American custom of describing Protestants as *evangélicos* (sometimes with a pejorative sense of 'Bible thumpers') has led bilingual reporters to use 'evangelical' as the English equivalent, overlooking its restriction to particular tendencies in Protestant history." In many Spanish-speaking Latin American countries, all Protestants are *evangélicos*, and the term cannot be easily translated to "evangelical." In addition to the distinction in terms of language, Evangelicals in the United States have in the past distanced themselves from Pentecostals, emphasizing Pentecostals' lack of education, their lack of financial support, and what is seen as their excessively effusive style of worship and emphasis on speaking in tongues, healing, and prophecy.[28] Ironically, what marginalizes Latin American and Caribbean Pentecostalism from Evangelicals in the

United States is exactly what makes it appealing in their own contexts. What distinguishes Evangelicals historically in the United States is their belief in heart-felt, transformative religious experience and the authority of the Bible in theological and moral issues. Pentecostals fit squarely here. However, Pentecostals also emphasize an expressive worship experience (including speaking in tongues) and physical healing. Pentecostalism is thus a particular subtype of Evangelicalism)

Pentecostal, Neo-Pentecostal, and Charismatic churches all exploded in popularity in the second half of the twentieth century across various denominations. Pentecostal churches trace their genealogy to the spiritual revival in Topeka, Kansas, in 1901, led by Charles Parham, and to the Azusa Street Mission in Los Angeles, California, between 1906 and 1910. Neo-Pentecostal churches, which are often not linked to a Pentecostal denomination and which are independent churches, are very closely connected to politics and economics, and followers are encouraged to be active participants in the public sphere. Charismatic movements are Pentecostal-like movements within mainline Christian denominations. Episcopal Charismatic Christianity emerged in 1959 when a congregation in Van Nuys, California, was baptized in the Holy Spirit. The birth of Charismatic Catholic Renewal (CCR) may be traced to Duquesne University in Pittsburgh in 1966 when a group of students and faculty had a similar experience of the Holy Spirit which they described as baptism in the Spirit. This Pentecostal-like movement, which spread to Latin America in the 1970s, emphasizes speaking in tongues and an individual connection with the Holy Spirit. CCR's first members were predominantly middle class and included a large number of women. Three trends shaped the movement during the 1980s: its growth among the working classes, its approval by the Episcopal leadership, and its primacy as a tool of evangelization. In the 1990s, CCR became institutionalized, becoming the face of the growing Charismatic/Pentecostal flavor of Latin American and Caribbean Catholic Christianity.

The presence of Pentecostalism in the Caribbean varies from nation to nation. While there was an explosion of evangelical revivals in the late 1800s and early 1900s in the Bahamas, Belize, Barbados, Suriname, and Guyana, today their traditional evangelical populations remain relatively small. Cuba also has a small evangelical population. However, in Haiti, Puerto Rico, and Jamaica, Pentecostalism is exploding. Furthermore, "Caribbean evangelicals are growing rapidly in the other traditionally Catholic countries—the Dominican Republic (in the 2 to 7 percent range), Haiti (15 to 20 percent), and Puerto Rico (7 to 30 percent)."[29] A direct correlation exists between the growth of Pentecostalism and the urbanization of the Caribbean. The Haitian scholar Laënnec Hurbon highlights that the growth of Pentecostalism in the Caribbean occurred in the urban centers and not the rural periphery.[30] Similarly, the anthropologist Sidney Mintz argues in *Worker in the Cane* that Puerto Ricans' conversion to Pentecostal churches can largely be attributed to island's change from a rural, agricultural setting to an urban environment.[31] Pentecostal churches, scholars argue, provide a much needed sense of family and community when individuals leave the rural settings where their families may have lived for generations and move to an anonymous existence in cities.

The presence of Pentecostalism in Latin America and the Caribbean demonstrates that the presence of Protestantism in these areas is not solely a result of of activity by missionaries from North America who were governed by the United States. Although it was introduced to the Caribbean from North America, Pentecostalism quickly took on the local flavor of the vernacular culture and developed local leadership and organizations. Breaking away from subordination to "foreigners in high national positions," Caribbean Pentecostals" "formed rapidly multiplying small communities rather than parishes and looked to themselves for organizing rather than to central headquarters in Stockholm or in Springfield, Missouri."[32] However, not all Pentecostal churches exist as independent entities; some remain connected to Pentecostal denominations in the United States.

The foundation of Pentecostalism is the Holiness and Revival traditions, which emphasize rebirth in the Holy Spirit and living within a community that counteracts the corruption of this world. In addition, Pentecostalism is able to negotiate between the modern and the traditional worlds, making it especially appealing in Latin America and the Caribbean:

> For example, it brings together the ancient layers of spiritism, in black Africa and indeed almost everywhere, with a modern sense of the union of psyche and soma. It brings together the ancient notion of illness as located in the community with the modern concept of community medicine. It unites the ancient layers of solidarity with the kinds of expansive organizational principles recommended by specialists in church growth. And the Pentecostal preference for stories, for gesture and oratory, belongs simultaneously to pre-literate and to post-literate society.[33]

Pentecostalism emphasizes the experience of the spirit, a predominant element in African diaspora religions and in Espiritismo. It also highlights one's individual experience of the sacred, connecting to the modern Western emphasis on the individual. It focuses on healing, testimony, and expressive rituals, all elements that connect with Caribbean worldviews.

Puerto Rico

Information on Pentecostalism in Puerto Rico in the early twentieth century is scarce. Data on Pentecostalism in Puerto Rico after the 1940s are more widely available. It is estimated that in 1942, Pentecostals made up 8.5 percent of the island's Protestant population and that that number grew to 25 percent in the following ten years.[34] In 1907, Juan Lugo, a Puerto Rican who was living in Hawaii, was converted to Pentecostalism by missionaries from the Azusa Street Mission. He returned to Puerto Rico in 1916. He ignored the geographic limitations set by other Protestant denominations and the opinion of pastors that he was untrained to do ministry. Ignoring the ministers' disapproval and enduring "harassment from the local authorities, within two years" he established "eight Pentecostal churches on the island, and by 1929 there were twenty-five churches called the Iglesia de Dios Pentecostal, associated today with the U.S. Assemblies of God." By 1942, Pentecostals churches accounted for most of the Protestant churches on the island and ranked first in number of pastors and candidates for baptism.[35] Juan Lugo's story highlights yet another distinction between Pentecostals and other Protestants: education. For Pentecostals one does not need a seminary degree in order to validate one's ministry; that validation comes from a sense of calling from God and of being gifted by the Spirit. This makes Pentecostal pastoral leadership much more accessible than similar positions in other Protestant denominations. Lugo's Pentecostal Church of God of Puerto Rico is the largest Protestant denomination on the island, followed by the Assemblies of God (with which Lugo was associated for some time) and the Iglesia Defensores de la Fe, founded by the Puerto Rican Juan Francísco Rodríguez Rivera.[36]

In the 1940s, a distinctive Puerto Rican religious tradition grounded in Pentecostalism emerged on the island in Arecibo. Known as Mita, today it counts devotees in the United States, Mexico, Venezuela, Haiti, Colombia, and the Dominican Republic. Its temple in San Juan holds more than five thousand people, and the religious organization owns several homes, businesses, schools, and a clinic in the surrounding area.[37] Mita's founder, Juanita Garcia Peraza, was a former Pentecostal who believed that she was the incarnation of the Holy Spirit and that her message was to return Christianity to its original roots. Mita (Juanita) is considered God's third revelation (the first being the Old and New Testaments). After her death, the Holy Spirit passed on to Teofile Vargas Stein, known as Aaron. Mita bears striking resemblances to Pentecostalism both in spirituality and in worship. Mita embodies a countercultural movement that pushes against modernity and that has clear boundaries between those who are chosen and those who are not. The movement represents an indigenous Pentecostal movement that was born on the island and has spread throughout the Americas. Puerto Rican Pentecostalism is distinctive not only in its prominence on the island but also in the manner in which it has shaped Pentecostalism in other parts of the Caribbean through missionary activity.

Dominican Republic

Puerto Rican Pentecostalism is connected to missionary activity in the Dominican Republic. In 1917, Salomón Feliciano Quiñones, a friend of Juan Lugo, arrived from Hawaii in the Dominican Republic. Salomón established his first mission in San Pedro de Macorís. His missionary work with other Puerto Ricans was eventually absorbed by the Assemblies of God twenty-four years later. The Church of God of Prophecy, another church with roots in the United States, and the Assemblies of God are the two largest Pentecostal churches in the Dominican Republic. Early Protestant missionaries in the Dominican Republic initially conducted the majority of their missionary activity in English, but the Pentecostal churches adopted Spanish as their missionary tongue. In addition, they worked and lived in their communities (especially among impoverished Dominicans) and had strong ties to the spirituality of the Dominican people.

The four largest Pentecostal denominations established themselves in the Dominican Republic during Trujillo's rule: the Assemblies of God, the Church of God, the Church of God of the Prophecy, and the Church of God Pentecostal. The missionary work of the Assemblies of God began in 1930 through the Puerto Rican Francisco Hernández González, who began the early stages of his ministry in Santo Domingo and San Pedro de Macorís. The Pentecostal Church of God also began its ministry with Puerto Rican preachers, but, lacking financial support, did not begin to thrive until missionaries arrived from the United States. The Church of God arrived in 1939 through the missionary work of Silvestre Jorge, a Bahamian, and the Church of God of the Prophecy, led by the Haitian Trajana Adrián, arrived in the same period. One marker of the difference between these recent Protestant missionary endeavors and earlier efforts is that the newer churches placed the leadership in the hands of the indigenous population: "In fact, since 1940, the superintendent of the church, the executive with the highest rank within the Assemblies of God has been a Dominican. Thus, early on, evangelicals sought to adapt to the local society and culture in their preaching style and acceptance of Dominican folkways."[38] Even when Pentecostal churches in the Dominican Republic have connections to Pentecostal churches in the United States, the leadership of churches on the island is left in the hands of the local population.[39]

Cuba

Pentecostalism in Cuba was limited initially by government control of religious places of worship and by a prohibition against conducting religious worship in private homes. In 1990, the Cuban government relaxed restrictions on house churches, which had been prohibited since 1962. This led directly to an explosion of Pentecostalism on the island. The Assemblies of God, which have been in Cuba since the 1930s, claim to have grown from 12,000 members and 89 congregations to 100,000 members and 756 congregations during the decade of the 1990s. These numbers are staggering, and they make Assemblies of God the largest Pentecostal church on the island.[40] Nonetheless, government restrictions keep most Pentecostal house churches connected to some degree to a traditional denomination. The Pentecostal storefront church phenomenon, in which churches appear on street corners in spaces formerly occupied by businesses, is not rampant in Cuba.[41]

The prosperity gospel, which emphasizes material wealth as a sign of God's blessing, is also beginning to thrive in Cuba. One group, Creciendo en Gracia, a Miami-based group whose founder, José Luis de Jesús Miranda, claims to be Jesus Christ, has thirty house churches in Cuba. With its emphasis on personal wealth, the prosperity gospel goes against the principles of Cuba's socialism. The charismatic style of this theology, more than its message, is what has appealed to Cubans. Notwithstanding the growth of the Assemblies of God and the attraction of the property gospel, Pentecostal churches overall have not thrived in Cuba, mainly because of the strength of the Cuban Council of Churches, which comprises "half of Protestant denominations (in addition to two more which participate as observers) and twelve ecumenical movements."[42] In addition to the historic limitations on house churches until fairly recently in Cuba's history, the strength and unity of mainline Protestant denominations, through the Cuban Council of Churches, have limited the growth of Pentecostalism on the island. Of the three former Spanish Catholic colonies of Cuba, Puerto Rico, and the Dominican Republic, it is in Cuba that the mainline Protestant denominations maintained their strongest hold.

Haiti

In 1997, 28.7 percent of the Christian population in Haiti claimed a Protestant religious identity. In urban centers such as Port-au-Prince, the number was as high as 39 percent. The majority of these Protestants are Pentecostal.[43] Most Pentecostal churches in Haiti have no international denominational affiliation and are instead independent entities ministered to by local pastors. Therefore, accurate statistics on the number of Pentecostal churches are difficult to obtain, and, because churches divide or merge frequently, their relationships are much more fluid than those of denominationally affiliated churches. Of the denominationally affiliated Pentecostal churches in Haiti, the Church of God in Christ is the largest. The next three largest denominational Pentecostal churches are Church of God of Prophecy, which arrived in Haiti in the 1930s; the Assemblies of God, which was transplanted to Haiti in 1957; and the United Pentecostal Church, which was organized in Haiti in 1968.[44]

The origins of Pentecostalism in Haiti are unknown. Most likely, Pentecostalism arrived via ad hoc missionary work and not through directed efforts from North American denominations.[45] The first Church of God in Christ pastor in Haiti was Paulceus Joseph, who converted in the United States and then arrived in Haiti in 1929. In 1933, one of his converts, Vital Herne, contacted the Church of God in Cleveland, Tennessee, reporting struggles with other pastors. His ministry was accepted by the Church of God in 1934. The organization infused money into his ministry, and two years later he reported having thirty congregations. Herne later split with the Church of God, and two North American missionaries, John and Stephanie Kluzit, were brought in to replace him. In the early 1940s, the Haitian government banned the Church of God for a two-year period because of "derogatory" comments made by a visiting pastor from the United States. Between 1941 and 1943, the years of the ban, the church lost two-thirds of its membership. By midcentury, the church had recovered, and by 1980 the Church of God (Tennessee) had 390 congregations. The Assemblies of God arrived in Haiti from the Dominican Republic. Lawrence Perrault, a missionary, attempted ministry in Haiti in the mid-1940s but was unsuccessful, and he left for the Dominican Republic; he returned to Haiti in 1957 and commenced a successful ministry. Other Haitian Pentecostal churches with North American connections include The Church of God of Prophecy (established in the 1930s), the Church of God in Christ, the Pentecostal Assemblies of the World, and the United Pentecostal Church.

Jamaica

Jamaica is distinct in that the history of Protestantism on the island is directly linked to the island's colonial past. In spite of the lengthy historical presence of mainline Protestant denominations on the island, the growth of Pentecostalism has drastically changed the face of Jamaican Christianity. The stage was set for Pentecostalism in Jamaica when churches identified with the Holiness Church movement in the United States began arriving in the island at the turn of the twentieth century. Holiness missionaries from the Church of God, Anderson (Indiana), arrived in Jamaica in 1907. A missionary society of the Holiness persuasion started a work in western Jamaica in 1912 that was eventually taken over by Wesleyan Methodists (now the Wesleyan Church). While Holiness churches emphasized a sanctifying experience by the Holy Spirit and a lively form of worship, they did not emphasize speaking in tongues or healing. Many Holiness churches in the United States became Pentecostal churches after the Topeka and Azusa Street revivals.

Pentecostalism arrived in Jamaica in the 1910s and took twenty years to take root. The growth of Pentecostalism represents the increased influence of North American culture on Jamaican culture, replacing the legacy of British colonialism. Though Pentecostalism in Jamaica was initiated by local preachers, many turned to Pentecostal denominations from the United States for missionary and financial support. For example, the two largest Pentecostal denominations started as a result of an invitation from J. Wilson Bell, a local independent preacher, to the Church of God, Tennessee, seeking affiliation.[46] In the 1920s, two local ministers were instrumental in the entrenchment of Pentecostalism in Jamaica. Rudolph Smith and Henry Hudson, of what later became the New Testament Church of God, established numerous congregations throughout the island. Hudson was made overseer of the New Testament Church of God in 1935. That same year, Smith, who had been instrumental in establishing the Bible Church of God, later known as the Church of God of Prophecy, was appointed its overseer.[47]

By 1950, various other Pentecostal groups had established themselves in Jamaica. The Pentecostal Assemblies of the World arrived in the 1920s, the Church of God in Christ in the 1920s, the Assemblies of God in 1941, and the United Pentecostal Church in 1947. In addition to these churches affiliated with denominations from the United States, numerous indigenous Pentecostal churches have appeared throughout the island. Pentecostalism flourished between the 1950s and the 1970s, when an independent Jamaica (it became independent in 1962) moved from an agricultural to an industrial economy.

This is similar to the trend throughout the Caribbean as a whole, where Pentecostalism accompanies urbanization. The growth of Pentecostalism has been accompanied by a corresponding decline in mainline Protestant denominations.[48]

By the 1960s, 20 percent of Jamaicans identified as Pentecostals. In a 1982 census, more than 400,000 Jamaicans identified themselves as belonging to the Church of God faith (probably various Pentecostal churches that have Church of God as part of their names). The next largest Protestant faith was the various Baptist groups, which had more than 217,000 adherents. The same census also showed that another 113, 570 people claimed to belong to other Pentecostal churches.[49] Given that Jamaica's population was about two million at the time, this indicates that almost 30 percent of Jamaicans were Pentecostal at that time. The charismatic awakening in Jamaica in the 1970s and 1980s had led to the establishment of a number of independent Pentecostal churches that appealed to people in the middle and upper classes of Jamaica. Along with an upswing in the independent Pentecostal churches of the traditional variety, the Charismatic Pentecostal churches had furthered stamped the Pentecostal character on ethos on Christianity in Jamaica.

Christianity in the Caribbean during the twentieth century was marked by the explosive growth of Pentecostalism. Though a late arrival in the history of Christianity, it has become the most significant Christian movement throughout the Caribbean. Pentecostal faiths arrived either through direct work by North American missionaries or through individuals who converted to a Pentecostal faith elsewhere and later returned to their homelands. For many a reflection of religion in the contemporary Caribbean, Pentecostalism "is by and large the new Christianity of black people, which in some measure is refuting the claim of those who speak for traditional European Christianity that divinity can only be perceived through the eye of the people of Europe, interpreted in their mythology and language, and represented visually through the imagery of their culture."[50] Pentecostalism created an indigenous Christianity that appealed greatly to the masses; through its incorporation of a Spirit-based Christianity and local leadership, Pentecostalism offered a religious ethos that appealed to poor Caribbean peoples that resonated with their African aesthetics and religious life.

However, Pentecostal and Charismatic Christianity are only one part of the story. The arrival of mainline Protestant denominations in the former Catholic Caribbean changed the religious landscape of these island nations, paving the way for the later growth of Pentecostal faiths. In addition, Catholicism remains strong in the region. Popular Catholic devotions to Mary, for example, and other local saints continue to flourish, and many of these devotions have become bridges to African diaspora religions, especially in Cuba and Haiti. Charismatic Catholicism is also growing. The complexity of Christianity in the twentieth-century Caribbean and in the Caribbean today reflects global Christianity, which is becoming increasingly supernatural in belief and more localized in terms of leadership and membership.

Migration and Revitalization

Hinduism, Islam, and Rastafarianism

The importation of indentured workers from Asia at the end of the nineteenth century deepened the religious diversity of the Caribbean with the introduction of Islamic and Hindu religious traditions. With the end of the transatlantic slave trade, the arrival of these new populations added a new layer to the religious worldviews of the Caribbean. While Islam had first arrived in the Caribbean via the transatlantic slave trade, the arrival of Muslim Asians gave it a visibility unseen in prior centuries. This had a significant impact on not only the religious life but also the culture and economic structure of Caribbean nations. The arrival of Asian immigrants also provoked questions of Caribbean identity and ethnicity.

Also at the turn of the twentieth century, people of African descent began to seek a revitalization of their African heritage by founding such groups as the Rastafarian movement. One of the most internationally recognized yet misunderstood Caribbean religious traditions, Rastafari shows us the manner in which Afro-Jamaicans sought to articulate a sense of African religion and identity while still being influenced by and struggling against the legacy of European colonialism. These three religious traditions reflect postemancipation colonial Caribbean religion and the negotiation of identity as the island nations finally achieved independence from European powers.

Hinduism

The story of the arrival of Hinduism in the Caribbean is inextricably linked to the demise of slavery in the regions and the arrival of Indian indentured workers to the British colonies. The largest concentrations of Hindus in the Caribbean live in Trinidad, Guyana, and Surinam. After the emancipation of slaves in 1838, the British began to import workers from their other colonies to work on sugar plantations. As we saw earlier, the majority of indentured laborers came from India. They were given three- to five-year contracts with the option of staying on in the Caribbean. The overwhelming majority, approximately 70 percent, remained. The indentureship program lasted from 1838 to 1917, with a brief three-year hiatus between 1848 and 1851. Close to 143,000 East Indians were brought to Trinidad alone between 1845 and 1917. The East India Association, founded in the 1890s, consisted primarily of the descendants of Brahmin priests.

By the turn of the century, the Caribbean-born Indian population outnumbered the Indian-born population.[1] At the time of Trinidad and Tobago's independence, in 1962, Indians represented 36 percent of the entire population, making them the islands' second largest ethnic group. Among the Indian poplation, 70 percent were Hindu, 15 percent were Christian, and 15 percent were Muslim. Hindus were 23 percent of the total population in 1960, and Muslims made up 6 percent.[2] The number of East Indians who arrived in Guyana was much larger, close to 240,000.[3]

The Indians who arrived in Trinidad and Tobago as indentured workers were from various economic castes and geographic regions in India. According to the records, "A majority of them emigrated from the states of Bihar and Uttar Pradesh. Small proportions of emigrants belonged to Bengal, Punjab, Himachal Pradesh, Kashmir, Tamil Nadu, Kerala and Andhra Pradesh. Some came from Nepal and some from Afghanistan. A small number of tribes from Bengal and Bihar also emigrated. Thus, a miniature of India and also of the Indian subcontinent was re-created in Trinidad."[4] However, the northern Indian Hindu tradition, which was the center of ancient Hinduism and had a rich theological history, came to dominate Indo-Trinidadian religious ethos. The Vedas (the oldest sacred texts of Hinduism) emerged from this region, and various prominent Hindu philosophers were northern Hindus. Within this context, Sanatan Dharma, the eternal law, developed and became the orthodoxy in the region. This legalistic northern Hindu tradition also shaped Caribbean Hinduism. However, the historian Brinsley Samaroo argues that, because the Indians who arrived in Trinidad were overwhelmingly from rural contexts, devotional Hinduism, which was more popular and less institutional, predominated. In Samaroo's words, "The general belief system of the majority of the religious groups that came here was Sanatanist; the main form of expression was bhaktic [devotion to a personal God], avoiding the intellectual discourse that so heavily characterizes Vedantic philosophy [philosophy of the Vedas]."[5]

The majority of Indians who arrived in Trinidad were Hindu, though there were some Muslims and, to a much smaller extent, Buddhist Indians.

The establishment of temples was fundamental to the preservation of Hinduism on the island, as was the development of an infrastructure to support Hindus who confronted various challenges in the diaspora. These developments included but were not limited to the legalization of Hindu marriages, the cremation of the dead, and the possibility of non-Christian education. Pundits (scholars of law and philosophy) were not recognized as marriage officers until 1945, a full ten years after imams (Muslim leaders, usually of a mosque) were permitted to marry Muslims. The state's refusal to recognize Hindu marriages led to the forced baptism of Hindus; those whose Hindu marriages were not recognized as legal by the state or the Catholic Church often had their estates repossessed by the government at the time of death of a spouse. In 1953, Hindus were given the right to cremate the dead. The Hindu mandate that bodies be cremated is grounded in the belief that cremation encourages the soul to pass into the realm of the dead.[6]

From as early as the 1860s, Hindus were celebrating public religious rituals in Trinidad. The Firepass festival, a south Indian ritual that culminated with walking over hot coals, was celebrated near Port of Spain. Twenty years later, however, laws were passed to restrict this public ritual. The Hosay ritual, a street festival that commemorates the martyrdom of Husayn (also spelled Hussein), Muhammad's grandson, became the major Indian religious festival in Trinidad, despite being a Muslim festival.[7]

Hinduism in Trinidad became quite distinct from Indian Hinduism, incorporating new myths, rituals, and festivals.[8] Moreover, the regional plurality of Indians and their distinctive styles of worship eventually came together in the Caribbean and formed a more generalized, less regionally specific Hinduism. The creation of temples cemented this consolidation process. With the construction of temples came an increase in the number, size, and importance of Hindu festivals. "Lengthy and elaborate plays (Ram, Lila, Krishna) depicting stories of the gods were performed in estates and villages in the nineteenth century, and Diwali [the festival of lights] and Phagwa (Holi) [the spring festival of colors] were the most popular annual events celebrated by Hindus in the colonies by the turn of the century."[9] Hinduism did not exist in a vacuum; it influenced other religious traditions in Trinidad. Hinduism influenced the Yoruba Shango/Orisha religion of Trinidad, as is evidenced primarily in its ritual life.[10]

Though the Indian caste system (an Indian system of social class and hierarchy) could not simply be transplanted to the Caribbean, elements of the caste system remained prominent and developed distinctively. Thus, a form of "Brahmanization" "occurred in the Caribbean, whereby throughout each

Hindu community, a core of Brahmanic ritual directed towards Sanskritic gods came into ascendency." Brahmins elite scholars and preachers gained a special prominence for their ritual leadership that was available to all castes, since the rigidity of the caste system could not be replicated in the diaspora. This Brahmanic Hinduism focused on the textual, Sanskritic tradition (also known as the Great Tradition). Rituals that rose to prominence under the Brahmans included offerings to deities (the *puja*), recitation of sacred texts (*kathas*), and officiation by Hindus, rather than Christians, at rites of passage (*samskaras),* weddings, and funerals.[11] Also contributing to this standardization was the arrival of the reformist movement Arya Samaj in the early twentieth century. Originating in north India, Arya Samaj called for reforms in doctrine and structure through Vedic purification and an emphasis on individual beliefs. The movement aggressively sent missionaries to the Caribbean in an effort to undermine Brahmanic authority.[12] The Brahmins responded to their presence with a unified front, establishing organization such as the Sanatan Dharma Association and the Sanatan Dharma Board of Control in Trinidad in order to affirm their role as the leaders of official Hinduism. Similar organizations were established in British Guiana and Surinam in the 1930s.

Initial Indian sites of worship in the Caribbean were small shrines. The diversity of the Hindu population led to a decline in the religion's more parochial practices. However, with the establishment of temples in the late nineteenth century, a more institutionalized ritual was established. Some of these temple spaces were encouraged by plantation owners, partly to maintain Indians as a close-knit and consequently marginalized indentured community. Hindu festivals always played a prominent role in Caribbean Hinduism. However, the core of colonial Caribbean Hinduism centered around everyday practices, otherwise described as popular or vernacular religion. Household shrines were at the center of this religiosity. Hinduism in the Caribbean eventually evolved into a mixture of temple life, domestic religion, and individual worship.

Islam

The first Muslims to arrive in this hemisphere came as early as Columbus's voyage in 1492, on which they served as crew members on his ships. Muslims began to arrive in larger numbers with the transatlantic slave trade, and their numbers grew during the nineteenth century. Muslims were no strangers to the Spanish and the Portuguese, for the almost eight-hundred-year occupation of the Iberian peninsula by Muslims ended the same year that Columbus set sail across the Atlantic. Unlike the British and the Dutch, the Spanish and Portuguese lived among Africans and, consequently, Muslims for centuries prior to the "discovery" of the Americas. Muslims were also among the one million Yoruba who were transported to the New World. Islam played a factor in constructing Yoruba identity, most notable in the fact that Yoruba is a term with Muslim origins.[13]

Studies of Afro-Caribbean religions in Spanish-speaking regions must take into account that encounters between the Spanish and African peoples long predated the transatlantic slave trade, which was itself preceded by the enslavement in medieval Spain and Portugal of people who were lighter-skinned than Africans. Thus, "Although there were some enslaved blacks there, slave status was identified with whites. The very word 'slave' is derived from 'Slav,' whites who were captured in eastern Europe and shipped into medieval Spain in large numbers."[14] Darker-skinned people were identified with conquerors and rulers. Black slaves who were exported during the trans-Saharan trade were primarily used as domestics by the Berber Arab aristocracy. In their quest for gold, Christians stumbled upon this slave trade. By 1090, the Moorish dynasty (Almoravides) conquered Spain, Portugal, Sudan, Morocco, and the Senegal River Valley; "Thus four centuries before the Atlantic slave trade began, black Africans from the Senegal region were quite familiar in the Iberian Peninsula. Many dark-skinned peoples appeared in the late eleventh century not as slaves but as warriors, conquerors, rulers, bards, and musicians."[15] The historian Gwendolyn Minlo Hall highlights the vast influence of Islamic law, culture, and language in shaping the Iberian Peninsula: "When African slavery was introduced to the English colonies in the Americas during the seventeenth century, Christianity, not race, continued to dominate discussions of legal slavery, just enslavement, and whether enslaved Africans who converted to Christianity had to be freed. The link between religion and race centering on the curse of Ham played a minor role in these early discussions. Racist justifications for enslavement and slavery of black Africans increased over time."[16] Religion was the initial justification for the transatlantic slave trade, not race, although, as that trade grew, slavery became associated with blacks. Thus, a religious and not a racial justification was the basis for the rejection, vilification, and persecution of practitioners of African religions by the Spanish.

The Portuguese and the Spanish appropriated the slave trade of the Moors, who practiced the enslavement of sub-Saharan blacks.[17] Once the Reconquista occurred, the Portuguese justified their enslavement of Moors by citing their war against Islam. The Portuguese, however, also enslaved white Christians. Papal bulls issued by Nicholas V (1454) and Calixtus II (1456) legitimized the enslavement of sub-Saharan Africans as a means of Christianizing them, thus ultimately benefiting the slaves. Slaves were considered captives taken during a just war. Because of the history of Muslim occupation, the Spanish were reluctant to import large numbers of Muslims to the Americas. A 1501 decree prohibited the entry of "Jews, Moors, heretics, and 'New Christians' from entering the Americas. The same decree, however, allowed for the passage of those 'born in the power of the Christians.'"[18] Nonetheless, sometimes through illegal trade with the British, Muslims continued to arrive in the Spanish Caribbean. The first Muslims to arrive in Jamaica came as enslaved Africans, the majority most likely coming from Senegambia and Sierra Leone. A significant Muslim Ashanti population was also brought to Jamaica. Drawing from colonial accounts, the historian Sultana Afroz highlights the presence of Ashanti and Mandinka practicing Muslims.[19] Jamaica still has an active Muslim presence. While Muslim slaves were brought to Haiti and the Dominican Republic, barely any trace of Islam remains in Hispaniola.[20] One place Afroz does find the remnants of Islam is in Haitian Vodou art.

Islam arrived in Trinidad through a process similar to the indentured-labor program that primarily drew from India and brought Hinduism to the Caribbean. The majority of Muslims were Sunni, though there were some Shi'ah, as well. The Hosay ritual in Trinidad, which is is the Shi'i Muslim commemoration of the martyrdom of the imam Husayn, grandson of Muhammad, is one example of public Muslim ritual life on the island. It occurs during the first ten days of the first month of the Islamic lunar calendar, Muharram. While it is a Shi'i ritual, it attracts individuals from a wide variety of religious backgrounds. The Islamist Frank Korom argues that the appeal of the ritual is in its vibrancy and healing powers. Debates over the "carnivalization" of the ritual, which can at times seem more festive than pious, continue today.[21] In 1882, Ordinance No. 9 was passed in Trinidad to limit the number of participants and routes of Hindu, Muslim, and Afro-Trinidadian religious processions. The normally peaceful Hosay ritual ended in bloodshed in 1884, demonstrating the repression of Islamic practices on the island. The military was called in to help control the procession, and, while the historical details are hazy, in the end 16 were killed and 107 injured.[22]

In addition to Indian Muslims, African Muslims have had a strong presence in Trinidad. As we have seen, some arrived through the transatlantic slave trade, while later arrivals came through the indentured-worker program. Within the island, Port of Spain had the first significant Muslim community on the island. Figures such as Muhammad Sisse, Muhammad Hausa, and "Jackson Harvey," in the first half of the nineteenth century, established a Muslim community after the British government demobilized its African troops at the end of the Napoleonic Wars. There is significant evidence to show that a sizable Muslim community existed in Port of Spain by the mid-1800s, led by an imam named Muhammad Bath. Communities were also established in Quaré and Manzanilla. The lack of Christian clergy in these settlements contributed to the free practice and relative growth of Islam. Muslims organized themselves into mutual aid societies, similar to *cabildos* in Cuba. They were extremely organized socially and financially. One report indicates that "[t]he Port of Spain Muslims not only collectively saved to purchase each other's freedom but also borrowed from one another to finance commercial and agricultural ventures."[23] They were very public in displaying their Muslim beliefs and practices. The Muslim community in Trinidad was probably one of the largest, most successful, and most visible in the Americas.

Rastafari

On November 2, 1930, Ras Tafari was crowned emperor of Ethiopia and took the following as part of his title: "Haile Selassie, King of kings and Lord of lords, Conquering Lion of the Tribe of Judea." This title is brimming with religious and biblical resonances. Haile Selassie means "power of the trinity"; "King of kings" and "Lord of lords" are titles of the Christ figure in the Book of the Apocalypse (Revelations) of the Christian Bible; and the Conquering Lion is a metaphor for the Jewish and Christian messianic figure (also mentioned in the Book of the Apocalypse). The appearance of these metaphors in the emperor's title may have been intended to show his preeminence over all other local leaders in Ethiopia, to proclaim the fact that Ethiopia is a profoundly Christian society, and to invoke the legend of the Kebra Negast, which traced Ethiopian royalty to Menelek, supposedly the son of the Queen of Sheba (Ethiopia) and Solomon, the Israelite King famous for his wisdom and multiple wives (I Kings 11). However, shortly after news of this event reached Jamaica (probably via a *Time* magazine article of November 18, 1930), preachers started appearing on the streets in various locations in Jamaica proclaiming that Haile Selassie was Christ returning as a black messiah to liberate Africans on the continent and in the diaspora from the centuries of oppressions to which they had been subjected.

According to oral traditions, the report of the crowning of Ras Tafari reminded these preachers of a prophecy made by Marcus Garvey some years before. Reportedly, Garvey had urged his followers, "Look to Africa; when you see a new king arise, you will know that your liberation is at hand." Consulting their Bible to see if this was a fulfillment of that prophecy, they found passages that echoed elements of Ras Tafari's new title, including a passage that seemed to refer to Christ as "the blessed and only Ruler, the King of kings and Lord of lords" (I Timothy 6:15). The Book of Revelation refers to the Christ figure as "the Lion of the tribe of Judah, the Root of David" (Revelations 5:5). Later, the writer of the Book of Revelations describes one of his visions of the Christ figure thus: "On his robe and on his thigh he has this name written: KING OF KINGS AND LORD OF LORDS" (Revelations 19:16). Matching these passages with the elements of title of the emperor provided convincing evidence to the first Rastas that he was indeed Christ reincarnated and the messianic figure who would restore Ethiopia's ancient glory and end the oppression of African peoples worldwide.

Precursors and Founders of Rastafari

The stage for the identification of Haile Selassie as messianic liberator, and hence the emergence of Rastafari, had been set by the religious and cultural resources that Afro-Jamaicans had employed in creating, preserving, and articulating an Afro-Jamaican identity in the face of British political, economic, and cultural hegemony. One element of these cultural resources was the folk religious ethos that had evolved among Afro-Jamaicans. From Myal to the Native Baptist Movement to Kumina to Revivalism (Zion and Pukumina), the common folk articulated a sense of their place in the cosmic drama and drew on the heritage of their African past and elements of Christianity that they encountered in Jamaica to deal with the exigencies of living under oppressive conditions. All of these traditions sought to connect people to spiritual and divine power in order to heal their personal and communal afflictions and to dismantle systems of oppression. As we have indicated in chapter 6, the spirit of resistance to European domination that pervaded Jamaican history drew inspiration from the folk religious ethos. Furthermore, this religious ethos appropriated the messianic and apocalyptic elements in the Bible to articulate a belief in the eventual defeat of the forces of oppression.

Closely related to the folk religious ethos but often articulated in more secular and intellectual terms is the tradition of Ethiopianism widely subscribed to in the African diaspora. In the broadest sense, Ethiopianism manifested itself in the practice of people in the African diaspora of identifying themselves with Ethiopia, which was sometimes thought of as interchangeable with Africa. Black churches, secret societies, and mutual aids societies often included Ethiopia in their names to express such identification. Part of this identification grew out of the recognition of Ethiopia as an ancient, highly developed civilization that was forged by Africans. It was also inspired by biblical references to Ethiopia and particularly by what sounds like a prophecy of Ethiopia's restoration to its former glory: "Princes shall come out of Egypt; Ethiopia shall soon stretch out her hands unto God" (Psalm 68:31). Ethiopianism thus posited a future restoration of Ethiopia and a future liberation of all those identified with it.

In the early 1900s, the Jamaican pan-Africanist Marcus Mosiah Garvey launched the most widespread and culturally and politically progressive black social movement of the early 1900s. He captured the aspirations of Afro-Jamaicans that had been preserved in their folk religious ethos and the desire for liberation that had been articulated through Ethiopianism throughout the African diaspora. Garvey founded a popular movement aimed at restoring Africans in the diaspora and Africans on the continent to their proper place in the world. Eventually settling in Harlem, in New York City, he formed the Universal Negro Improvement Association (UNIA), which was built on the twin premises of black pride and black self-reliance. To inspire black pride, Garvey turned to history to argue that Africans had built great civilizations while Europeans were still primitive if not savage. He noted, "Africa was peopled with a race of cultured black men, who were masters in art, science and literature; men who were cultured and refined; men who, it was said, were like the gods. Even the great poets of old [Greeks] sang in beautiful sonnets of the delight it afforded the gods to be in companionship with the Ethiopians." He continues, "Why, then, should we lose hope? Black men, you were once great; you shall be great again. Lose not courage, lose not faith, go forward."[24] To encourage self-reliance, Garvey advocated the establishment of a black government in Africa to oversee the affairs and well-being of blacks everywhere, the repatriation of educated and skilled blacks to Africa to develop its society and economy, and the acquisition of technical skills and the establishment of business by blacks in the Americas. To achieve this vision, Garvey established a shipping line called the Black Star Line to facilitate trade and travel between Africa and the Americas. Unfortunately, the failure of the Black Star Line was his undoing. The U.S. government, already wary of his influence, accused and convicted him of mail fraud for using the U.S. Postal Service to solicit the buying of shares in the shipping company. Deported to Jamaica in 1927, Garvey never regained the prominence he had once held in Harlem. He spent the rest of life in relative obscurity, dying in England in 1940.

The currents of Jamaica's folk religious ethos, Ethiopianism, and Garveyism converged in Rastafari when the founders of the movement identified Haile Selassie as the messianic redeemer of the black race. Between 1930 and 1933, the Jamaicans Henry Archibald Dunkley, Joseph Nathaniel Hibbert, and Leonard Percival Howell independently came to this conclusion and started proclaiming the divinity of Haile Selassie and the imminent liberation of blacks everywhere. They were soon joined by their fellow Jamaican Robert Hinds. It was Howell, in partnership with Hinds, who catapulted Rastafari into the public arena through his acerbic criticism of Jamaica's colonial order, his doctrine of black superiority and white inferiority, his advocacy for black repatriation from the hopeless situation in Jamaica to the African homeland, and his call for allegiance to Haile Selassie instead of the British Crown. For his inveighing against whites and the Jamaica's colonial government, Howell was arrested and convicted of sedition and imprisoned for two years, initiating a conflictual relationship with Jamaica authorities that continued to dog him for more than twenty years.

After his release from prison, Howell decided to withdraw from the public gaze to establish what amounted to a self-governing Rastafarian commune, called Pinnacle, which was situated in a somewhat remote area in the parish of St. Catherine. Howell and his followers supported themselves by subsistence farming and by growing ganja (marijuana) as a cash crop. Rumors that Pinnacle was a guerrilla training camp and repeated complaints that the Rastas were harassing their neighbors led the authorities to execute periodic raids on the commune, arresting and jailing its occupants, including Howell. In 1954, the government decided to deal with this "nuisance" once and for all. The police moved in, razed the buildings in the commune, arrested Howell and other leaders, and dispersed the residents. Though Howell was again convicted, his conviction was eventually overturned. By this time, he was proclaiming himself to be Jesus Christ, sent to Jamaica by his father, Haile Selassie, to bring enlightenment and redemption to black people. He was deemed mentally unstable and committed to a mental institution. This marked his exit from the center stage of Rastafari; after his release, he spent the rest of his life in virtual anonymity.

Radical Rastas and Cultural Innovations

Even before Howell's departure from the forefront of the movement, a young brigade of Rastas was already moving Rastafari beyond the boundaries set forth by the faith's founding fathers. The young Rastas formed groups with names such as "House of Youth Black Faith" (HYBF) and "I-gelic House" or "Higes Knots." They congregated in the Back O' Wall slum in West Kingston and in Wareika Hills east of Mountain View Avenue. These Young Rastas, in a manner more radical than their predecessors, took on a pose of "dreadness" and uncompromising rejection of the Jamaican establishment and even elements of Jamaica's folk tradition. They were responsible for initiating or "institutionalizing" many of the cultural elements that are characteristic trademarks of Rastafari. As Barry Chevannes, an esteemed scholar of the Rastafarian movement, points out, the first generation of Rastas concentrated on establishing the status of Haile Selassie as an incarnated divine liberator.[25] These adherents were also caught up in the social ferment of the 1930s, which manifested itself in widespread strikes for better wages, the formation of local trade unions, and the establishment of the People's National Party and the Jamaica Labor Party, both seeking self-governance and independence. Some leading Rastas, especially Robert Hinds, seem to have supported the charismatic and populist politician and trade union leader Alexander Bustamante.[26] Furthermore, the nascent Rastafari movement had not sufficiently separated itself from Jamaica's religious folk ethos. Their rituals (singing, preaching, dancing, lighting candles, holding street meetings), their style of leadership, their dress (wearing white), their symbols (e.g., the staves carried by leaders), and their healing or conjuring practices all smacked of Revivalism, an Afro-Christian folk tradition. The new vanguard of the young Rastas sought to create a distinctive identity for Rastafari by repudiating involvement in the machination of local politics (*politricks*) and seeking to purge Rastafari of elements of Revivalism, especially those seen as superstitious (lighting candles) or as involving contact with spirits.[27]

The oral nature of the Rastafarian tradition has given rise to multiple claims concerning the origin of particular elements of what has become the Rastafarian ethos. The provenance of dreadlocks is a case in point. One oral tradition traces the origin of dreadlocks to Howell's "guardsmen," who were posted as sentinels at Pinnacle.[28] Chevannes's informants from the HYBF claimed that they instituted the hairstyle to accentuate their "dreadness."[29] And John P. Homiak's informants from I-gelic House claimed responsibility for initiating the uncombed locks as a mark of believers' return to the original state of nature.[30] Whatever may have been its inception, the new vanguard of Rastafari from the late 1940s to the 1950s elevated dreadlocks to a place of centrality in the movement. The name of the style, dreadlocks, was supposed to indicate the awful and dire conditions of their lives as well as to communicate the fear they wished to generate in the hearts of their oppressors. By forswearing the use of scissors and combs, those with dreadlocks also indicated their commitment to natural living and to African beauty, as opposed to what they perceived as the unnaturalness of the proffered European standard of beauty.

These young Rastas also took the practice of ganja smoking, long prevalent among young Jamaica males, including Howell's followers, and elevated it to the quintessential Rastafarian ritual. In the hands of HYBF and I-gelic House, ganja became the psychoactive agent whose ritual ingestion assists in the journey to discover the true self or I-n-I consciousness, the discovery that a divine essence is really at the core of one's being. Beyond its ritual efficacy, ganja use became a means of challenging the Jamaican establishment, whose laws proscribed the use of the "holy weed." When arrested on charges related to ganja or on other alleged infraction of the law, Rastas and their supporters used the courts to contest not only the legitimacy of the law but also the authority of the judicial system itself. Their disruption of court proceedings often resulted in their being sent to jail for contempt of court before their cases could be properly adjudicated.

The young radical Rastas were also responsible for the development of an in-group dialect called "dread talk," "Rasta talk," or "I-ance." Dread talk emerged spontaneously in "reasoning" sessions, dialogical conversations undertaken in conjunction with ganja smoking. During these sessions, Rastas explore their understanding of self and the world around them. Dread talk became a means of distinguishing followers from those who used the oppressive language of Babylon and the popular dialect that showed they had no consciousness of their self-worth. The Jamaican scholar Velma Pollard identifies three processes at work in dread talk. The first constitutes an assignment of new meanings to well-known words. For example, "chant" takes on the meaning "to discuss," especially religious issues; "sight ("siit") comes to mean "I agree or understand what is said"; and "sound" ("sounz") means "words or powerful truths." In the second process, Rastas reject certain syllables in words and replace them with syllables they deem more appropriate to the meaning of the words. In this case, the new sounds of the words carry the weight of their meanings. Thus, the word "understand" becomes "overstan," "oppress" becomes "downpress," and "dedicate" becomes "livicate." The third process involves the removal of the initial syllable of a word and replacing it with the letter I. In this process, "elected" become "ilected, "brethren" becomes "idren," and "natural' or "vital" become "ital."[31] These processes not only indicate the emerging Rastafarian consciousness but constitute a rejection of standard English as corrupt in its very linguistic forms. The Rastafarian poet Bongo Jerry expresses this powerfully in his poem *Mabrak*:

> Save the YOUNG
> From the language that MEN teach,
>
> . . .
>
> SILENCE BABEL TONGUES; recall and
> recollect BLACK SPEECH.
> Cramp all double meaning
> And all that hiding behind language bar,
> For that crossword speaking
> When expressing feeling
> Is just English language contribution to increase confusion in
> Babel-land tower—
>
> . . .
>
> Ever now communicate—for now I and I come to recreate:
> Sight sound and meaning to measure the feeling
> Of BLACK HEARTS.[32]

The radicalism of the young vanguard was matched by a kind of austerity, sometimes bordering on asceticism, that produced the "ital" lifestyle and the patriarchal orientation of the movement. Ital is dread talk for "natural and "vital" and can even be understood as "organic." For the radical Rastas, this meant a commitment to a diet (or "livet") of natural foods. Drawing on the Levitical laws of the ancient Israelites, they forswore the eating of pork, shellfish, fishes without scales, and other food proscribed in those laws. Processed foods, especially those in cans, were also rejected as "deaders" (that which is dead or has lost its vitality). The use of refined salt was also proscribed. Some went so far as to become strict vegetarians, eating only grains, fruits, ground provisions, and vegetables. Their conviction was that health and vitality were ensured through natural living (ital livity). This led to the belief in "everliving life"—that is, the belief that an ital lifestyle, including the use of healing herbs, would ensure that Rastas would live forever.

HYBF and I-gelic House made Rastafari into a virtual cult of black male redemption that relegated women to the margins of the movement. Women were not allowed to join circles of men as they partook of the "chalice" (smoked the ritual ganja pipe) and could not participate in the accompany-ing "reasoning." Elaborating a patriarchy, these brethren elevated themselves to the status of "kingmen," and their women were placed in the subordinate status of queens or dawtas (daughters), who could come to the conscious-ness of Rastafari only through the sponsorships of their kings. Women were considered not only weak, like the first biblical woman, Eve, but also pollut-ing, particularly during menstruation. For this reason, some Rastas had only minimal dealing with women in general—not even allowing them to prepare food and certainly not dealing with them during their menstrual periods. Some became the ultimate ascetics by adopting a celibate lifestyle.

The radical Rastas of the late 1940s and 1950s were not only busy shap-ing a distinct identity for Rastafari; they also brought a new militancy to the denunciation of and confrontation with Jamaican authorities. While there was an implicit and explicit rejection of the Jamaican colonial status quo in early Rastafari, the new vanguard accentuated this by the new lifestyle we have described and by their constant haranguing of Jamaica's colonial society and its agents. These radicals marched frequently in the streets of Kingston calling down "blood and fire" on the guardians of what they perceived as an oppressive society. The term "Babylon" was introduced to designate the oppressive state of affairs in Jamaica in particular and the West in general. Jamaica was regarded as Babylon because Africans were taken from their ancestral homeland and deposited there against their will and because its social institutions were built on the exploitation of the masses of Afro-Jamai-cans even as they were excluded from whatever bounty the society had to offer. Thus, their situation had parallels to the conditions of the ancient Isra-elites during their exile in Babylonia. The word "babilan" (Babylon) came to designate the oppressors and their frontline agents, the police.

The general societal reaction to these militants was profoundly negative. Their unkempt hair, their ragged clothes (some wore crocus, a coarse mate-rial used to make sacks), and their unintelligible speech were all evidence of mental deterioration in the eyes of many. They were considered by some to be lunatics. Their disregard for the laws against ganja cultivation and use and their constant vitriol against the government were considered indicative of their criminal disposition, and criminality came to be considered an essen-tial trait of Rastafari among many members of society. The smoking of ganja was believed to stimulate this disposition. The militancy of the Rastas in gen-eral and of the radical Rastas in particular was met with violent suppression by the state. Arrests, imprisonments, harassments, destruction of dwellings, and shearing of their locks became prevalent as the 1950s wore on.

Repatriation Fever, Nyabinghi Issembly, and Nyabinghi Drumming

In the 1950s, the Rastafarian call for repatriation became increasingly prominent. While this call went back to Howell, it reached a fever pitch during this decade. Several factors contributed to this. The militancy of the young vanguard and the repressive activities of the Jamaican authority accentuated the sense of exile and alienation and thus the desirability of returning to Africa, the ancestral homeland. A kind of "migration fever" was also sweeping Jamaica in the post–World War II era as many Jamaicans emigrated to England and North America to work in the rebuilding efforts that followed the end of the war. The founding of the modern state of Israel, in 1948, and the migration of Jews to take up residence there may have also contributed to the intensification of desire for repatriation. Probably most significant was Haile Selassie's announcement, in 1954, through the Ethiopian World Federation, of a land grant to members of that group who wished to settle in Ethiopia. Members of the Federation had supported the emperor in his struggle against Italy, which invaded Ethiopia in 1935. To Rastas in Jamaica, this was proof that His Imperial Majesty was making provision for their repatriation.

Prince Emmanuel Edwards and Claudius Henry, the most notable Rastafarian leaders to emerge in the 1950s in Jamaica, stoked the fires of repatriation. When Prince Emmanuel Edwards called on Rastas from all across the country to gather at his Ackee Walk camp to discuss repatriation, rumors swelled that the passage to Africa was imminent. Some of those attending the convention may have expected to board ships headed for Africa after the convention. The convention catapulted Edwards into national prominence, but he and his followers became increasing reclusive. After setting up camps in several locations, they eventually established a commune in the hills overlooking Bull Bay, east of Kingston. Edwards, as unquestioned leader of the commune, claimed and was accorded divine status; he positioned himself as part of a trinity composed of Haile Selassie, Marcus Garvey, and Prince Emmanuel Edwards.[33] The followers of Edwards became known as Bobo Dreads or Bobo Shanti and are widely known for their flowing robes and their characteristic head wrap, as well as for selling brooms door to door.

Henry came to prominence in 1959 when he organized a convention at his Rosalee Avenue compound and sold tickets that were purportedly for passage to Africa. Thousands reportedly sold their possessions and descended on Kingston expecting to embark for Africa. This convention created high drama and much publicity but ended in disappointment for those who came to Kingston expecting to repatriate. Probably because of the publicity that attended the convention, the fact that its promoters were selling tickets for repatriation that did not materialize, and the denunciation of the Jamaica establishment during the convention, the police raided Henry's compound and found a stash of small arms and explosives. Henry was convicted of treason and sentenced to six years imprisonment. Not long after, Henry's son, Ronald, was implicated in a plot against the Jamaican government and was executed.[34]

A significant aspect of Rastafari that arose in the 1950s was the Rasta convention, the Nyabinghi Issembly. The conventions led by Edwards and Henry brought these meetings to the public's attention, but the mass gatherings seem to have first developed in the Rastafarian camps in Wareika Hills. Initially, they had the twin purpose of preparing for repatriation and "chanting down Babylon."

The conventions were called Nyabinghi or 'Binghi, meaning "death to all oppressors." The ritual singing, dancing, and "flashing" of dreadlocks were meant to unleash cosmic forces for the destruction of oppressive systems and institutions. These movement-wide assemblies have become a major means for Rastas to show their solidarity despite the heterogeneity of the movement. Also known as "grounding" or "groundation," they also help cement the commitment of adherents to the movement and its principles through the affective attachment (a kind of collective consciousness) engendered by such mass gatherings and the expounding of the principles of Rastafari by leading brethren.

Yet another component of the Rastafarian ethos that emerged in the 1950s was the Nyabinghi drumming tradition. Howell seemed to have adopted Revivalist song tradition and Kumina drumming for his religious ceremonies. Rastas in West Kingston and on the periphery of the city turned to Burru, a drumming tradition carried over from the days of slavery. Burru had evolved into a Christmas tradition during which drummers and singers march through their communities singing topical songs about events transpiring and rumors circulating in these communities. Rastas were exposed to Burru drumming in West Kingston and were attracted to it because it was deemed to be an authentic African tradition preserved in Jamaica. Brother Job and Count Ossie are the two figures usually associated with this exposure and the eventual adoption of Burru drumming by Rastas. Brother Job was an expert Burru drummer who started showing up in the yards and camps of Rastas with his drum. Count Ossie became enamored of Brother Job's virtuosity and prevailed on him to give him lessons. Count Ossie had tremendous musical aptitude and soon mastered Burru drumming techniques. He proceeded to add his own experimentations and innovations to the Burru tradition, producing what has become the Nyabinghi drumming tradition of Rastafari. Like Burru drumming, Nyabinghi drumming is performed on a three-drum set: the bass lays down the basic rhythm; the funde carries the syncopated tempo; and the repeater (peta) is free to improvise within the context of the rhythm and tempo laid down by the other drums. Once he had mastered the drums, Count Ossie and the group of Rastafarian drummers he gathered around himself were much sought after to provide drumming accompaniment to ceremonies in Rastafarian camps and at Nyabinghi Issemblies.

Changing Fortunes for Rastafari

After the turbulence of the 1950s, the 1960s became something of a watershed for the Rastafari movement. While tensions with Jamaican authorities persisted and sometimes erupted into confrontations, the Jamaican government pursued a policy of conciliation and rehabilitation with regards to Rastas. The most infamous incidents that escalated into violence and repression were the Coral Gardens riots and the bulldozing of Shanty Town in Back O' Wall. The Coral Gardens incident erupted near Montego Bay in 1963, arising from a dispute over whether Rastas would be allowed to continue using a footpath across the famed Rose Hall Estate, which was being restored as a tourist attraction. When the police were called in, the situation degenerated into a riot in which property was destroyed and a number of people, including Rastas and police men, lost their lives. The public reaction was a stereotypical condemnation of Rastafari as a criminal subculture fueled by ganja smoking. Perceiving that criminality was getting out of control in the mid-1960s and associating Shanty Town with endemic criminality, Hugh Shearer, who was prime minister at the time, ordered it razed by bulldozers, displacing the poor squatters who lived there, including a sizable contingent of Rastas.

Despite these incidents, change had already begun in the relationship between Rastafari and the wider Jamaican society. The catalyst for this change was the 1960 study of the Rastafari movement carried out by the scholars M. G. Smith, Roy Augier, and Rex Nettleford from University College of the West Indies at Mona.[35] When the study was published, it took on the character of a public policy document. Contrary to popular perception that posited laziness, violence, and lunacy as the salient attributes of Rastas, the study found that most Rastas were basically peace-loving people seeking to survive in a society that afforded them few opportunities and accorded them little humanity. The paper contended that Rastas should not be subjected to systemic repression by the police. Furthermore, the study suggested that the assumption of an African identity was legitimate in light of the African background of most Jamaicans and also concluded that the possibility of repatriation should be investigated by the government.[36]

A number of initiatives flowed from the recommendations of the 1960s study, the most significant of which were missions to Africa to investigate the possibility of repatriation, an effort to develop ties with African countries, and an invitation to the Ethiopian Orthodox Church to establish congregations in Jamaica. Following up on the recommendations of the study, the government of Premier Norman Manley appointed a delegation, which was composed primarily of leaders from civic and activist organizations committed to the welfare and uplift of Afro-Jamaicans but which also included the famous Jamaican journalist Victor Reid and three Rastas, Mortimo Planno, Philmore Alvaranga, and Douglas Mack, to travel to Africa to investigate the possibility of repatriating Rastas.[37] The delegation traveled to Ethiopia, Nigeria, Ghana, Liberia, and Sierra Leone and had audiences with various officials, including Haile Selassie and the Ghanian leader and pan-Africanist Kwame Nkrumah. On its return to Jamaica, the delegation presented an official report to Premier Manley. Authored by Vic Reid, the report highlighted the warm reception the delegation had received in the various African countries but pointed out that since these countries were in a nation-building phase, they were interested in receiving only skilled people who could contribute to such a task and were not prepared for any large-scale repatriation from the African diaspora. Refusing to sign the official report, the Rastafarian delegates compiled their own report, painting a rosier picture of the prospects for repatriation. They highlighted Haile Selassie's desire to receive "the right people" and Liberia's open welcome of "all people of African descent."[38]

In 1962, Jamaica became independent from Britain, and the government of Premier Norman Manley was replaced by that of Prime Minister Alexander Bustamante. Bustamante was not as favorably disposed to the issue of repatriation as Manley had been. In addition, the Coral Garden incident in 1963 eroded much of the sympathy for Rastafari generated by the 1960 study. Frustrated by the lack of any further government action on the issue of repatriation, the Rastas raised their own funds and undertook another mission to Africa, visiting Nigeria, Kenya, and Ethiopia. According to Douglas Mack, one of the Rastafarian delegates, Nigerian officials refused to meet with the delegation, but the governments of Kenya and Ethiopia provided accommodation for lengthy stays, granted audiences with government officials, and issued promises to assist with repatriation.[39] Despite these missions, neither the Jamaican government nor any African government undertook any official program of repatriation.

The second initiative to flow from the 1960 report converged with the desire of the newly independent Jamaica to forge ties with the newly independent nations of Africa. One manifestation of this desire was the issuance of invitation to African dignitaries to visit Jamaica. This initiative continued throughout the 1960s and reached it culmination in the historic visit of Haile Selassie to Jamaica in April 1966. This visit brought Rastafari into the public limelight in a positive manner. To begin with, thousands of Rastas (and others) descended on the Palisados Airport (now Norman Manley International) to welcome the man they perceived as their messiah. When Haile Selassie's plane landed, the crowd broke the security barrier and surrounded the plane on the tarmac, holding placards and voicing chants proclaiming the divinity of the African emperor. Perceiving a security problem, the emperor refused to deplane. The efforts of police, the military, and government officials failed to calm the crowd or to convince them to step back from the plane. The day was saved by a Rastafarian elder, Mortimo Planno, who mounted the steps of the plane and appealed to the crowd to pull back. Planno's request was heeded, and Haile Selassie disembarked. During the visit, Rastas participated in various official functions, including a luncheon at the prime minister's official residence; a reception at Kings House, the governor general's official residence; and a ball at the swanky Sheraton Hotel. Many who would cross to the other side of the street at the approach of a Rasta rubbed shoulders with the brethren at these official functions. The dignity and poise with which the Rastas conducted themselves did not go unnoticed by local officials and the general public. The Rastas reportedly had a private meeting with the emperor from which emerged the phrase "liberation before repatriation." Supposedly, the emperor charged the Rastas with liberating Jamaica before repatriating to Ethiopia. While repatriation remained a central tenet of Rastafari, after Haile Selassie's visit the repatriation fever that had gripped the movement since the 1950s subsided.

The third initiative to emerge from the 1960 study was an invitation from the Jamaican government to the Ethiopian Orthodox Church to start ministering in Jamaica. After his 1966 visit, Haile Selassie commissioned the Church to commence its ministry in Jamaica. The first congregation was established on Maxfield Avenue in Kingston in 1970. Since then, several other congregations have been established in other towns. Both the Jamaican government and Haile Selassie seem to have envisioned the ministry of the

Ethiopian Orthodox Church as a means of channeling Rastafarian veneration from the emperor himself into a more acceptable Christian form. Given the African provenance of the Church, a number of Rastas became members. Even the singer Bob Marley received Christian baptism in the Ethiopian Orthodox Church shortly before his death, and its ministers officiated at his funeral. However, Rastafarian convictions, especially those concerning the divinity of Haile Selassie, have often come into conflict with traditional Ethiopian Orthodox teachings.[40]

While the conciliation measures were working themselves out, other social processes were weaving elements of Rastafari into the texture of Jamaica society. These included the growing influence of Rastafari on Jamaica's emerging musical culture, the adoption of elements of Rastafari into youth culture, especially among poor disenchanted youths, and the convergence of social criticism offered by young, radical intellectuals and the Rastafarian critique of the Jamaican status quo. We have already mentioned the insertion of elements of Rastafari into Jamaican popular music via the music of the drummer Count Ossie. In 1960, Count Ossie arranged and provided part of the accompaniment for "Oh Carolina," a hit record produced by the legendary Prince Buster and sung by the Folkes Brothers. On this song, the Nyabinghi drumming style appeared for the first time on a popular recording. As the musicologist Lloyd Bradley argues, the message of "Oh Carolina" itself was not particularly significant, but the inclusion of Nyabinghi drumming was significant "as a piece of cultural legislation." He suggests that it initiated "a bond between Rastafari and Jamaican music business that is still in place today, with each side doing as much for the other—while reggae gives Rasta access to the world's stage, Rasta's depth of spirituality means that reggae will always have something to say."[41] Much of this Rastafari spirituality was brought to Jamaica's popular music by the musicians who fashioned its unique sounds from the days of ska to emergence of reggae. Of note are such artists as Don Drummond, Jah Jerry, Bra Gaynair, and Bunny Gaynair, who were members of the Skatalites, the band that provided the accompaniment for most of the local recording before 1966. In the late 1960s and throughout the 1970s, Bob Marley and the Wailers came to exemplify the marriage of Rastafari and Jamaican popular music. Not only were the Rastafari rhythms employed liberally, but Marley and other turned the popular form into the mouthpiece for Rastafarian philosophy and spirituality.

By the late 1960s, disillusionment about the promise of Jamaican independence was growing. Self-government has been achieved, but the material circumstances of the majority of Jamaicans had not changed appreciably, if at all. The Rastafari notion of Jamaica as Babylon was appearing more like a reality to an increasing number of people. As a result, what had once been the Rastafarian critique of the establishment was becoming the criticism voiced by Jamaica's poor. In addition, at the street level, young people began to adopt Rastafarian lingo and to wear the Rastafari colors of red, green, and gold as expressions of their commitment to "roots" culture.

Within the same context of disillusionment, the Black Power movement from the United States spread to the Caribbean with its embrace of African identity and radical politics. Taking hold among the young intelligentsia on college and university campuses, Black Power challenged the European orientation of the Caribbean's newly independent governments and the dominant status accorded European culture. In Jamaica, some young intellectuals established links with Rastafari. This is best exemplified by the Guyanese historian Walter Rodney, who was teaching at the Mona campus of the University of the West Indies. Rodney frequently "reasoned" with Rastas and taught them African history. Because of his advocacy of Black Power philosophy and his frequent visits to the depressed areas of Jamaica, Rodney was banned from Jamaica in 1968. Another example of the coalescing of Rastafari and other progressive forces in Jamaica was the formation of group called Abeng and the publication of a magazine with the same name. Abeng was composed of radical intellectuals, artists, writers, trade unionists, and Rastas. Unfortunately for Rastas, both Black Power and Abeng had very short life spans.

As Rastafari moved into the 1970s and 1980s, several salient issues came to the fore. As early as the late in 1960s, young people from the middle and even the upper class had started to embrace Rastafari. As the 1970s progressed more young Jamaicans started to embrace their African heritage and, with that, the outlook of Rastafari. Even those who did not actually embrace Rastafari were often described as or accused of being "Rasta-minded." One of the most celebrated cases of upper-class conversion to Rastafari was Stephen "Cat" Coore, son of David Coore, a deputy prime minister and minister of finance in the Jamaican government of Prime Minister Michael Manley in the 1970s. Cat Coore became a "dreadlocks" guitar player in the internationally famous reggae band named Third World.

Many of the young middle-class Rastas eventually coalesced around the charismatic Rastafarian prophet called Gad, whose real name is Vernon Carrington. This group formed the Twelve Tribes of Israel, the third major sect of Rastafari, along with traditional Nyabinghi and the Bobo Dreads. Prophet Gad famously urged his followers to read "a chapter [of the Bible] a day." Their interpretation of the Bible is regarded as being closer to that of traditional Christians than that of either the Nyabinghis or the Bobo Dreads. For this they are derisively referred to as "Christian Rastas." As the name suggests, each member of the sect was assigned to one of twelve tribes based on the names of the sons of the biblical patriarch Jacob. This reflected the Rastas' belief that they are the descendants or reincarnations of the ancient Israelites. Twelve Tribes is also known for raising funds to repatriate those of its members who wish to go to Sheshamane, Ethiopia. Educated Rastas tend to identify with this Rastafarian sect, and a number of famous reggae artists, including Bob Marley, Dennis Brown, and Freddy McGregor, were or are members of this group.

Political Cooptation and Commercial Exploitation

During the 1970s, the Rastafarian image, symbols, language, and ideas, along with reggae music, were all exploited for their political appeal. While many politicians of both political parties did this, Michael Manley was the master at co-opting Rastafari. As the leader of the People's National Party, he ran a populist campaign in which he painted himself as the biblical Joshua committed to "beat down Babylon" and to lead Jamaica's oppressed to the state of freedom and plenty. His campaign speeches were peppered liberally with Rastafarian expressions such as "I and I," "Hail the man," and "peace and love," and he quoted frequently from reggae songs that were critical of the present state of affairs in Jamaica. The most egregious and theatrical exploitation of Rastafari symbolism was Manley's "rod of correction." According to the lore that developed, Manley acquired a walking stick as a gift from Emperor Haile Selassie I when he visited Ethiopia in the late 1960s. Dubbing it the rod of correction, he displayed it prominently during campaign speeches, promising to "beat down Babylon" and bring "power to the people." Interpreted through the lens of Rastafari, which sees Selassie as the messiah of black liberation, the rod became a symbol of Manley's divine anointing and his commission to correct the wrongs of Jamaican society. Rastas, who generally stayed on the sidelines of party politics, warmed to Manley's campaign and supported him, helping him achieve success at the polls in 1972. Even Bob Marley reportedly joined the musical bandwagon that often traveled with Manley. However, Manley's government proved to be utterly unable to improve the material conditions of the majority of Jamaicans during the oil crisis and the economic recession of the 1970s. Many Rastas felt exploited and betrayed, especially when Manley did nothing to change the laws criminalizing ganja possession and use.

Rastafari not only moved fully into the public sphere in Jamaica but also moved onto the world stage with the international success of the Jamaican crime film *The Harder They Come* and with the ascendancy of Bob Marley as a third-world superstar and Rastafari ambassador. Though Rastas were not featured prominently in *The Harder they Come*, at least one Rasta appeared as a low-level ganja dealer. More significant, the tone of resistance in many of the songs, especially the theme song, which had the same name as the film, accurately reflected the Rastafarian critique of the Jamaican status quo. Of course, the influence of Marley in spreading awareness of Rastafari far outstripped the impact of *The Harder They Come*. Marley was the living incarnation of Rastafari, and his lyrics were suffused with Rastafarian spirituality and philosophy, often sung to unmistakable Nyabinghi rhythms, as in *Rastaman Chant* and some renditions of *Babylon System*. Having gained super stardom, Marley became something of national hero in Jamaica. He was awarded the Order of Merit, the second highest honor given by the Jamaican government, and, on his passing, he was granted a state funeral.

Ebb and Flow in Rastafari Influence

During the 1980s and into the 1990s, the influence of Rastafari ebbed in Jamaica's popular music and Jamaican society. It probably started with the election campaign of 1980. Because Manley had failed to deliver on his promises, Rastas withdrew their support for his progressive politics, making it difficult to use reggae and Rastafari to appeal to the Jamaican populace. The leader of the opposition, Edward Seaga, with his long fascination with Jamaica's folk religions, appealed to the grassroots via the Revivalist traditions. His slogan "Deliverance Will Come" came from a hymn long popular in Revival and Pentecostal Churches.

The death of Haile Selassie, in 1975, and of Bob Marley, in 1981, contributed to this muted phase of Rastafarian history. Other leading Rastas were dying, as well. Jacob Miller, a Rasta and a rising reggae star, died in car crash in 1980. The founding Rastas, including Howell, were aging and passing from the scene. Since then, other well-known Rastas have passed away: Prince Emmanuel Edwards, leader of the Bobo Dreads; Gad (Vernon Carrington), the leading elder of the Twelve Tribes of Israel; and Mortimo Planno, one of the Rastafarian representatives on the 1960 government delegation to Africa to study the prospects for repatriation. Rastas had longed claimed that Haile Selassie was not subject to death; only the unrighteous Babylonians had death as their end. Now Rastas had to deal with the reality of death, and they had no coherent and convincing response. This fact must have had some effect on their psychological disposition, contributing to their lack of militancy during the 1980s. In addition, they must have lost some credibility with outsiders, especially the young, who either embraced the Pentecostal/Charismatic type of Christianity or became immersed in the dance hall ethos, which was less political and less religious than reggae. Furthermore, in the mid-1990s, some famous Rastas, including Judy Mowatt of the I-Threes, that did backup vocals for Marley, and the reggae promoter and emcee Tommy Cowan, converted to evangelical Christianity.

However, since the mid-1990s, Rastafari has sought to reinsert itself in the public sphere in Jamaica, both in the sphere of music and in politics. The rise of a new generation of Rastafarian reggae artists, some of whom are versed in the conventions of the dance hall culture, has returned a "conscious" discourse to the center of Jamaican popular music. Such artists as Anthony B. Capleton, and Buju Banton have focused the critical eye of Rastafari on continued inequities and exploitation in Jamaican society. Artists such as Luciano and Garnet Silk have returned Rastafarian spirituality to a central place in their music. With regard to politics, while Rastas have traditionally eschewed participation in electoral politics with the exception of the Rastafarian Ras Sam's run for a city council seat in the early 1960s, Rastas have contested a few seats in recent elections in Jamaica. In each case, they garnered only a few votes, but this newfound political involvement may signal a new desire to insert Rastafarian perspectives into the social and political process. Back in the 1980s, the Rastafarian intellectual Leachim Semaj called for Rastas to move beyond symbolism and cultural activism and to embrace social and political theory in the service of transforming Jamaican society. Could these recent Rastafarian politicians be heeding this call and setting the stage for a serious of engagement of Rastafari with the political process in Jamaica?

Like the mustard seed that Jesus spoke of in one of his parables, Rastafari has grown from small beginnings to become a religion known and embraced around the world. It spread to other locations first via travel and immigration: individuals from other Caribbean islands traveling to and studying in Jamaica, encountering Rastafari, and taking it back to their home countries; Jamaican students studying in Barbados, Trinidad, Cuba, and elsewhere and sharing their Rastafarian convictions and their reggae music; and Jamaican Rastas emigrating to North America, Europe, and Africa, practicing their faith in their new location. Many second-generation Jamaicans and other Caribbean and African youths, especially in England, turn to Rastafari and reggae in the face of the alienation they experience in their new lands. The international reach of reggae through the communications media has also contributed to the spread of Rastafari to disparate places and the acceptance of some of its elements by individuals who have never met a Jamaican Rasta face to face. Today Rastafari has a significant, if not massive, presence in North America, Europe, Africa, New Zealand, and Brazil. While no official numbers are available, various estimates now place the number of Rastas around the world at between 700, 000 and one million. A quick check on the Internet reveals Rastafarian groups in Costa Rica, Nicaragua, Russia, Israel, Japan, Fiji, and a host of other countries. Of course, Rastafari gains new flavor as it spreads. For some, what appeals to them is the Rastafarian commitment to a natural way of life; for others, Rastafari offers an Afrocentric identity and a critique of colonial and imperialist powers; for others, it is the spirituality with which it infused reggae music; for yet others, it offers the spirit of rebellion and nonconformity to hegemonic culture.

The arrival of Hinduism and Islam forever changed Caribbean religion. Though Christianity and African diaspora religion often receive all the attention, the presence of these religious traditions alters the religious and cultural landscape of the region. These traditions have also changed and evolved in their new environment, for, as we have seen, the Hinduism and Islam of the Caribbean have taken on the flavor of the region in their expressions and their ritual life. Rastafarianism is representative of an African-centered Caribbean religion that was itself born in the Caribbean. Unlike Santería or Vodou, whose roots are found in Africa, Rastafarianism is Jamaican. However, its mixture of pan-Africanism and elements of Christianity exemplifies the religious transformation that characterizes the evolution of religion throughout Caribbean history. These three religious tradition represent the growing diversity of the religions and peoples of the Caribbean and the dynamic process that continues to shape the religious landscape.

Legitimation, Indigenization, and Contextualization

Caribbean religions entered the twenty-first century as established religious traditions at the defining moment for legitimation, growth, and globalization. No longer relegated to their island nations, religions that are either indigenous to the Caribbean or have been imported and now flourish in the Caribbean are world religions. Whether it is the Jamaican grassroots religion of Rastafarianism or the global movement of Pentecostalism, the Caribbean has become a microcosm of global religion. However, with growth and globalization come questions of identity, authenticity, and tradition.

Legitimation

The late twentieth century revealed a Caribbean religious landscape where the question of religious legitimation came to be a pressing concern as Caribbean populations became global and their religious traditions spread along with them. The question of legitimation is fundamentally a question of identity. For many religions that have traditionally been spread through ritual and oral transmission, the legitimation of their practices and beliefs leads to a radical shift in the manner in which these religions exist. Cuba is of particular note in this process, for here legitimation has taken on a different character in light of the antireligious stance of the early Castro government. The religious landscape of Cuba has changed dramatically since the 1990s. Cuba has witnessed a revival in public religious beliefs and practices, in part because of the 1980 policy of *convivencia* (coexistence of religion and government in Cuba). This constructive coexistence allows for a more public face for Cuban religion, which, as we have seen, went underground for the first decades after the revolution. Protestant denominations have become more prominent on the island, partly because many bring aid to the island. For the Catholic Church, the question of syncretism and the relationship between Catholicism and Afro-

Cuban religions dominates, for ecclesial leaders are troubled by the elements of Catholicism incorporated into Afro-Cuban religions. Cubans historically have not been attached to the institutional Catholic Church and have instead practiced a popular piety that is located primarily in the domestic sphere yet is also manifested in pilgrimages and patronal festivals to Our Lady of Charity and Saint Lazarus. The influence of African diaspora religion and its effect on Cuban Catholicism is indeed a characteristic of Cuban Catholicism.[1] Indeed, one of the hallmarks of contemporary Cuban belief is the facility with which Cubans can exist in multiple religious worldviews without contradiction. Santeros (Santería practitioners), for example, participate in various Catholic rituals as part of their initiation. More important, the Catholic feast days that are most prominent in Cuba are those also associated with Santería. As the Afro-Cuban religious scholar Christine Ayorinde thoughtfully points out, "Because many practitioners of *santería* depend on the Catholic Church for certain sacraments, until recently, the churches tended to be packed on the annual festivals of Saint Lazarus and Saint Barbara rather than at Christian feasts such as Christmas and Easter."[2] In spite of these associations, or perhaps because of them, the Catholic Church in Cuba continues to maintain an antagonistic relationship with Afro-Cuban religions. This stance was exemplified in the refusal to allow Santería priests to meet with the pope when he visited Cuba in 1998.

Despite the ongoing Catholic discontent, this new openness to religion as a whole in Cuba has turned Santería into a more public religion. Practitioners now publicly display their necklaces to the *orishas*, and rituals can be performed in public. In addition, the government actively incorporates religion into its presentations of Afro-Cuban culture. The establishment, in 1991, of the Yoruba Cultural Association (*Asociación Cultural Yoruba*) also marks the public face of Afro-Cuban religion in contemporary Cuba. Its membership is in the thousands. The Ifá Iranlowo is a group of more than one hundred *babalowos* (high priests) on the island.[3] Santeros in Cuba are now establishing ties with Yoruba priests in Nigeria, and questions of syncretism and orthodoxy are at the forefront of contemporary Santería, especially in light of the Roman Catholic elements that are present in Cuban Santería but absent in Nigerian Yoruban religion.

Financial considerations for religious services have also entered the contemporary discussion of religion in Cuba. That Santería priests have profited financially from expensive initiations costing thousands of dollars has been a point of contention on the island, especially with many foreigners coming to the island for religious initiation and guidance. As the economic climate took a downturn, many Cubans turned to Espiritismo as a more economical spiritual path. The Cuban government has also recognized the financial benefits of Santería, and Santería tourism has become part of the culture of the island, where tourists can take a tour and visit an "authentic" Santería ritual.

The legitimation of Santería is now an issue on the minds of many practitioners. Since the 1990s, *babalowos* have tried to unify, arguing that this would enable them to ensure orthodoxy and to decrease fragmentation within the religion. This move toward centralization is clearly seen in the consolidation of the practice of the yearly Ifá predictions offered by *babalowos* at the beginning of each year. In 1997, five different *letras* (predictions) were issued; by 2003, there were only two groups of *babalowos*, both issuing predictions as a collective, a reflection of the ties that are growing among practitioners.[4] Part of the motivation behind the unification of the religion is a desire to give Afro-Cuban religions a more public political voice in the face of Christianity. Along with the concern for unity, there are also efforts in Cuba to promote the Yorubization of Santería, emphasizing its African foundation. For example, in 1992, the Workshop on Yoruba Culture in Cuba proposed removing the Roman Catholic elements of the religion, abandoning the name Santería, and returning to a more "orthodox" Nigerian religion.[5] Others disagree with these efforts, stating that Yoruba religion in Cuba is just as authentic as African practices, which are fluid and have transformed themselves over the course of history.

Haitian Vodou is another Afro-Caribbean religion seeking legitimation as an acceptable religious tradition. After the co-optation of certain Vodou sectors during the Duvalier regime, practitioners moved toward reclaiming the authenticity of Vodou by taking power back into their own hands. After *oungans* (priests) who had been associated with the regime were persecuted by the Vodou community and Vodou itself was maligned for its association with the Duvalier regimes, cultural activists "formed the *Zantray* movement in the late 1980s which aimed to create a public organization devoted to defending the presence of Vodou in Haitian society."[6] The Bode Nasyonal organization was similarly created. Bode Nasyonal, which has close to fifteen thousand members globally, focuses on defending the rights of Vodou practitioners.[7] Its goals are to create a registry of Vodou practitioners and practices and to engage Vodou as a more public religion around certain social issues, such as education and the environment. Central to the mission of organizations such as Zantray and Bode Nasyonal is a desire to educate the broader population about Vodou. These Vodou organizations also at times attempt to regulate Vodou practices and prayers. Similar to the efforts to re-Yorubanize

Santería, attempts are being made to re-Africanize Vodou: "Within the past ten years, with the advent of the 'root culture' movement [a movement that attempts to return to the African roots of Vodou practices] driven by the progressive wing of culturalists (Vodou organizations such as Zantray, Bode Nasyonal, New Rada Community, and the Congress of Santa Barbara, which emerged around or after the fall of Duvalier in 1986), efforts to drop the first part of the prayer Dyó have been resisted by many *oungan* and *manbo*."[8] The Dyó prayer, which begins Vodou ceremonies, incorporates Roman Catholic prayers (the Our Father, the Hail Mary, and the Apostle's Creed). The attempt at re-Africanization is driven by the belief that returning Vodou to its "pure" African roots will bestow more authenticity and legitimacy on the traditions. This debate reveals that the question of the role of Roman Catholicism in African diaspora religion is not exclusive to Cuba.

Vodou practitioners today are public about their beliefs and practices, and Vodou is seen as a constitutive element of Haitian culture. However, as Laënnec Hurbon warns, the popularization of Vodou can also lead to its dilution. Vodou elements are often taken up and appropriated by those seeking to experiment with the tradition with little regard to the religion's core beliefs.[9]

Spiritual Baptists in Trinidad are even further down the road of receiving legitimation and uniting themselves in a common front. Many congregations have begun to affiliate, creating the sense of being a denomination, though the leaders' authority is limited to enforcing orthodoxy or orthopraxy. Spiritual Baptists' effort to organize is in part an effort to distinguish their practice from Shango, in spite of the fact that these traditions are interrelated and members are known to participate in each others' religious practices.[10] As indicated in chapter 6, both Spiritual Baptists and Shango (Orisha religion) have received the imprimatur of the government of Trinidad and Tobago as legitimate religious traditions after decades of repression, malignment, and marginalization.

As Caribbean religions become more and more globalized, it will be essential to create a sense of what authentically constitutes each religious tradition. These religions as they currently exist are fairly new developments within the history of religions. While African religions, for example, have existed for centuries, the particularity of Santería, Palo Monte, and Vodou, with their Roman Catholic elements, is of recent origin. Yoruba religion has existed for centuries; Santería has not. Similarly, religions such as Rastafarianism and Christian Pentecostalism are twentieth-century phenomena. As all these religious traditions seek legitimation and probably move toward institutionalization, questions of identity will become increasingly decisive in their efforts at self-definition.

Caribbean Theology

The emergence in the second half of the twentieth century of distinctive theological voices that have focused on the Caribbean context have given rise to Caribbean theology. This development must be understood in light of the explosion of liberation and contextual theologies in the 1960s and 1970s. These theological voices emerged from "the underside of history," taking as their starting point the sociopolitical context and the spirituality of marginalized peoples. The variety of voices that claim a liberationist and/or contextual theological hermeneutic include theologies from the global South, those of U.S. minorities, and those that have a feminist perspective. Each of these struggles against various types of social injustice. Black liberation theology takes race as the starting point from which it constructs contemporary Christian theology. Latin American liberation theology privileges poverty as its primary hermeneutic.[11] Within the Caribbean, the most influential theological schools have been those of black theology and Latin American liberation theology.

Caribbean theology reflects the particular concerns of Caribbean populations. Broadly, Caribbean theology can be categorized as emanations from three groups of scholars: those scholars writing in the Caribbean, those writing in the United States, and those writing in Europe. A distinction that runs through all three categories is the rather stark division between those who are engaged in the Spanish-speaking Caribbean and those who are not.

Caribbean theologians first gathered in the mid-1950s at a meeting sponsored by the World Council of Churches. A 1993 conference on Caribbean theology at the United Theological College of the West Indies sought to define the central concerns of Caribbean theology. In his keynote address, Adolfo Ham, a Caribbean Church historian, outlined three features of this theology: Caribbean theology as a contextual theology, one that reflects the diversity of Caribbean cultures, a "decolonized" theology; as a missiological and ecumenical theology; and as one that is in dialogue with other Caribbean diaspora and "third-world" populations.[12] Central to Caribbean theology written in the Caribbean is that it engages the Caribbean sociopolitical and cultural landscape by emphasizing questions of poverty, culture, and race. This theology may also be geared toward preparing students for ministry within the specific Caribbean context.

Caribbean diaspora theology developed in the late twentieth century partially in direct response to African American (i.e., black and womanist theology, the latter reflecting black women's theological reflections) and liberationist discourses in the Americas. Caribbean theologians, especially black Caribbean theologians, often note the marginalization they feel when reading and attempting to dialogue with black theology. Too often, they claim, these black theological voices construct a normative understanding of black Christianity that is African American in culture and outlook. In a similar vein, non-black Spanish-speaking Caribbean theologians often find their context and particularity eclipsed by the overwhelming prominence of Latin American liberation theology.

As the Caribbean theologian Delroy A. Reid-Salmon asserts, "African American theology neither considers the Caribbean Diasporan experience as an appropriate starting point for theological inquiry nor does it address the issues and concerns of the Caribbean Diaspora despite this phenomenological entity being in existence in America for more than one hundred years."[13] Black theology from the United States excludes Caribbean black theology as a vital interlocutor and even ignores black Caribbeans in their midst within the United States. Critiquing first-generation black theologians such as James Deotis Roberts and James H. Cone for their complete inattention to black Caribbeans, Reid-Salmon notes that when even second-generation black theologians such as Dwight Hopkins do engage in dialogue outside the United States, they often address African theologians and not others in the African diaspora. The normativity of liberation within black theology is also questioned by Caribbean theologians, for they find that liberation is not the only paradigm through which to understand the theological landscape of blacks. The religious diversity of the Caribbean is one theme that is consistently addressed by Caribbean theologians. Scholars such as Anthony Pinn, whose scholarship decentralizes Christianity in the study of black religion, do not escape Reid-Salmon's critique. Pinn, he argues, conflates black theology and black religion by equating academic reflection on black religion (theology) with actual black religious practices, thereby making his discursive inclusion of non-Christian traditions problematic.

Nor does womanist theology escape a similar critique from Caribbean theologians. However, within womanist theology, Dianne Stewart has emerged as a significant voice, drawing from African diaspora religions in her own research. As she observes, "Given the rich African religious heritage of the Caribbean and the role women play in its preservation, it is unfortunate that, even in the twenty-first century, Caribbean women of African descent have yet to partake in this wellspring of womanist/feminist theological reflection."[14] Stewart's research focuses on Jamaican Kumina women as a vital resource for womanist theology. However, the challenge of incorporating non-Christian religious traditions into Christian theological discourse remains. Stewart's response to the Christian-centered discourse of womanism is at times too strong, for she ignores Caribbean women's Christian experiences. Caribbean religion is reduced at times in her work to non-Christian religious beliefs that are juxtaposed with Christian womanism in the United States.

Not all Caribbean theology has directly engaged in dialogue with black theologies of the United States. Emerging from the Puerto Rican context, the Puerto Rican theologian Luis Rivera-Pagán highlights the importance of postcolonialism for understanding Puerto Rican theology.[15] Many Spanish-speaking Caribbean theologians and those living in the diaspora are likely to dialogue with U.S. Latino/a and Latin American theologians before their "Anglo" Caribbean colleagues. Much that emerges from the Spanish-speaking Caribbean is classified as Latino/a or Latin American theology. Those authors who write explicitly under the heading of Caribbean theology are overwhelmingly non-Hispanic. For Puerto Ricans, the question of identity and "fitting" into contemporary theological discourse as Caribbean or Latino/a is especially difficult, given Puerto Rico's status as a dependency of the United States.

Linked to the articulation of a distinctive Caribbean theology is the establishment of Christian theological schools that emphasize ministry in and for the Caribbean context. The second half of the 1900s began a new chapter in the development of theological education in the Caribbean with the establishment of various theological seminaries focusing on Christian Protestant education. Many of these seminaries are ecumenical in establishment and focus. In 1960, the American missionary Zenas Gerig founded the Jamaica Theological Seminary. Though sponsored by the Missionary Church, it has always has an ecumenical flavor, training ministers from across the Caribbean for various denominations that consider themselves evangelical. Gerig established the Caribbean School of Theology under the auspices of the Caribbean Evangelical Association on the same site as the Jamaica Theological Seminary. United Theological College of the West Indies in Jamaica (now the theological school of the University of the West Indies, Mona) was established in 1966 through the merger of several denominational ministerial training schools. Founding denominations included the Anglican Church, the Disciples of Christ, the Evangelical Lutheran Church, the Guyana Presbyterian Church, the Jamaica Baptist Union, the Methodist Church in the Caribbean and the Americas, the Moravian Church (East West Indies and Jamaican Provinces), the Presbyterian Church of Trinidad and Guyana, and the United Church of Jamaica and Grand Cayman.[16] This ecumenical seminary focuses on training Protestant ministers and has a relationship with Columbia Theological Seminary in Atlanta, Georgia.

The Seminario Evangelico de Puerto Rico (Evangelical Seminary of Puerto Rico) opened its doors in 1919. It was founded by the Puerto Rican Theological Seminary (Presbyterian), in Mayaquez; the Grace Conway Institute (Baptist), in Rio Piedras; the Robinson Institute (Methodist), in Hatillo; and the Disciples of Christ Institute (Christian Church), in Bayamon. Located in San Juan, the seminary offers master's and certificate programs for Protestants on the island and has trained most of its Protestant leaders. The seminary is currently supported by six denominations: Baptist churches of the United States, the Methodist Church, the Disciples of Christ, the Evangelical Lutheran Church, the Presbyterian Church (USA), and the Iglesia Evangélica Unida (Puerto Rico).[17] The student body, however, is broader than the six supporting denominations. With their emphasis on the Caribbean context and their vibrant growth in the last fifty years, Protestant seminaries, along with a host of denominational bible schools and colleges, are at the forefront of creating indigenous ecclesial leadership throughout the Caribbean and training Caribbean scholars in theological reflection appropriate for the Caribbean context. In 1973, the Caribbean Council of Churches was founded; it now has thirty-three member churches in thirty-four territories. The Council brings Caribbean churches together across national, denominational, linguistic, and cultural lines. Its focus is the renewal and development of the region.[18] Collaborations between Protestant Caribbean churches, in which the Roman Catholic Church does not participate, are also creating a more rigid line between Catholics and Protestants. Roman Catholicism in the Caribbean often aligns itself with Latin American Catholic churches rather than its Caribbean neighbors. With the explosion of Pentecostalism and other forms of Protestantism described as *evangélico*, manifestations of Protestantism that clearly reject Roman Catholicism as part of their identity, the future of true ecumenism in the Caribbean remains unclear. These theological institutions, linked with the development of Caribbean theology, mark the birth of an authentic academic and pastoral Caribbean voice in the twentieth century.

Music, the Arts, and Liturgy

Perhaps nowhere does the pervasive influence of Caribbean religion on Caribbean culture as a whole reveal itself as clearly as in the world of music and the arts. The incorporation of secular black music into African diaspora religion is a central feature of Caribbean religious music. Whether it is reggae, dance hall, jazz, or salsa, the beats that move bodies outside the churches and religious gathering spaces have now entered directly and intentionally into the realm of religion. In the case of African diaspora Christianity, as the theologian Robert Beckford thoughtfully articulates, influence flows in both directions between secular and sacred cultures: "This process is reciprocal, as musical styles from hip-hop to reggae also take inspiration, if not literal guidance, from the music and culture of African diasporan Christianity."[19] This relationship between the "church hall" and the "dance hall," as Beckford describes it, is fundamental for understanding how religion and popular culture mutually influence and challenge each other in the contemporary Caribbean. In the case of Jamaica, the proximity of the dance hall to the church hall among the working class and within working-class movements contributes to their cross-fertilization.

The centrality of drumming within African traditional religions has replicated itself in the diaspora. Whether within Vodou, Santería, or Rastafarianism, drumming remains a fundamental dimension of ritual life. Within Jamaican Christianity, the religious awakenings (or revivals) of the 1860s brought African-styled music, singing, and drumming within a Christian framework. The Revival Zion tradition that emerged from these awakenings merged a Christian worldview with a worship style that privileged African music and dance. This in turn came to influence other Jamaican religious traditions. More specifically, "Revival styles of music were appropriated by Rastafarian religion and subsequently became a part of the music culture that had shaped and influenced reggae and dance hall into the present."[20] In a similar manner, local folk and popular music styles have influenced the worship style of Jamaica's Pentecostalism. African religion comes to influence Jamaican Christianity, which in turn becomes influential in other Jamaican religions and in the broader popular culture. Ultimately, however, the "dancehall" and the "church hall" share a common cultural heritage that predates any explicit contemporary influence. One would be remiss not to mention the intersection of religion, music, and popular culture in Jamaica without mentioning Rastafarianism. The international popularity of reggae has in many ways globalized it as a musical genre that transcends Jamaica, yet its roots in Jamaica and its connection to Rastafarianism are uncontested. While not all reggae music is Rastafarian, many of the dominant themes of Rastafarianism appear in reggae.

The popularity of Rastafari and reggae in Jamaica and abroad opened up both to commodification and commercial exploitation. Bob Marley himself became a gold mine for Chris Blackwell's Island Records through a spate of successful albums and frequent live concerts. The tourist interest in Jamaica also capitalized on reggae and Rastafari. In 1978, Reggae Sunsplash was started as a music festival featuring many popular reggae acts that took place in hot July, the slowest month for Jamaican tourism. This event attracted thousands of visitors from as far away as Japan, boosting hotel occupancy and foreign exchange in an otherwise lean period. Sunsplash was also exported abroad to major cities in North America, Europe, and even Japan. Reggae Sunsplash had a rather rocky history and was replaced in 1992 by Reggae Sumfest as the premiere reggae festival in Jamaica. In addition to the commercialization of reggae music, the Rastafarian image and Rastafari symbols have become the common fare in tourist arts and crafts. By far the most prevalent image in the crafts markets in Montego Bay, Ocho Rios, and Kingston are the carvings of Rastafarian heads and the image of Bob Marley on tee-shirts, plaques, and paintings; popular too are personal accessories, tee-shirts, and jewelry featuring the Rastafarian colors of red, green and gold.[21] The 1980s also saw the eclipse of classic reggae with its "conscious," Rasta-inspired lyrics and the rise in popularity of the dance hall genre with its stance of braggadocio, its valorization of gun violence, and its sexually explicit lyrics. Not that Rastas disappeared from the music scene, but they were relegated to the sidelines. The most telling incident that exemplified the eclipse of Rastafari during this period was the stoning of the reggae artist Bunny Wailer at a concert by a crowd eager to hear the dance hall artist they had come to see.

Reggae, however, is not limited to Rastafarianism. In recent years, Christian reggae has emerged on the Caribbean scene. Gospel reggae bands are mostly unknown in the international music scene, and often their fame extends only to their Christian communities. The existence of Evangelical Protestant reggae music signals that reggae has transcended Rastafarianism and entered into the popular culture of Jamaica through an unlikely, path. The symbols and images of reggae Rastafarianism have been translated into an evangelical Christian setting via popular music. In the process, gospel reggae artists have tried to Christianize reggae. These efforts have not always been well received by Jamaican evangelicals, who are uncertain whether reggae can ever truly be divorced from Rastafarianism. However, gospel artists have defended their use of reggae, arguing that the Christian gospel should be presented to Caribbean youths in a medium that is culturally relevant and accessible. For many, reggae (and dance hall) is that medium.

Since Pentecostalism's birth in the early twentieth century, music has played a pivotal role in its enthusiastic worship style. Generally speaking,

Pentecostal worship is not as ritually structured as that in mainline Protestant denominations, and the personal experience of the Spirit is central. Within that Spirit centeredness is the belief that the Holy Spirit guides the musical expressions of worship. Until the 1950s and 1960s, Pentecostal music was characterized by hymns and choruses, although black Pentecostalism throughout the Americas remains deeply influenced by the spirituals and by black folk music. The 1960s ushered in a new era, with youth driving Pentecostal music into new genres. The emergence of Christian rock, which was followed in the contemporary Caribbean by Christian salsa, merengue, and dance hall, marked a new phase in Pentecostal music. Not only has the genre changed, being updated to include music that is popular in youth culture, but Pentecostal music has moved out of the churches through recording contracts, performances, and outdoor festivals.

In the 1970s, members of the Youth for Christ organization in Trinidad and Tobago coined the term "gospelypso" to refer to a new music style that combines calypso rhythms with Christian messages. Gospelypso became a means of indigenizing the musical expressions of Pentecostal worship on the island for young Christians, replacing the usual acceptance of North American worship styles as somehow more legitimate expressions. Fueled by the cultural nationalism of the local Black Power movement, gospelypso artists sought an authentically Trinidadian form of Christian music. Calypso itself had been heavily influenced by the Orisha and Spiritual Baptist religions on the island. Given the Baptist roots of calypso, gospelypso artists were able to claim that their genre was a return to authentic, local Christian music.[22] However, resistance from powerful church leaders has prevented Gospelypso from gaining much prominence within churches or in popular culture. Jamaican gospel dance hall and gospel music influenced by Soca (dance music influenced by calypso) are also found in Pentecostal settings in Trinidad. Unlike gospelypso artists who attempt to seek some legitimization within churches, Gospel dance hall and Soca musicians tend to perform in dance hall settings.[23] Gospel dance hall artists take religion to the "world" and do not want to be constrained by ecclesial settings.

Music is foundational to Vodou ritual. As noted by the musicologist Gerdès Fleurant, "The music is the central element of the Vodun ceremony, and as such, drummers and song leaders are indispensable individuals chosen as much for their artistic talent as for their liturgical knowledge." Fleurant argues that Vodun music also serves as a moral barometer for the community for the *lwa* are present in the music, whether manifest or not. Popular artists have appropriated the use of Vodou rhythms, most notably in the 1970s "Freedom Culture" movement that included artists such as Boukman Eksperyans and Azor.[24] Some Vodou fusion rock artists even go to the extreme of simulating Vodou rituals and ritual space onstage.[25]

Within Yoruba religion, the importance of the aesthetic is fundamental to ritual life. As the anthropologist David Brown has highlighted, the creation of altars is not only part of ritual life but also a system of giftgiving to the *orishas*; art is a medium through which to please the *orishas* and a means by which to cultivate one's relationship with them.[26] Outside the context of religion explicitly, the influence of Yoruban religion is found throughout the arts in Cuba. Perhaps the most well-known example of this is in the surrealist art of Wilfredo Lam (1902–1982). Lam depicted the *orishas* Eleggua and Ogun in his artwork, and paintings such as *The Warrior* reveal an Afro-Cuban cosmology.[27] Other prominent Cuban artists who draw from Afro-Cuban religion include Juan Boza and Ana Mendieta.

Popular rap music has developed into a central site for debates on race in contemporary Cuba. Led by young Afro-Cubans, the hip-hop movement in Cuba has created a space for youth to articulate their frustrations and to critique the resurgent racism on the island beginning in the 1990s. Artists such as Hermanos de Causa draw on the Cuban poetic and artistic tradition and rewrite lyrics to speak to the situation of race in contemporary Cuba. Central to this hip-hop movement is a retrieval of Afro-Cuban culture as fundamental to Cuban identity as a whole. As Alejandro de la Fuente observes, this takes the form of highlighting and retrieving the value of African religion as a means of affirming one's Afro-Cuban identity: "Many have used Afro-Cuban religious symbols to highlight the need to fully acknowledge African contributions to Cubanidad. Some rappers play an active role in this process of recovery and affirmation by using Yoruba terms in their songs, an effort that seeks to arrest and perhaps even reverse the process of cultural destruction associated with slavery and the Middle Passage."[28] The connection between one's African roots and one's religious identity has become central to contemporary Cuban hip-hop. The most well known of hip-hop artists is the Orishas, whose very name is obviously the same as that of the spirits of Yoruban religion. On their first studio CD, *A Lo Cubano*, the rhythms and *orishas* of Santería figure prominently. Rap is not the only genre of Cuban music that incorporates Afro-Cuban religions. Popular music as a whole makes references to Afro-Cuban religious practices. Artists such as Adalberto Álvarez y su Son, Elio Revé, and NG La Bandas all sing of Afro-Cuban religion.[29]

Music also opens a window into Afro-Cuban religious practices that have been historically extremely secretive in terms of rituals and beliefs.

In his excellent study of the influence of Abakuá on popular Cuban music, the musicologist Ivan Miller argues that Abakuá chants and rhythms have saturated all genres of Cuban music. Practitioners were able to facilitate this development since the true nature and the significance of these chants were unknown to outsiders.[30] Artists such as Beny Moré drew from Abakuá chants and rhythms in their music. Popular music as a whole, Miller argues, is fundamental for the study of African diaspora religion in the Caribbean, for here we find the oral history of African peoples, whether rhythmic or lyrical. African religion came to saturate Cuban and Cuban-American popular culture.[31] Many U.S. audiences, listening to Desi Arnaz chant to "Babalú" on *I Love Lucy*, were completely unaware that he was chanting to an *orisha*. For the scholar of African Diaspora religion, the study of popular culture becomes an essential focus. Similarly, the study of Caribbean popular culture is enriched by the study of African diaspora religion.

New Religious Movements

The study of new religious movements in the Caribbean has been fairly limited, and there is scant academic scholarship on them. Nonetheless, it is important to document their presence and growth in the Caribbean, especially as they seem poised to change the face of Caribbean religion in the future. Laënnec Hurbon documented the growth of the Jehovah's Witnesses, Mahikari, the Adventists, the Apostles of Infinite Love, and transcendental meditation on the island of Guadeloupe in the 1970s.[32] The number of Jehovah's Witnesses nearly doubled in that decade, from four thousand to seven thousand. The number of Seventh-Day Adventists also grew steadily in Martinique and Guadeloupe in the 1970s. A staunch rejection of Roman Catholicism accompanied both of these religious shifts.

The Mahikari movement was founded in Japan in the late 1950s and arrived in Martinique and Guadeloupe in the mid-1970s, while the Apostles of Infinite Love are a quasi-Roman Catholic movement founded in Canada in the early 1950s; because of legal issues with the Canadian government, it later relocated to Guadeloupe. Believers claim that they are the authentic Roman Catholic Church. Members are found primarily in rural areas and among the lower economic classes. The Church has also begun to establish itself in Puerto Rico. La Palma Sola, in the Dominican Republic, was established in the late 1960s and has established a significant membership on the Haitian border. This movement has been successful among rural populations through its combination of Roman Catholic ritual imagery and its acceptance of Vodou practices. Its association with Vodou made it suspect to the Dominican government, and in 1962 its compound was attacked by the military; after the attack, estimates of the number of dead varied from two hundred to five hundred.

Predicting the potential growth of all of these movements is difficult, and their future in the Caribbean remains to be seen. Some, such as the Jehovah's Witnesses, position themselves as directly rejecting Catholicism and thus offer an alternative form of Christian spirituality. Others, such as La Palma, draw from Catholicism yet also incorporate elements of African diaspora religion. What is clear is that, through their connection with the urban and the rural poor, these religious movements provide an alternative religious way of life, especially for populations in economic and political turmoil.

The Earth People of Trinidad emerged in the mid-1970s when the Spiritual Baptist Jeanette Baptiste began to have visions of Mother Earth as primordial Mother, a contrast to the male God of Christianity.[33] The Earth People's racialized mythology associates whiteness (the race of the Son) with masculinity, war, and technology. The true path is that of blacks (the race of the Mother), nature, nakedness, a close relationship with the earth, and non-oppressive human relationships. Jeanette prophesized that the current era is that of the Son and that it will end destructively in order to usher in a new era of the Mother. The goal of the Earth People is to prepare for this new era and to spread the truth to blacks as the children of the Mother. Jeanette's visions signify that the beginning of the end for the manifestation of the Mother must occur during her lifetime. This is a small movement in Trinidad, whose membership is estimated around fifty.

Neo-Pentecostals constitute the third wave of global Pentecostalism. In the first wave, churches and denominations emerged from classic Pentecostal churches, such as the Church of God in Christ and the Assemblies of God; in the second wave came the rise of Charismatic movements within mainline Christian denominations, such as the Charismatic movement within Roman Catholicism. Neo-Pentecostals are independent and, in some cases, postdenominational (having split from a first-wave church) churches that are spreading rapidly across the globe, including in the Caribbean. They have no denominational ties to Pentecostal churches and are often indigenous to particular countries and contexts. Prosperity theology or the prosperity gospel is found in some Neo-Pentecostal megachurches, where the emphasis is on the belief that poverty does not equal humility and that material wealth is a sign of divine love.

Gender

The question of women's religious participation and the manner in which they have been sidelined and ignored by many religious institutions are at the forefront of contemporary scholarship on feminism within the field of religious studies. Many of the Caribbean religions we have discussed offer some alternative spaces for women that expand their leadership roles beyond what has tended to be possible within mainline Christianity. Yet, as a whole, the issue of patriarchal control of religion is one that has not escaped contemporary Caribbean religions. While Rastafarianism is often depicted as a liberationist, decolonial religion of empowerment for black Jamaicans, when it comes to the issue of women it remains extremely patriarchal and oppressive, and women represent a minority population in Rastafarianism. This patriarchal stance is based largely on the broader Jamaican culture and on Rastafarianism's privileging of Old Testament Levitical laws, which render the domination of women in a form of sacred discourse. Women do not have leadership positions in Rastafarianism, and men are understood as the patriarchal head of a household. Since the 1970s, however, the entry of women from different economic classes, as well as a more liberated generation of male Rastas, has opened more spaces for women within the religion. The scholar Loretta Collins has argued that most scholarship on Rastawomen has taken a too simplistic approach, not taking seriously their everyday lives and engaging Rastafarianism through an imperialistic "First World" assessment.[34] Since the 1970s, various Rastawomen's organizations have been formed, such as the King Alpha and Queen Omega Daughters Theocracy I, in order to educate and empower women, as well as to explore notions of women's identity and sexuality within Rastafarianism.

The influx of young middle-class Jamaicans into the Rastafarian movement also brought the issue of gender to fore. As we saw earlier, the radical Rastas of the 1940s and 1950s marginalized women and women could "trod" Rastafari only through their kingmen. Now that young educated women who are accustomed to arguing with men in classrooms are embracing Rastafari, it is becoming difficult for men to exclude them from "reasoning" sessions. What is more, many of these are independent women who are pursuing Rastafari on their own terms and are not dependent on Rasta men to lead them in their growth within Rastafarianism. This turn of events has initiated a discussion of women's status in the movement, a discussion that is continuing today. Many brethren agree that women should participate equally in the rituals and activities of Rastafari, while others still hold to the precepts established in the 1950s. Among the Bobo Dreads, for example, ritual laws exclude woman from many activities and traditional practices, subordinating them to men.

While Pentecostalism is often depicted in Latin American theological scholarship as a patriarchal religion with little space for women's leadership and authority, in actuality women do achieve leadership positions within its churches. As Diane Austin-Broos has persuasively argued, not only the institution of Pentecostalism but also the theology behind possession by the Spirit creates an empowering environment for women. Focusing her research on Jamaica, Austin-Broos highlights that women often serve as pastors on Pentecostal churches. The leadership, nonetheless, remains overwhelmingly male, with elders in a church almost always being men. In addition, Pentecostal women pastors are infrequent in rural settings. Women can also serve as evangelists and deacons.[35] Drawing from sexual imagery, Pentecostals often interpret women's bodies as more appropriate "vessels" for the reception of the Spirit. Since in Pentecostalism adherents are feminine before the sacred as receivers of God's spirit, the female body has been perceived as having a privileged status in the reception of that Spirit.

African Diaspora religions in Cuba have created an ambiguous space for women in which they are both included and marginalized in ritual leadership. In Palo Monte, for example a woman can achieve the status of *tata nganga* only after menopause, when the "impurity" of menstruation has ended. Women are entirely excluded from Abakuá. In her excellent study of gender in Santería, Mary Ann Clark, a scholar of religious studies, argues that Yoruba religion offers a more fluid understanding of gender, calling on both male and female practitioners to take on female roles. In other words, practitioners experience a female normativity within the religion.[36] While Clark's argument is sound, women nonetheless are still ritualistically excluded from many leadership positions. Within Santería, women are excluded from the status of *babalawo*, priest of Ifá. Though this is a distinct tradition within Yorubaland, within Cuba and the United States it has become absorbed as part of Santería. Women are unable to play the *batá* drums, they are unable to sacrifice various types of animals, and they are prohibited from serving as *osainista*, herbal experts who specializes in the plants offered to the *orishas*.[37] It is both saddening and troubling that, while Caribbean religions do create more ritual leadership possibilities for women in some cases, overwhelmingly there still exists a "glass ceiling" for women in terms of true ritual leadership and authority.

Caribbean Religions in the United States

Caribbean religions in the diaspora (outside the Caribbean) are clearly marked by the diversity of their adherents. In the United States, they have taken on a multiracial and multi-ethnic character. Vodou is not only Haitian in the United States; Santería is no longer Cuban. The practitioners of Afro-Caribbean diaspora religions are no longer black. Instead, we find in the United States a diversity of races and ethnicities practicing Afro-Caribbean religions. For many Caribbean peoples in the United States, Caribbean religions have become a means by which to stay connected with their homeland and culture. White Cubans in the United States, for example, who perhaps balked at the practice of Santería in their homeland, are now turning to the religion as a way of reconnecting with their Cuban roots. However, the legal struggle between the Church of Lukumi Bablú Ayé (founded by Ernesto Pichardo) in Hialeah, Florida, as the first public Santería worship site in the United States and the City of Hialeah, a predeominantly Cuban area whose council members were overwhelmingly Cuban, demonstrates that not all Cuban-Americans are comfortable with Santería. The 1993 U.S. Supreme Court decision to grant the Church the right to perform animal sacrifice marks the legal recognition of Santería as an authentic religion.

Santería established itself in New York first among Afro-Cubans musicians and then among Puerto Ricans and African Americans.[38] The appeal of Santería for African Americans is rooted in 1960s pan-Africanism coupled with Black Nationalism. African Americans distilled the African elements of Santería and made it their own. The attention given to Yorubaland and Nigeria outweighs that given to Cuba, and the Caribbean context is ignored. Within the United States, the conversion of African Americans to Santería has posed some challenges to traditionally Cuban practitioners. For many African Americans, conversion to Santería is seen as a way to return to their African roots. Therefore, as we have seen within the Cuban context, the question of the incorporation of Roman Catholic elements in the religion has become a matter of contention among religious practitioners. These practitioners claim they are practicing an authentic Yoruba religion that is free from the "corruptions" of Catholicism within Santería. Fundamental to African American Yoruba religion in the United States is a rejection of Catholic influences and Cuban cultural elements.

Though some feel that authentic Yoruba religion in the United States should be stripped of its Catholic elements and become a "pure" African religion, others recognize that Santería draws not only drawn from Yoruba religion but from the crucible of the Afro-Cuban experience, making it a distinct religion that incorporates dimensions of Catholic ritual life and symbolism into its religious practice and iconography. Santería in the United States, unlike in Nigeria, is a house religion that has no formal temple site and is often practiced in secrecy. It is also radically different in structure and transmission from contemporary Yoruba religion. Clear tensions exist between white Cubans and Afro-Cubans regarding the manner in which they approach the religion. The question of race plagues not only Santería but also other traditionally black Caribbean religions that now have white adherents. The inclusion of whites in certain contemporary Rastafarian groups is also a signal of the changing racial make-up of these religious traditions.

These now multinational religions will surely be confronted with questions of identity and race as they continue to be practiced and grow outside their homelands. In addition to the diverse backgrounds of adherents, many Afro-Caribbean religions have had to adapt to the urban settings in which many Caribbeans in the United States now live. Rituals that occurred in rural settings now have to be transformed and accommodate the walk-ups, apartments, and small back yards that house urban Caribbean religions in the United States.

Conclusion

Throughout this text, we have offered some broad brushstrokes of the history of religions in the Caribbean. At the center of this history is the unequal and often violent encounter between cultures and traditions: European, African, indigenous, and Asian. The children of the Caribbean, much like their religions, are the products of these encounters. What emerges from the Caribbean is a rich tapestry of diverse religious traditions that reflects the richness of the peoples that inhabit its islands. The study of religion is one entry point, an essential one, that reveals the complexity and diversity of the historical and contemporary Caribbean.

While much of this book has focused on African religious traditions and the manner in which slaves and their descendants have marked the religious landscape of the Caribbean, to reduce the Caribbean to its African influences would be misleading. As the essayist Antonio Benítez-Rojo has written, "Does this mean that the Caribbean rhythm is African? If I had to answer this question, I would say not entirely. I would say that the crossed rhythm that shows up in Caribbean cultural forms can be seen as the expression of countless performers who tried to represent what was already here, or there, at times drawing closer and at times farther away from Africa." Basing his insights on the Cuban reality, Benítez-Rojo reminds us that the Caribbean is "a polyrhythmic space that is Cuban, Caribbean, African, and European at once, and even Asian and Indoamerican, where there has been a contrapuntal and intermingled meeting of the biblical Creator's *logos*, of tobacco smoke, the dance of the *orishas* and *loas*, Chinese bugle, Lezama Lima's *Paradiso*, and the *Virgen de la Caridad de the Cobre* and the boat of the Three Juans."[1] This creolized, dynamic reality reflects the long history of encounter and adaption to the Caribbean context.

This volume is in no way exhaustive and should be understood as an entry point into the rich world of Caribbean religious history. To fully cover the history of *every* religion in the Caribbean over the past five hundred years would require multiple volumes. However, the broad historical trajectories and the social history that ground this book speak to the historical rhythm of the Caribbean as a whole. The major religious traditions we have covered, as well as the minor ones, reflect the Caribbean's complex, creolized religious landscape. The encounter of indigenous peoples, Europeans, and various diaspora populations created a vibrant religious world that continues to transform itself as new religious movements and peoples both enter and exit these islands.

Notes

CHAPTER 1

1. See Carlos Moore's discussion of Cuban census data in "Afro-Cubans and the Communist Revolution," in *African Presence in the Americas*, ed. Carlos Moore, Tanya R. Saunders, and Shawna Moore (Trenton, NJ: Africa World Press, 1995), 199–239.

2. Franklin W. Knight and Colin A. Palmer, "The Caribbean: A Regional Overview," in *The Modern Caribbean*, ed. Franklin W. Knight and Colin A. Palmer (Chapel Hill: University of North Carolina Press, 1989), 3.

3. Rex Nettleford, *Mirror Mirror: Identity, Race and Protest in Jamaica* (Kingston, Jamaica: Collins and Sangster, 1970), 171–72.

4. O. Nigel Bolland, *Struggles for Freedom: Essays on Slavery, Colonialism and Culture in the Caribbean and Central America* (Belize City, Belize: Angelus Press, 1997), 7.

5. E. Franklin Frazier, *The Negro Family in the United States* (Chicago: University of Chicago Press, 1940).

6. Prem Misir, "Introduction," in *Cultural Identity and Creolization in National Unity: The Multiethnic Caribbean*, ed. Prem Misir (Latham, MD: University Press of America, 2006), xxi.

7. Bolland, 8.

8. M. G. Smith, *The Plural Society in the British West Indies* (Berkeley: University of California Press, 1965), 112. Also see Bollland, 8–10.

9. M. G. Smith, "Social and Cultural Pluralism," *Annals of the New York Academy of Science*, 83 (January 1960): 763–85.

10. Bolland, 3.

11. Edward Braithwaite, *The Development of Creole Society in Jamaica, 1770–1820* (Oxford: Clarendon Press, 1971), 296.

12. Braithwaite, 298–99.

13. Bolland, 13–14.

14. Donald J. Cosentino, "Introduction: Imagine Heaven," in *Sacred Arts of Haitian Vodou*, edited by Donald J. Cosentino (Los Angeles: UCLA Museum of Cultural History, 1995), 47.

15. Bolland, 18.

16. Misir, xxii, xxiv. See also Brinsley Samaroo, "India and the Indian Diaspora: The Continuing Links," and Percy C. Hintzen, "The Caribbean: Race and Creole Ethnicity," both in Misir. See Carlos Moore's discussion of Cuban census data in Moore, 199–239.

17. Patrick Taylor, "Dancing the Nation: An Introduction," *Nation Dance: Religion, Identity, and Cultural Difference in the Caribbean*, ed. Patrick Taylor (Bloomington: Indiana University Press, 2001), 11–12.

18. Victor Turner, *The Ritual Process: Structure and Anti-Structure* (New York: Aldine, 1969), 95.

CHAPTER 2

1. The Lesser Antilles is divided into two groups of Island. The southern group, called the Windward Islands, consists of Martinique, Dominica, Grenada, Saint Lucia, and St. Vincent and the Grenadines. Though close to the Windward Islands, Barbados and Trinidad and Tobago are not grouped with them. The northern group, the Leeward Islands, consists of the U.S. Virgin Islands, Guadeloupe, St. Eustatius, Saba, St. Martin, St. Kitts and Nevis, Antigua and Barbuda, Anguilla, Montserrat, and the British Virgin Islands. A number of smaller islands and cays are also to be found in the Leeward Islands.

2. Irving Rouse, *The Tainos: Rise and Decline of the People Who Greeted Columbus* (New Haven: Yale University Press, 1992), 5–9.

3. Arnold R. Highfield, "Some Observations on the Taino Language," in *The Indigenous People of the Caribbean*, ed. Samuel M. Wilson (Gainesville: University Press of Florida, 1997), 155.

4. Rouse, 26–48; Miguel Rodriguez, "Religious Beliefs of the Saladoid People," in *The Indigenous Peoples of the Caribbean*, ed. Samuel A. Wilson (Gainsville: University Press of Florida, 1992), 81–82.

5. Rouse, 12.

6. Rouse, 12.

7. S. Lyman Tyler, *Two Worlds: The Indian Encounter with the European, 1492–1509* (Salt Lake City: University of Utah Press, 1988), 175.

8. D. J. R. Walker, *Columbus and the Golden World of the Island Arawaks: The Story of the First Americans and Their Caribbean Environment* (Lewes, Sussex : Book Guild, 1992), 57–58.

9. Douglas Hall, *The Caribbean Experience: An Historical Survey, 1450–1960,* (Kingston, Jamaica: Heinemann Educational Books, 1982), 4–5.

10. Tyler, 146.

11. Rouse, 20.

12. Rouse, 22–23.

13. Rouse, 9; William F. Keegan, "'No Man [or Woman] Is an Island': Elements of Taino Social Organization," in *The Indigenous People of the Caribbean*, ed. Samuel M. Wilson (Gainesville: University Press of Florida, 1997), 109.

14. Tyler, 7.

15. Keegan, 114–16; "The Taino World." elmuseo.org/taino/tainoworld.html, June 10, 2007.

16. Walker, 51; Tyler, 46.

17. Walker, 66.

18. Alissandra Cummins, "European Views of the Aboriginal Population," in *Indigenous People of the Caribbean*, ed. Samuel M. Wilson (Gainesville: University Press of Florida, 1997), 48.

19. Fray Ramón Pané, *An Account of the Antiquities of the Indians*, ed. José Juan Arrom and trans. Susan C. Griswold (Durham, NC: Duke University Press, 1999), 3–4.

20. Rouse, 13; Henry Petijean Roget, "Notes on Ancient Caribbean and Mythology," in *The Indigenous People of the Caribbean*, ed. Samuel M. Wilson (Gainesville: University Press of Florida, 1997), 105.

21. Rouse, 121.

22. Pané, 21.

23. Pané, book XIX.

24. Tyler, 148; Bartolomé de las Casas, *History of the Indies*, trans. Andrée Collard (New York: Harper and Row, 1971), 55.

25. José R. Oliver, "The Taino Cosmos," in *The Indigenous People of the Caribbean*, ed. Samuel M. Wilson (Gainesville: University Press of Florida, 1997), 149.

26. Pané, 5.

27. Roget, 104–5.

28. Pané, 6.

29. Roget, 104–5; Pané, 6.

30. Pané, 14.

31. Oliver, 144–51.

32. Elizabeth Righter, "Ceramics, Art, and Material Culture of the Early Ceramic Period in the Caribbean Islands," in *The Indigenous People of the Caribbean*, ed. Samuel M. Wilson (Gainesville: University Press of Florida, 1997), 74.

33. Roget, 101.

34. Rodríguez, 84.

35. Roget, 105.

36. Roget, 108.

37. Rouse, 119; Roget,105, 107.

38. Rodríquez, 85–86.

39. Similar ball games were played in Mexico and in Central and South America. The Mayans are duly reputed for the ball game they played.

40. Rouse, 15; Ricardo E. Alegría, "The Ball Game Played by the Aborigines of the Antilles," *American Antiquity* 16, no. 4 (April, 1952): 348.

41. Rodríquez, 82–84.

42. Pané, 21–22. Pané believes the *behique* used subterfuge during these ceremonies to get the *zemis* to speak and to produce the object supposedly from the body of the sick. He describes how a tube ran from the *zemis* to someone in another place. The supposed communication from the *zemi*, he believes, was produced by someone speaking through the tube.

43. Pané, 23–25.

44. Tyler, 33–34.

45. Tyler, 30–31.

46. Walker, 51, Tyler, 74-91.

47. Tyler, 46.

48. Walker, 61.

49. Tyler, 38, 46; Walker, 51.

50. Walker, 50.

51. Tyler, 110–11.

52. Tyler, 109.

53. las Casas, 107.

54. Tyler, 111.

55. Tyler, 98–99, 112–15.

56. Tyler, 116–18.

57. Tyler, 126.

58. Tyler, 131.

59. Tyler, 138–39.

60. Tyler, 139.

61. Tyler, 139–40.

62. Rouse, 7–8; Massimo Livi-Bacci, "Return to Hispaniola: Reassessing the Demographic Catastrophe," *Hispanic American Historical Review* 83, no. 1 (2003): 3.

63. Tyler, 220–22.

64. Walker, 276.

65. Tyler, 208–9.

66. Tyler, 225; Walker, 306.

67. Tyler, 235–36.

68. Walker, 310; Tyler, 237–40.

69. Bartolomé de las Casas, *Bartolomé de las Casas: A Selection of His Writings*, trans. and ed. George Sanderlin (New York: Knopf, 1973), 38–39.

70. Justo L. González, *The Development of Christianity in the Latin Caribbean* (Grand Rapids, MI: Eerdmans, 1969), 44.

71. González, 35, 43.

72. González, 22–24.

73. Las Casas, *Bartolomé de las Casas: A Selection of His Writings*, 80–85; Gonzalez, 21.

74. Walker, 32.

75. Walker, 33.

CHAPTER 3

1. Laura de Mello e Souza, *The Devil and the Land of the Holy Cross: Witchcraft, Slavery, and Popular Religion in Colonial Brazil*, trans. Diane Grosklaus Whitty (Austin: University of Texas Press, 2006; 1986), 46.

2. De Mello e Souza, 48.

3. Anthony M. Stevens-Arroyo, "The Contribution of Catholic Orthodoxy to Caribbean Syncretism: The Case of la Virgen de la Caridad del Cobre in Cuba," *Des Sciences Sociales des Religion* 117 (January-March 2002): 42.

4. William A. Christian, *Local Religion in Sixteenth-Century Spain* (Princeton: Princeton University Press, 1981), 3.

5. Linda B. Hall, *Mary, Mother and Warrior: The Virgin in Spain and the Americas* (Austin: University of Texas Press, 2004), 19.

6. Armando Lampe, "Christianity and Slavery in the Dutch Caribbean," in *Christianity in the Caribbean: Essays on Church History*, ed. Armando Lampe (Kingston, Jamaica: University of the West Indies Press, 2001), 130.

7. Angus MacKay, "Religion, Culture, and Ideology of the Late Medieval Castilian / Granadan Frontier," in *Medieval Frontier Societies*, ed. Robert Bartlett and Angus McKay (Oxford: Clarendon Press, 1989), 23, cited in Hall, 27.

8. Octavio Paz, *Sor Juana Or, the Traps of Faith, Margaret Sayers Peden*, trans. (Cambridge, MA: Harvard University Press, 1988), 338.

9. Fernando Ortiz, *Los cabildos y la fiesta afrocubano* (Havana: Editorial de Ciencias Sociales, 1992), 4. See also Ortiz, "La Fiesta Afro-Cubana del 'Dia de Reyes,'" *Revista Bimestre Cubana* 15, no. 1 (January-February 1921): 5–26. Jorge and Isabel Catellanos

argue that, while *cabildos* did originate in Spain, in Cuba, they took on a decidedly more "American" flavor that makes them their own specific entity. Jorge Castellanos and Isabel Castellanos, *Cultura Afrocubana*, vol. 1: *El Negro en Cuba, 1492–1844* (Miami: Ediciones Universal, 1988), 110.

10. Castellanos and Castellanos,110.

11. George Brandon, *Santería from Africa to the New World: The Dead Sell Memories* (Bloomington: Indiana University Press, 1993), 71.

12. Rafael Ocasio, "Babalú Ayé: Santería and Contemporary Cuban Literature," *Journal of Caribbean Studies* 9, no. 1–2 (Winter 1992-Spring 1993): 29–40.

13. For an excellent account of the influence of three African priestesses and their role in the preservation of Lukumí religion in Cuba, see Miguel W. Ramos, "La Division de la Habana: Territorial Conflict and Cultural Hegemony in the Followers of Oyo Lukumí Religion, 1850s–1920s," *Cuban Studies* 34 (2003): 38–69.

14. Joan Cameron Bristol, *Christians, Blasphemers, and Witches: Afro-Mexican Ritual Practice in the Seventeenth Century* (Albuquerque: University of New Mexico Press, 2007), 66.

15. Bristol, 77.

16. Irene Wright, "Our Lady of Charity," *Hispanic American Historical Review* 5 (1922): 709–17.

17. Terry Rey, "The Politics of Patron Sainthood in Haiti: 500 Years of Iconic Struggle," *Catholic Historical Review* 88, no. 3 (2002): 521.

87. Rey, 533.

19. Ramón Torreira Crespo, "Breve Arcercamiento Histórico a la Iglesia Católica en Cuba: Conquista, Colonización y Pseudorrepuública," in *Religiosidad Popular: México Cuba*, ed. Noemí Quezada (México: UNAM: 2004), 190–92.

20. Torreira Crespo, 200.

21. Torreira Crespo, 210.

22. Johannes Meier, "The Beginnings of the Catholic Church in the Caribbean," in *Christianity in the Caribbean: Essays on Church History*, ed. Armado Lampe (Kingston, Jamaica: University of the West Indies Press, 2001), 32.

23. Michael A. Gomez, "African Identity and Slavery in America," *Radical History Review* 75 (1999): 117. Gomez builds on the research of Carlos Larrazábal Blanco, *Los negros y la esclavitud en Santo Domingo* (Santo Domingo, Dominican Republic: Editora de Colores, 1975), and Franklyn J. Franco, *Los negros, los mulatos, y la nacion dominicana* (Santo Domingo, Dominican Republic: Editorial Nacional, 1969).

24. José Luis Saez, S.J., *La iglesia y el negro esclavo en Santo Domingo: Una historia de tres siglos* (Santo Domingo, República Dominicana: Patronato de la Ciudad Colonial de Santo Domingo, 1994), 43–44.

25. Gwendolyn Midlo Hall, *Slavery and African Ethnicities in the Americas* (Chapel Hill: University of North Carolina Press, 2005), 82.

26. Larrazábal Blanco, 129–30.

27. William Wipfler, "The Catholic Church and the State in the Dominican Republic, 1930–1960," in *Christianity in the Caribbean: Essays on Church History*, ed. Armando Lampe (Kingston, Jamaica: University of the West Indies Press, 2001), 197.

28. Meier, 35.

29. Meier, 36.

30. John M. Kirk, *Between God and the Party: Religion and Politics in Revolutionary Cuba* (Tampa: University of South Florida Press, 1989), 18.

31. Terry Rey, *Our Lady of Class Struggle: The Cult of the Virgin Mary in Haiti* (Trenton, NJ: Africa World Press, 1999), 29.

32. Rey, *Our Lady of Class Struggle*, 32.

33. Leslie G. Desmangles, *The Faces of the Gods: Vodou and Roman Catholicism in Haiti* (Chapel Hill: University of North Carolina Press, 1992), 26.

34. Hein Vanhee, "Central African Popular Christianity and the Making of Haitian Vodou Religion," in *Central Africans and Cultural Transformations in the American Diaspora*, ed. Linda M. Heywood (New York: Cambridge University Press, 2002), 243.

35. Vanhee, 255.

36. Jason R. Young, *Rituals of Resistance; African Atlantic Religion in Kongo and the Lowcountry South in the Era of Slavery* (Baton Rouge: Louisiana State University Press, 2007), 50.

37. Young, 54.

38. Young, 57.

39. John Thornton, "The Development of an African Catholic Church in the Kingdom of Kongo, 1491–1750," *Journal of African History* 25, no. 2 (1984): 148.

40. Thornton, 154.

41. Thornton, 152

42. Thornton, 156.

43. John Thornton, "On the Trail of Voodoo: African Christianity in Africa and the Americas," *The Americas* 44 (1988): 262.

44. Thornton, "On the Trail of Voodoo," 269.

45. Vanhee, 258.

46. Terry Rey, "Kongolese Catholic Influences on Haitian Popular Catholicism: A Sociohistorical Exploration," in *Central Africans and Cultural Transformations in the American Diaspora*, ed. Linda M. Heywood (New York: Cambridge University Press, 2002), 266.

47. Rey, "Kongolese Catholic Influences," 269.

48. Rey, "The Politics of Patron Sainthood in Haiti," 523.

49. George Breathett, "Catholic Missionary Activity and the Negro Slave in Haiti," *Phylon* 23, no. 3 (3rd Qtr., 1962): 279.

50. Breathett, 282.

51. François-Marie Kersuzan, "Conférence populaire sur le vaudoux," 22, cited in Kate Ramsey, "Legislating 'Civilization' in Postrevolutionary Haiti," in *Race, Nation, and Religion in the Americas*, ed. Henry Goldschmidt and Elizabeth MacAlister (New York: Oxford University Press, 2004), 247.

CHAPTER 4

1. Edwin Gaustad and Leigh Schmidt, *The Religious History of America* (San Francisco: HarperSanFrancisco, 2002), 31–35.

2. Dale Bisnauth, *History of Religions in the Caribbean* (Kingston, Jamaica: Kingston, 1989), 33.

3. F. R. Augier, D. G. Hall, and S. C. Gordon, *Making of the West Indies* (London: Longman, 1960), 26–27.

4. Augier et al., 28.

5. Augier et al., 33.

6. Armando Lampe, "Christianity and Slavery in the Dutch Caribbean," in *Christianity in the Caribbean: Essays on Church History,* ed. Armando Lampe (Kingston, Jamaica: University of the West Indies Press, 2001), 126–28.

7. Lampe, 131.

8. Lampe, 133.

9. Lampe, 135–38.

10. Lampe, 142–43.

11. Lampe, 133–34, 144–46.

12. Lampe, 132.

13. Bisnauth, 42.

14. Bisnauth, 43.

15. Bisnauth, 45.

16. Bisnauth, 46.

17. Bisnauth, 50.

18. Fitzroy Richard Augier and Shirley Courtnay Gordon, compilers, *Sources of West Indian History* (London: Longman, 1962), 143.

19. Keith Hunte, "Protestantism and Slavery in the British Caribbean," in *Christianity in the Caribbean: Essays on Church History,* ed. Armando Lampe (Kingston, Jamaica: University of the West Indies Press, 2001), 89–91.

20. Hunte, 74–75; Bisnauth, 54.

21. Bisnauth, 48–49.

22. Hunte, 95.

23. Alfred Caldecott, *The Church in the West Indies* (London: Frank Cass, 1970 [originally published in 1898]), 58–59.

24. Augier and Gordon, 143.

25. Caldecott, 58.

26. Caldecott, 59–60.

27. See Caldecott's note on p. 57.

28. Robert Worthington Smith, "Slavery and Christianity in the British Caribbean," *Church History* 19, no. 3 (September 1950): 173.

29. Caldecott, 61.

30. Caldecott, 62.

31. Augier and Gordon, 158.

32. Caldecott, 62; Augier and Gordon, 159.

33. Caldecott, 52–55.

34. Augier and Gordon, 157–58.

35. Caldecott, 56.

36. Hunte, 96–97.

37. Smith, 172; Hunt, 91.

38. Augier and Gordon, 146.

39. Caldecott, 63–68; Hunte, 91–92.

40. Bisnauth, 53.

41. Augier and Gordon, 144.

42. J. Taylor Hamilton and Kenneth G. Hamiltion, *History of the Moravian Church: The Renewed Unitas Fratrum, 1722–1957* (Winston-Salem, NC: Interprovincial Board of Christian Education, Moravian Church of America, 1967), 44–49; Hunte, 98–99.

43. Edward Bean Underhill, *The West Indies: Their Social and Religious Condition* (Westport, CT: Negro Universities Press, 1970 [1862]), 98–100.

44. Hamilton and Hamilton, 150–51.

45. Caldecott, 73; Hamilton and Hamilton, 150–51, 256–59.

46. Caldecott, 73.

47. Hewlester A. Samuel, Sr. *The Birth of the Village of Liberta, Antigua* (Antigua: Hewlester Samuel, 2007), 89–90.

48. Caldecott, 73.

49. Augier and Gordon, 154–55.

50. Caldecott, 74.

51. Caldecott, 74.

52. Augier and Gordon, 147.

53. Milton C. Sernett, *African American Religious History: A Documentary Witness*, 2d ed. (Durham, NC: Duke University Press, 1999), 44–46.

54. Sernett, 47.

55. Hunte, 102–3.

56. Augier and Gordon, 154, 157; Hamilton and Hamilton, 257.

57. Smith, 174.

58. Augier and Gordon, 151–52.

59. Augier and Gordon, 147–48; Smith, 175; Caldecott, 76.

60. Hunte, 104–105.

61. Augier and Gordon, 149; Smith, 175.

62. Hunte, 103.

63. Caldecott, 81, 88.

64. Caldecott, 86; Augier and Gordon, 161.

65. Caldecott, 83.

66. Caldecott, 80, 82–85.

67. Caldecott, 92; Hunte 106.

68. Hunte, 107–8.

69. Jean Besson, "Religion and Resistance in Jamaican Peasant Life: The Baptist Church Revival," in *Rastafari and Other African-Caribbean Worldviews*, ed. Barry Chevannes (New Brunswick, NJ: Rutgers University Press, 998), 48–51; Augier and Gordon, 213–14.

70. Hunte, 110–11.

71. Hunte, 112–13; Augier and Gordon, 135.

72. Hunte, 114.

73. Hunte, 115–16; Caldecott, 136.

74. Augier and Gordon, 232–33.

75. Caldecott, 139–40.

76. Caldecott, 146–47.

77. Caldecott, 144–45.

78. Hunte, 117–18.

79. Hunte, 118–20.

80. Hunte, 121.

CHAPTER 5

1. Mercedes Cros Sandoval, *Worldview, the Orichas, and Santería: Africa to Cuba and Beyond* (Gainesville: University of Florida Press, 2006), 48.

2. Joseph Murphy, *Santeria: African Spirits in America* (Boston: Beacon Press, 1993), 7.

3. George Brandon, *Santeria from Africa to the New World: The Dead Sell Memories* (Bloomington: Indiana University Press, 1993), 141.

4. Murphy, 67–68.

5. Michael Atwood Mason, "'I Bow My Head to the Ground': The Creation of Bodily Experience in Cuban American Santeria," *Journal of American Folklore* 107 (Winter 1994): 30.

6. James R. Curtis, "Santeria: Persistence and Change in an Afrocuban Cult Religion," in *Objects of Special Devotion: Fetishism in Popular Culture*, ed. Ray B. Brown (Bowling Green: Bowling Green University Popular Press, 1982), 347.

7. Román Orozco and Natalia Bolivár Aróstegui, *Cuba Santa: Comunistas, Santeros, y Cristianos en la isla de Fidel Castro* (Madrid: El País Aguilar, 1998), 97.

8. Rafael Ocasio, "Babalú Ayé Santeria and Contemporary Cuban Literature," *Journal of Caribbean Studies* 9, no. 1-2 (Spring 1993): 30.

9. Curtis, 339–40; Lydia Cabrera, "Religious Syncretism in Cuba," *Journal of Caribbean Studies* 10, no. 1–2 (Winter 1994-Spring 1995): 85.

10. Miguel W. Ramos, "La Division de la Habana: Territorial Conflict and Cultural Hegemony in the Followers of Oyo Lukumí Religion, 1850s–1920s," *Cuban Studies 34 (2003): 51–52.*

11. See Fernando Ortiz, *Los Negros brujos* (Miami, FL: Ediciones Universal, 1973 [first published in 1906]).

12. Michael L. Conniff and Thomas J. Davis, *Africans in the Americas* (New York: St. Martin's Press, 1994), 275–76.

13. David H. Brown, *Santería Enthroned: Art, Ritual, and Innovation in an Afro-Cuban Religion* (Chicago: University of Chicago Press, 2003), 67.

14. Brown, 81–82.

15. Murphy, 35.

16. Mary C. Curry, *Making the Gods in New York: The Yoruba Religion in the African American Community* (New York: Routledge, 1997), 5; Marta Moreno Vega, "The Yoruba Tradition Comes to New York City," *African American Review* 29 (Summer 1995): 202.

17. Vega, 201–3.

18. Curtis, 336.

19. Curtis, 337.

20. Vega, 203; Curry, 7–8.

21. Curry, 68; Vega, 204; Brandon, 114–16.

22. Vega, 205; Brandon, 117–19.

23. Curry, 1–10.

24. "Ninguno conserva la pureza de su origen geográfico, ninguna ha sido resistente al efecto de factores externos. Por el contrario, y debido a la poca consistencia filosófica de estos cultos, a su carácter animista y mágico, y no a sus fundamentos mitológicos—como asi ocurre con los lucumí –, las religions congas han sido más permeables que ninguna otra." Miguel Barnet, *Afro-Cuban Religions* (Princeton: Markus Wiener, 1995), 81–82.

25. Natalia Bolívar Aróstegui and Carmen Gonzalez de Villegas, *Ta Makuende Yaya y Las Reglas de Palo Monte: Mayombe, Brillumba, Kimbisa, Shamalongo* (Havana, Cuba: Ediciones Unión, 1998), 20.

26. Jesús Fuentes Guerra and Grisel Gómez Gómez, *Cultos Afrocubanos: Un estudio etnolingüístico* (Havana, Cuba: Editorial de Ciencias Sociales, 1996), 23–26.

27. Maureen Warner-Lewis, *Central Africa in the Caribbean: Transcending Times, Transforming Cultures* (Kingston, Jamaica: University of the West Indies Press, 2004),145–46.

28. Jesús Fuentes Guerra and Armin Schwegler, *Lengua y ritos del Palo Monte Mayombe: Dioses cubanos y sus fuentes Africanas* (Madrid, Spain: Iberoamericano, 2005), 28–30.

29. Barnet, 79.

30. David H. Brown, "Annotated Glossary for Fernando Ortiz's 'The Afro-Cuban Festival: Day of the Kings,'" in *Cuban Festivals: An Illustrated Anthology*, ed. Judith Bettelheim (New York: Garland, 1993), 85.

31. Barnet, 118.

32. Margarite Fernández Olmos and Lizabeth Paravisini-Gebert, *Creole Religions of the Caribbean: An Introduction from Vodou and Santería to Obeah and Espiritismo* (New York: New York University Press, 2003), 80.

33. Fernández Olmos and Paravisini-Gebert, 84.

34. Robert Farris Thompson, *Flash of the Spirit: African and Afro-American Art and Philosophy* (New York: Random House, 1983), 110.

35. Farris Thompson, 116.

36. Brown, "Annotated Glossary for Fernando Ortiz's 'The Afro-Cuban Festival: Day of the Kings,'" 52–53.

37. George Reid Andrews, *Afro-Latin America: 1800–2000* (New York: Oxford University Press, 2004), 72.

38. Reid Andrews, 81.

39. Lydia Cabrera, "Ritual y simbolos de la iniciación en la sociedad secreta Abakua," *Journal de la Société des Américanistes* 58 (1969): 140.

40. Ekue rejects anything having to do with the feminine. It is said that Sikán, considered the spiritual mother of the Abakuá, betrayed her people by revealing a deep religious secret and because of this was condemned to death. All women are punished because of Sikán's betrayal. Another explanation that is given for women's exclusion is that, at one time, the true owner of all power was a woman and so, to ensure that men remain in control of sacred power ,men excluded women from the society.

41. "The voice of Ekue (uyo) is sounded during *plantes* (initiatory, funerary, or general ceremonies which include drumming, singing, and processions) and marvelous masked figures called *íreme*—pejoratively referred to as '*diablitos*'—emerge from the sacred temple space (*famba*) too dance and perform ritual duties." Brown, "Annotated Glossary for Fernando Ortiz's 'The Afro-Cuban Festival: Day of the Kings,'" 52–53.

42. Fernández Olmos and Paravisini-Gebert, 93.

43. In most of the literature, *lwa* is used as both singular and plural. This seems to reflect the common usage in Haiti. Instead of anglicizing it in the plural by addition an "s" (as some have done), we maintain the convention of using the same form for both singular and plural.

44. Donald J. Cosentino "Introduction: Imagine Heaven," in *Sacred Arts of Haitian Vodou*, ed. Donald J. Cosentino (Los Angeles: UCLA Museum of Social History, 1995), 32.

45. Selden Rodman and Carole Cleaver, *Spirit of the Night: The Vaudun Gods of Haiti* (Dallas: Springs, 1992), 53–55; Gerdès Fleurant, "Introduction," in *Vodou: Visions and Voices of Haiti*, by Phyllis Galembo (Berkeley, CA: Ten Speed Press, 1998), xix,

46. Fleurant, xviii.

47. Cosentino, 45; Fleurant, xxv ; Rachel Beauvoir-Dominique, "Underground Realms of Being: Vodou Magic," in *Sacred Arts of Haitian Vodou*, ed. Donald J. Cosentino (Los Angeles: UCLA Fowler Museum of Social History, 1995), 162–63.

48. Cosentino, 28.

49.Sidney Mintz and Michel-Rolph Trouillot, "The Social History of Haitian Vodou," in *Sacred Arts of Haitian Vodou*, ed. Donald J. Cosentino (Los Angeles: UCLA Museum of Social History, 1995)135.

50. Laënnec Hurbon, *Vodoo, Search for the Spirit* (New York: Harry N. Abrams, 1995), 34.

51. Mintz and Trouillot, 135.

52. Cosentino, 38.

53. Hurbon, 41–42.

54. Beauvoir-Dominique, 162; Hurbon, 42–43.

55. Leslie G. Desmangles, *The Faces of the Gods: Vodou and Roman Catholicism in Haiti* (Chapel Hill: University of North Carolina Press, 1992), 45.

56. Hurbon, 51.

57. Desmangles, 43–44.

58. Mintz and Trouillot, 142; Rodman and Cleaver, 100.

59. Mintz and Trouillot, 144–46; Rodman and Cleaver, 102–2.

60. Mintz and Trouillot, 146–47; Rodman and Cleaver, 104.

61. "The influence of these ignorant spirits can also produce physical disturbances, ranging from headaches to major illness. Every person is born with a guiding spirit who protects him or her from the influence of ignorant spirits." Mario A. Núñez Molina, "Community Healing Among Puerto Ricans: Espiritismo," in *Healing Cultures: Art and Religion as Curative Practices in the Caribbean and Its Diaspora*," ed. Margarite Fernández Olmos and Lizbeth Paravisini-Gebert (New York: Palgrave, 2001), 119.

62. David J. Hess, *Spirit and Scientists: Ideology, Spiritism, and Brazilian Culture* (University Park: Pennsylvania State University Press, 2001), 2–3.

63. Orozco and Bolívar Aróstegui, 287.

64. Andrés I. Pérez y Mena, "Understanding Religiosity in Cuba," *Journal of Hispanic/ Latino Theology* 7, no. 3 (2000): 24.

65. Reinaldo L. Román, "Governing Mad-Gods: Spiritism and the Struggle for Progress in Republican Cuba," *Journal of Religion in Africa* 37 (2007): 11.

66. Christine Ayorinde, *Afro-Cuban Religiosity, Revolution, and National Identity* (Gainesville: University Press of Florida, 2005), 20–21.

67. Núñez Molina, 117–18.

CHAPTER 6

1. Margarite Fernandez Olmos and Lizabeth Paravisini-Gebert, *Creole Religions of the Caribbean: An Introduction from Vodou and Santeria to Obeah and Espiritismo* (New York: New York University Press, 2003), 131; Dianne M. Stewart, *Three Eyes for the Journey: African Dimensions of the Jamaican Religious Experience* (New York: Oxford University

Press, 2005), 49; Diane J. Austin-Broos, *Jamaica Genesis: Religion and Politics of the Moral Orders* (Chicago: University of Chicago Press, 1997), 43. We are little surprised that the Yoruba word *obi*, which refers to a type of divination and the pieces of coconut or kola nuts used in this system of divination, has not been suggested as a possible root for *obeah*. Interestingly, the Orisha (Shango) tradition of Trinidad and Tobago uses obi seeds in its divination practices.

2. Stewart, 49–51.

3. Stewart, 44–49.

4. Stewart, 46.

5. Monica Schuler, "Myalism and the African Religious Tradition in Jamaica," in *African and the Caribbean: The Legacies of a Link*, ed. Margaret E. Crahan and Franklin W. Knight (Baltimore: Johns Hopkins University Press, 1979), 71.

6. Schuler, 73–74.

7. Fernandez Olmos and Paravisini-Gebert, 136.

8. Stewart, 44, 46; See also James M. Phillippo, *Jamaica: Its Past and Present State* (Freeport, NY: Books for Library Press, 1971 [1843]), 248.

9. Stewart, 45–47.

10. Schuler, 66.

11. Phillippo, 280.

12. Monica Schuler, *"Alas, Alas, Kongo": A Social History of Indentured African Migration to Jamaica, 1841–1865* (Baltimore: Johns Hopkins University Press, 1980), 40.

13. Schuler, *"Alas, Alas, Congo,"* 40–41.

14. Schuler, *"Alas, Alas, Congo,"* 41, 43.

15. Schuler, *"Alas, Alas, Congo,"* 41–43.

16. Stewart, 149; Schuler, *"Alas, Alas, Congo,"* 4, 7.

17. Schuler, *"Alas, Alas, Congo,"* 1; Cheryl Ryman, "Kumina: Stability and Change," *ACIJ Research Review* 1 (1984): 86.

18. Ryman, 86.

19. Ryman, 88. The Maroons in St. Thomas lived in proximity to the Central Africans and their descendants who practice Kumina. Cultural exchanges and influences have flowed both ways between these two groups.

20. Ryman, 90.

21. Stewart, 150–51; Ryman, 87.

22. Schuler, *"Alas, Alas, Congo,"* 77.

23. Stewart, 51–53. Also see Kenneth Bilby, "Gumbay, Myal, and the Great House: New Evidence of the Religious Background of Jonkonnu in Jamaica," *ACIJ Research Review: 25th Anniversary Edition* (1999/4): 47–70; and Kenneth Bilby, "The Koromanti Dance of the Windward Maroons of Jamaica," *Nieuwe West Indische Gids* 55, no. 1-2 (August 1981): 52–101.

24. Mervyn Alleyne, *Roots of Jamaican Culture* (London: Pluto Press, 1988), 100; Austin-Broos, 58.

25. Alleyne, 100.

26. Quoted by Austin-Broos, 57; Also see W. J. Gardner, *A History of Jamaica from its Discovery by Christopher Columbus to the Year 1872* (London: Frank Cass, 1873), 465.

27. Barry Chevannes, "Introducing the Native Religions of Jamaica," in *Rastafari and other African-Caribbean Worldviews*, ed. Barry Chevannes (New Brunswick, NJ: Rutgers University Press, 1998), 8.

28. Alleyne, 101; George Eaton Simpson, *Black Religions in the New World* (New York: Columbia University Press, 1978), 111.

29. Simpson, 116.

30. Chevannes, 6.

31. Austin-Broos, 83–86; Martha Warren Beckwith, *Black Roadways: A Study of Jamaican Folk Life* (New York: Negro Universities Press, 1969 [1929]), 169–68.

32. Chevannes, 9; Beckwith, 1968–71.

33. Austin-Broos, 98; Mary R. Olson, "The Early Years," http://churchofgodinjamaica.org/index.php?pageId=2.2, March 29, 2009.

34. http://vikratistos.com/jh.html, March 29, 2009.

35. Austin-Broos, 102.

36. Austin-Broos, 101, 110.

37. This information came from research done over the past three years by Ennis Edmonds, one of the authors of the present volume. The research includes interviews and participant observations, mostly in two former Revival Zion churches in a rural community in St. Elizabeth, Jamaica.

38. Chevannes, 9.

39. Bridget Brereton, *A History of Modern Trinidad 1783–1962* (Jordan Hill, Oxford: Heinemann, 1981), 12–13; James T. Houk, *Spirit, Blood and Drums: The Orisha Religion in Trinidad* (Philadelphia: Temple University Press, 1995), 50.

40. Houk, 51; Brereton, 16.

41. Brereton, 33.

42. "Orisha" with an upper-case "O" denotes an Afro-Trinidadian religious tradition, while "*orisha*" with a lower-case "o" refers to the spirits or deities that are venerated in this tradition.

43. Stephen D. Glazier, "African Cults and Christian Churches in Trinidad: The Spiritual Baptists Case," *Journal of Religious Thought* 39, no. 2 (Fall-Winter 1982–1983): 17–18.

44. Houk, 8.

45. Rudolph Eastman and Maureen Warner-Lewis, "Forms of African Spirituality in Trinidad and Tobago," in *African Spirituality: Forms, Meanings, and Expressions*, ed. Jacob K. Olupona (New York: Crossroad, 2000), 409–10.

46. Houk, 36–37, 90–96; Frances Henry, *Reclaiming African Religions in Trinidad: The Socio-Political Legitimation of the Orisha and Spiritual Baptist Faiths* (Kingston, Jamaica: University of the West Indies Press, 2003), 7.

47. Houk, 86–90.

48. Henry, 34.

49. Henry, 49–50; These developments are more fully discussed by Henry in chapters 3 and 4.

50. Houk, 149–54; Warner-Lewis, 407; Henry, 2–3.

51. Henry, 9–10.

52. Henry, 80.

53. Henry, 81–83.

54. Henry, 83–86.

55. Henry, 2–6; Houk, 158–66.

56. Houk, 12–14.

57. Stephen D. Glazier, *Marchin' the Pilgrims Home: A Study of the Spiritual Baptists of Trinidad* (Salem, WI: Sheffield, 1983), 3; Houk, 71.

58. Houk, 71.

59. Houk, 72; Glazier, *Marchin' the Pilgrim Home*, 34–35; Eudora Thomas, *A History of the Shouter Baptists in Trinidad and Tobago* (Tacarigua, Trinidad: Calaloux, 1987), 30–31.

60. Houk, 74–75; Glazier, *Marchin' the Pilgrim Home*, 37–39; Lorna McDaniel, "Memory Spirituals of the Ex-Slave American Soldiers in Trinidad's 'Company Villages,'" *Black Music Research Journal* 14, no. 2 (Autumn 1994): 134.

61. Houk, 75.

62. McDaniel, 134.

63. Henry, 46.

64. Thomas, 23.

65. Melville J. Herskovits and Frances S. Herskovits, *Trinidad Village* (New York: Knopf, 1947), 218.

66. Thomas, 24–25.

67. Earl Lovelace, *The Wine of Astonishment* (London: Heinemann, 1982, and New York: Vintage, 1984).

68. Henry, 34–35.

69. Henry, 35–36; Thomas, 25–28.

70. Henry, 73.

71. Henry, 52–60.

72. Herskovits and Herskovits, 193–197; Glazier, *Marchin' the Pilgrims Home*, 52–53; Houk, 77–78.

73. Thomas, 47–48.

74. Houk, 36, 84.

75. George Eaton Simpson, "Baptismal, 'Mourning,' and 'Building' Ceremonies of the Shouters in Trinidad," *Journal of American Folklore* 79, no. 314 (October-December 1966): 538–42; Herskovits and Herskovits, 201–4.

76. Warner-Lewis, 411.

77. Glazier, *Marchin' the Pilgrims Home*, 59.

78. Herkovits and Herskovits, 190–92; Glazier, *Marchin' the Pilgrims Home*, 44.

79. Glazier, *Marchin' the Pilgrims Home*, 43.

80. Stephen D. Glazier. "Embedded Truths: Creativity and Context in Spiritual Baptist Music," *Latin American Music Review/Revista de Musica Latinamericana* 18, no. 1 (Spring-Summer 1997): 47.

81. Glazier, "Embedded Truths," 53–54.

82. Thomas, 37–38.

CHAPTER 7

1. Olga Portuondo Zúñiga, *La Virgen de la Caridad del Cobre: Simbolo de la Cubanía*, rev. ed. (Madrid, Spain: Agualarga Editores, 2002), 10.

2. For an excellent overview of the Cobre slave community see María Elena Díaz, *The Virgin, the King, and the Royal Slaves of El Cobre: Negotiating Freedom in Colonial Cuba, 1670–1780* (Stanford: Stanford University Press, 2000).

3. Moreno's role in the slave community is not limited to this religious apparition. At the age of seventy-seven, he was given the position of captain of the local militia, a role that entailed military and religious duties. Moreno represented the slaves of Cobre when

the Crown attempted to transfer them to Havana. He was an advocate for the slaves and a mediator between them and Spanish authorities. Moreno played an active political role among the Cobre slaves and was for some time seen as their leader and representative to the Spanish. It is interesting to note that the recording of his testimony occurred while he occupied a prominent position. Juan Moreno is not the only Afro-Cuban to whom La Caridad appeared. Onofre de Fonseca, who was chaplain of the shrine of El Cobre from 1683 to 1710, introduces the narrative of the girl Apolonia to his written account of Cachita's presence among the Cobre community. Daughter of one of the miners, Apolonia was on her way to visit her mother when La Caridad appeared before her, telling her where she wanted her temple to be built. This second "apparition" story is not as well known within Cuba, and its later date, coupled with a lack of firsthand testimony, makes its historical validity questionable.

4. Joseph M. Murphy, "YéYé Cachita: Ochún in a Cuban Mirror," in *Òsun across the Waters: A Yoruba Goddess in Africa and the Americas*, ed. Joseph M. Murphy and Mei-Mei Sanford (Bloomington: Indiana University Press, 2001), 88. For a study of the iconographic lightening of La Caridad see Portuondo Zúñiga.

5. Murphy, 87. *Òsun across the Waters* provides an excellent introduction to the *orisha* Oshun in the African and American contexts. There are various ways to spell Oshun in English; we have chosen Oshun.

6. Terry Rey, *Our Lady of Class Struggle: The Cult of the Virgin Mary in Haiti* (Trenton, NJ: Africa World Press, 1999), 171.

7. Christian Lalive d'Epinday, "Dependance Sociale et Religion: Pasteurs et Protestantismes Latino-Americains," *Archives de Sciences Sociales de Religions* 26 (July-September 1981): 86–87.

8. Samiri Hernández-Hiraldo, *Black Puerto Rican Identity and Religious Experience* (Gainesville: University of Florida Press, 2006), 20.

9. Hernández-Hiraldo, 69–70.

10. For a detailed account of the first Protestants on the island see Luis Martínez-Fernández, *Protestantism and Political Conflict in the Nineteenth-Century Hispanic Caribbean* (New Brunswick, NJ: Rutgers University Press, 2002), ch. 5.

11. Anna Adams, "*Brincando el Charco* / Jumping the Puddle: A Case Study of Pentecostalism's Journey from Puerto Rico to New York to Allentown, Pennsylvania," in *Power, Politics, and Pentecostals in Latin America*, ed. Edward L. Cleary and Hannah W. Stewart-Gambino (Boulder, CO: Westview Press, 1997), 165.

12. Dale Bisnauth, *History of Religions in the Caribbean* (Kingston, Jamaica: Kingston, 1989), 216.

13. Samuel Silva Gotay, "Historia social de las iglesias en Puerto Rico," in *Historia general de la Iglesia en America Latina*, vol. 4: *Caribe* (Salamanca, Spain: Ediciones Sígueme, 1995), 271.

14. Ana María Díaz-Stevens, *Oxcart Catholicism on Fifth Avenue: The Impact of the Puerto Rican Migration on the Archdiocese of New York* (Notre Dame, IN: University of Notre Dame Press, 1993), 53.

15. Emilio Betances, *The Catholic Church and Power Politics in Latin America: The Dominican Case in Comparative Perspective* (Lanham, MD: Rowman and Littlefield, 2007), 212–13.

16. Bisnauth, *History of Religions in the Caribbean*, 217.

17. For a detailed account see William Wipfler, "The Catholic Church and the State in the Dominican Republic, 1930–1960," in *Christianity in the Caribbean: Essays in Church History*, ed. Armando Lampe (Kingston, Jamaica: University of the West Indies Press, 2001), 191–228.

18. Justo González, *The Development of Christianity in the Latin Caribbean* (Ann Arbor, MI: University Microfilms International, 1969), 68.

19. González, 70.

20. Adolfo Ham Reyes, "An Ecumenical Perspective on the Cuban protestant Missionary Heritage," *International Review of Mission* 74, no. 295 (July 1985): 329.

21. Ham Reyes, 329.

22. Ham Reyes, 333.

23. Martínez-Fernández, 145.

24. Theron Corse, *Protestants, Revolution, and the Cuba-U.S. Bond* (Gainesville: University of Florida Press, 2007), 2.

25. Louis A. Pérez, Jr., *On Becoming Cuban: Identity, Nationality, and Culture* (Chapel Hill: University of North Carolina Press, 1999), 255.

26. Corse, 29.

27. Corse, 62–65.

28. Edward L. Cleary, "Introduction: Pentecostals, Prominence, and Politics," in *Power, Politics, and Pentecostals in Latin America*, ed. Edward L. Cleary and Hannah W. Stewart-Gambino (Boulder, CO: Westview Press, 1997), 7–8.

29. David Stoll, *Is Latin America Turning Protestant? The Politics of Evangelical Growth* (Berkeley: University of California Press, 1990), 8.

30. Laënnec Hurbon, "Pentecostalism and Transnationalisation in the Caribbean," in *Between Babel and Pentecost: Transnational Pentecostalism in Africa and Latin America*, ed. André Corten and Ruth Marshall-Fratani (Bloomington: Indiana University Press, 2001), 125.

31. Sidney W. Mintz, *Worker in the Cane: A Puerto Rican Life History* (New Haven: Yale University Press, 1960).

32. Cleary, 5.

33. David Martin, *Tongues of Fire: The Explosion of Protestantism in Latin America* (Cambridge, MA: Blackwell, 1990), 282.

34. Anthony L. LaRuffa, "Pentecostalism in Puerto Rican Society," in *Perspective on Pentecostalism: Case Studies from the Caribbean and Latin America*, ed. Stephen D. Glazier (Washington, DC: University Press of America, 1980), 50.

35. Adams, 166.

36. Allan Anderson, *An Introduction to Pentecostalism: Global Charismatic Christianity* (New York: Cambridge University Press, 2004), 79.

37. Laënnec Hurbon, "Religious Movements in the Caribbean," in *New Religious Movements and Rapid Social Change*, ed. James A. Beckford (Beverly Hills, CA: Sage, 1986), 146–76.

38. Betances, 218–19.

39. D. D. Bundy, "Dominican Republic," in *The New International Dictionary of Pentecostal and Charismatic Movements*, ed. Stanley Burgess and Eduard M. Van der Maas, rev. and expanded ed. (Grand Rapids, MI: Zondervan, 2002), 82.

40. Anderson, 80.

41. Corse, 139–40.

42. Ana Celia Perera Pintado, "Religion and Cuban Identity in a Transnational Context," *Latin American Perspectives* 32 (2005): 159.

43. Hurbon, "Pentecostalism and Transnationalisation in the Caribbean," 126.

44. Anderson, 80.

45. The following historical information is found in D. D. Bundy, "Haiti," in *The New International Dictionary of Pentecostal and Charismatic Movements*, ed. Stanley Burgess and Eduard M. Van der Maas, rev. and expanded ed. (Grand Rapids, MI: Zondervan, 2002), 116–17.

46. Diane J. Austin-Broos, *Jamaica Genesis: Religion and the Politics of Moral Order* (Chicago: University of Chicago Press, 1997), 102.

47. Austin-Broos, 103–9.

48. William Wedenoja, "Modernization and the Pentecostal Movement in Jamaica," in *Perspective on Pentecostalism: Case Studies from the Caribbean and Latin America*, ed. Stephen D. Glazier (Washington, DC: University Press of America, 1980), 29–30.

49. Austin-Broos, 245.

50. Ashley Smith, "Mainline Churches in the Caribbean: Their Relationship to the Cultural and Political Process," *Caribbean Journal of Religious Studies* 9 (1998): 32.

CHAPTER 8

1. Leslie G. Desmangles, Stephen D. Glazier, and Joseph M. Murphy, "Religion in the Caribbean," in *Understanding the Contemporary Caribbean*, ed. Richard S. Hillman and Thomas J. D'Agostino (Boulder, CO: Lynne Rienner, 2003), 271–72.

2. Frank J. Korom, *Hosay Trinidad: Muharram Performances in an Indo-Caribbean Diaspora* (Philadelphia: University of Pennsylvania Press, 2003), 99.

3. Malcom Cross, "East Indian-Creole Relations in Trinidad and Guiana in the Late Nineteenth Century," in *Across the Dark Waters: Ethnicity and Indian Identity in the Caribbean*, ed. David Dabydeen and Brinsley Samaroo (Basingstoke: Macmillan Caribbean, 1996), 17.

4. Satnarayan Maharaj, "Sanatan Dharma Maha Sabha in Context: A Note," in *The Construction of an Indo-Caribbean Diaspora*, ed. Brinsley Samaroo and Ann Marie Bissessar (St. Augustine, Trinidad and Tobago: University of the West Indies, 2004), 115.

5. Brinsley Samaroo, "Reconstructing the Identity: Hindu Organization in Trinidad during Their First Century," in *The Construction of an Indo-Caribbean Diaspora*, ed. Brinsley Samaroo and Ann Marie Bissessar (St. Augustine: Trinidad and Tobago: University of the West Indies, 2004), 48.

6. Samaroo,119–20. 7. Bridget Brereton, *Race Relations in Colonial Trinidad (1870–1900)* (New York: Cambridge University Press, 1979), 183.

8. Desmangles, Glazier, and Murphy, 272.

9. Steven Vertovec, "'Official' and 'Popular" Hinduism in the Caribbean: Historical and Contemporary Trends in Surinam, Trinidad, and Guyana," in *Across the Dark Waters: Ethnicity and Indian Identity in the Caribbean*, ed. David Dabydeen and Brinsley Samaroo (Basingstoke: Macmillan Caribbean, 1996), 117.

10. Noorkumar Mahabir and Ashram Maharaj, "Hindu Elements in the Shango/Orisha Cult of Trinidad," in *Across the Dark Waters: Ethnicity and Indian Identity in the Caribbean*, ed. David Dabydeen and Brinsley Samaroo (Basingstoke: Macmillan Caribbean, 1996), 90–107.

11. Vertovec, 120.

12. Vertovec, 121.

13. Paul E. Lovejoy, "The Yoruba Factor in the Trans-Atlantic Slave Trade," in *The Yoruba Diaspora in the Atlantic World*, ed. Toyin Falola and Matt D. Childs (Bloomington: Indiana University Press, 2004), 40–55; Silviane Diouf, *Servants of Allah: African Muslims Enslaved in the Americas* (New York: New York University Press, 1998).

14. Gwendolyn Minlo Hall, *Slavery and African Ethnicities in the Americas: Restoring the Links* (Chapel Hill: University of North Carolina Press, 2005), 1.

15. Hall, 4.

16. Hall, 7.

17. Leslie B. Rout, Jr., *The African Experience in Spanish America* (Princeton: Marcus Wiener, 2003; 1976), 11.

18. Michael A. Gomez, *Black Crescent: The Experience and Legacy of African Muslims in the Americas* (New York: Cambridge University Press, 2005), 14.

19. Sultana Afroz, "As-Salaamu-Alaikum: The Invincibility of Islam in Jamaican Heritage," *Wadabagei* 10, no. 2 (Spring-Summer, 2007): 5–39.

20. Benson LeGrace, "'Quismat' of the Names of Allah in Haitian Vodou," *Journal of Haitian Studies* 8, no. 2 (Fall 2002): 160–64.

21. Korom, 101.

22. Korom,116.

23. Gomez, 71.

24. Marcus Mosiah Garvey, *Philosophy and Opinions of Marcus Garvey: Africa for the Africans*, 2nd ed., ed. Amy Jacques Garvey (New York: Routledge, 1967), 57.

25. Barry Chevannes, *Rastafari: Roots and Ideology* (Syracuse, NY: Syracuse University Press, 1994), 145–46.

26. See Chevannes, 146–52, for a discussion of this social ferment and Rastafarian involvement.

27. Chevannes argues that Rastafari has never fully escaped the pervasive folk religious ethos in Jamaica. Elements of Revivalism still persist in its ideology and ritual practices. See Chevannes, 145, 170, and Barry Chevannes, "A New Approach to Rastafari," in *Rastafari and other African-Caribbean Worldviews*, ed. Barry Chevannes (New Brunswick, NJ: Rutgers University Press, 1998), 20–42.

28. Theodore Malloch, "Rastafarianism: A Radical Caribbean Movement/Religion," *Center Journal* 4, no, 4 (Fall 1985): 74.

29. Barry Chevannes, "The Origin of Dreadlocks," in *Rastafari and other African-Caribbean Worldviews*, ed. Barry Chevannes (New Brunswick, NJ: Rutgers University Press, 1998), 88–93.

30. John P. Homiak, "Dub History: Sounding of Rastafari Livity and Language," in *Rastafari and Other African-Caribbean Worldviews*, ed. Barry Chevannes (New Brunswick, NJ: Rutgers University Press, 1998), 151–54.

31. Velma Pollard, *Dread Talk: The Language of Rastafari* (Kingston, Jamaica: Canoe Press, 1994), 3–10.

32. Bongo Jerry, "Mabrak," in *The Penguin Book of Caribbean Verse in English*, ed. Paula Burnett (London: Penguin Books, 1986), 69–71.

33. Chevannes, *Rastafari: Roots and Ideology*, 173–74.

34. Nathaniel Samuel Murrell, "Introduction: The Rastafari Phenomenon," in *Chanting Down Babylon: The Rastafarian Reader*, ed. Nathaniel Samuel Murrell, William David Spencer, and Adrian Anthony McFarlane (Philadelphia: Temple University Press, 1998), 7–8.

35. M. G. Smith, Roy Augier, and Rex Nettleford, *The Rastafari Movement in Kingston, Jamaica* (Mona, Jamaica: Institute of Social and Economic Research, 1960).

36. See Smith et al., 33–38, for the recommendations made to the government of Jamaica.

37. Douglas R. A. Mack. *From Babylon to Rastafari: Origin and History of the Rastafarian Movement* (Chicago: Research Associates School Times Publications, 1999), 93–94.

38. Ibid., 114.

39. Ibid., 117–45.

40. Ennis Barrington Edmonds, *Rastafari: From Outcasts to Culture Bearers* (New York: Oxford University Press, 2003), 87.

41. Lloyd Bradley, *This Is Reggae Music: The Story of Jamaica's Music* (New York: Grove Press, 2001), 61.

CHAPTER 9

1. This was the main argument of Michelle A. Gonzalez, *Afro-Cuban Theology: Race, Religion, Culture, and Identity* (Gainesville: University Press of Florida, 2007).

2. Christine Ayorinde, *Afro-Cuban Religiosity, Revolution, and National Identity* (Gainesville: University Press of Florida, 2005), 153–54.

3. Ayorinde, 166.

4. Ayorinde, 164.

5. Christine Ayorinde, "Writing Out Africa? Racial Politics in Cuban *regal de ocha*," in *The African Diaspora and the Study of Religion*, ed. Theodore Louis Trost (New York: Palgrave Macmillan, 2007), 158.

6. Laurent Dubois, "Filming the Lwa in Haiti," *Caribbean Studies* 36, no. 1 (January-June 2008): 215–19.

7. See its Web site at http://homepage.mac.com/intersocietal/interso/Vodoun/vodoun. html.

8. Phyllis Galembo, *Vodou Visions and Voices of Haiti* (Berkeley, CA: Ten Speed Press, 2005).

9. Laënnec Hurbon, "Globalization and the Evolution of Haitian Vodou," in *Orisa Devotion as World Religion*, ed. Jacob K. Olupona and Terry Rey (Madison: University of Wisconsin Press, 2008), 268.

10. Stephen D. Glazier, "Contested Rituals of the African Diaspora," in *New Trends and Developments in African Religions,* ed. Peter B. Clarke (Westport CT: Greenwood, 1998), 105–20.

11. In many ways these are simplistic caricatures of both theological schools. However, within black theology, race remains the primary analytic category, and, within Latin American liberation theology, class analysis predominates. However, both these theologi-

cal schools have expanded their analyses to offer a broader and more comprehensive understanding of humanity, oppression, and social justice. See *Liberation Theologies in the United States: An Introductory Reader*, ed. Stacey M. Floyd-Thomas and Anthony B. Pinn (New York: New York University Press, 2010).

12. Adolfo Ham, "Caribbean Theology: The Challenge of the Twenty-First Century," in *Caribbean Theology: Preparing for the Challenges Ahead*, ed. Howard Gregory (Kingston, Jamaica: Canoe Press, 1995), 4.

13. Delroy A. Reid-Salmon, "Sin of Black Theology: The Omission of the Caribbean Diasporan Experience from Black Theological Discourse," *Black Theology* 6, no.2 (2008): 154–73.

14. Dianne M. Stewart, "Womanist Theology in the Caribbean Context: Critiquing Culture, Rethinking Doctrine, and Expanding Boundaries," *Journal of Feminist Studies in Religion* 20, no. 1 (Spring 2004): 61.

15. Luis Rivera-Pagán, "Doing Pastoral Theology in a Post-Colonial Context: Some Observations from the Caribbean," *Journal of Pastoral Theology* 17, no. 2 (Fall 2007): 1–27.

16. The Web site is www.utcwi.edu.jm.

17. The Web site is www.se-pr.edu.

18. Kortright Davis, *Emancipation Still Comin': Explorations in Caribbean Emancipatory Theology* (Maryknoll, NY: Orbis Books, 1990), 47.

19. Robert Beckford, *Jesus Dub: Theology, Music, and Social Change* (New York: Routledge, 2006), 1.

20. Beckford, 19.

21. Ennis B. Edmonds, *Rastafari: From Outcasts to Culture Bearers* (New York: Oxford University Press, 2003).

22. Timothy Rommen, "Nationalism and the Soul: Gospelypso as Independence," *Black Music Research Journal* 22, no.1 (2002): 48.

23. Timothy Rommen, *"Mek Some Noise": Gospel Music and the Ethics of Style in Trinidad* (Berkeley: University of California Press, 2007), 23.

24. Gerdès Fleurant, "The Music of Haitian Vodou," in *African Spiritualities: Forms, Meanings, and Expressions*, ed. Jacob K. Olupona (New York: Crossroad, 2000), 443.

25. Hurbon, 270.

26. David H. Brown, "Toward an Ethnoaesthetics of Santería Ritual Arts: The Practice of Altar-Making and Gift Exchange," in *Santería Aesthetics in Contemporary Latin American Art*, ed. Arturo Lindsay (Washington, DC: Smithsonian Institution Press, 1996), 78.

27. Julia P. Herzberg, "Rereading Lam," in *Santería Aesthetics in Contemporary Latin American Art*, ed. Arturo Lindsay (Washington, DC: Smithsonian Institution Press, 1996), 149–69.

28. Alejandro de la Fuente, "The New Afro-Cuban Cultural Movement and the Debate on Race in Contemporary Cuba," *Journal of Latin American Studies* 40 (2008): 700.

29. Ayorinde, Afro-*Cuban Religiosity, Revolution, and National Identity*, 155.

30. Ivan Miller, "A Secret Society Goes Public: The Relationship between Abakuá and Cuban Culture," *African Studies Review* 43, no. 1 (April 2000): 161–88.

31. Rafael Ocasio, "Dancing to the Beat of Babalu Aye: Santería and Popular Cuban Culture," in *Fragments of the Bone: Neo-African Religions in the New World*, ed. Patrick Bellegrade-Smith (Champaign: University of Illinois Press, 2005), 90–102.

32. Much of the information on new religious movements is found in Laënnec Hurbon, "Religious Movements in the Caribbean," in *New Religious Movements and Rapid Social Change*, ed. James A. Beckford (Beverly Hills, CA: Sage, 1986), 146–76.

33. See Roland Littlewood, "From Mimesis to Appropriation in Shouter Baptism and Shango: The Earth People of Trinidad," in *New Trends and Developments in African Religions*, ed. Peter B. Clarke (Westport, CT: Greenwood, 1998), 121–39.

34. Loretta Collins, "Daugters of Jah: The Impact of Rastafarian Womanhood in the Caribbean, the United States, Britian, and Canada," in *Religion, Culture, and Tradition in the Caribbean*, ed. Henchand Gossai and Nathaniel Samuel Murrell (New York: St. Martin's Press, 2000), 227–56.

35. Diane J. Austin-Broos, *Jamaica Genesis: Religion and the Politics of Moral Orders* (Chicago: University of Chicago Press, 1997), 127.

36. Mary Ann Clark, *Where Men Are Wives and Mothers Rule: Santería Ritual Practices and Their Gender Implications* (Gainesville: University Press of Florida, 2005).

37. María Margarita Castro Flores, "Religions of African Origin in Cuba: A Gender Perspective," in *Nation Dance: Religion, Identity, and Cultural Difference in the Caribbean*, ed. Patrick Taylor (Bloomington: Indiana University Press, 2001), 58–59.

38. Marta Moreno Vega, "The Dynamic Influence of Cubans, Puerto Ricans, and African Americans on the Growth of Ocha in New York City," in *Orisa Devotion as World Religion*, ed. Jacob K. Olupona and Terry Rey (Madison: University of Wisconsin Press, 2008), 320–36.

CONCLUSION

1. Antonio Benítez-Rojo, *The Repeating Island: The Caribbean and the Postmodern Perspective*, 2nd ed. (Durham, NC: Duke University Press, 1996), 81.

Bibliography

Afroz, Sultana. "As-Salaamu-Alaikum: The Invincibility of Islam in Jamaican Heritage." *Wadabagei* 10, no. 2 (Spring-Summer 2007): 5–39.

Agosto Cintrón, Nélida. *Religion y Cambio Social en Puerto Rico (1898–1940)*. Río Piedras, Puerto Rico: Ediciones Huracán, 1996.

Alegría, Ricardo E. "The Ball Game Played by the Aborigines of the Antilles." *American Antiquity* 16, no. 4 (April, 1952): 348–52.

Alleyne, Mervyn. *Roots of Jamaican Culture*. London: Pluto Press, 1988.

Anderson, Allan. *An Introduction to Pentecostalism: Global Charismatic Christianity*. New York: Cambridge University Press, 2004.

Andrews, George Reid, *Afro-Latin America: 1800–2000*. New York: Oxford University Press: 2004.

Augier, Fitzroy Richard, and Shirley Courtnay Gordon, compilers. *Sources of West Indian History*. London: Longman, 1962.

Augier, F. R., D. G. Hall, and S. C. Gordon. *Making of the West Indies*. London: Longman, 1960.

Austin-Broos, Diane J. *Jamaica Genesis: Religion and the Politics of Moral Orders*.Chicago: University of Chicago Press, 1997.

Ayorinde, Christine. *Afro-Cuban Religiosity, Revolution, and National Identity*. Gainesville: University Press of Florida, 2005.

———. "Writing Out Africa? Racial Politics in Cuban *regla de ocha*." In *The African Diaspora and the Study of Religion*. Edited by Theodore Louis Trost, 151–66. New York: Palgrave Macmillan, 2007.

Barnes, Sandra, ed. *Africa's Ogun: Old World and New*. Bloomington: Indiana University Press, 1989.

Barnet, Miguel. *Afro-Cuban Religions*. Princeton: Markus Wiener, 1995.

Beckford, Robert. *Jesus Dub: Theology, Music, and Social Change*. New York: Routledge, 2006.

Beckwith, Martha Warren. *Black Roadways: A Study of Jamaican Folk Life*. New York: Negro Universities Press, 1969 [1929].

Bellegarde-Smith, Patrick. *Fragments of Bone: Neo-African Religions in a New World*. Champaign: University of Illinois Press, 2005.

Besson, Jean. "Religion and Resistance in Jamaican Peasant Life: The Baptist Church Revival." In *Rastafari and Other African-Caribbean Worldviews*. Edited by Barry Chevannes. New Brunswick, NJ: Rutgers University Press, 1998.

Betances, Emilio. *The Catholic Church and Power Politics in Latin America: The Dominican Case in Contemporary Perspective*. Lanham, MD: Rowman and Littlefield, 2007.

Bilby, Kenneth. "The Koromanti Dance of the Windward Maroons of Jamaica." *Nieuwe West Indische Gids* 55, no. 1-2 (August 1981): 52–101.

———. "Gumbay, Myal, and the Great House: New Evidence of the Religious Background of Jonkonnu in Jamaica." *ACIJ Research Review: 25th Anniversary Edition* (1994): 47–70.

Bisnauth, Dale. *History of Religions in the Caribbean.* Kingston, Jamaica: Kingston, 1989.

Bolívar Aróstegui, Natalia. *Sincretismo religioso: Santa Bárbara, Changó.* Havana, Cuba: Pablo de la Torriente, 1995.

Bolívar Aróstegui, Natalia, and Carmen Gonzalez de Villegas. *Ta Makuende Yaya y las reglas de Palo Monte: Mayombe, Brillumba, Kimbisa, Shamalongo.* Havana, Cuba: Ediciones Unión, 1998.

Bolland, O. Nigel. *Struggles for Freedom: Essays on Slavery, Colonialism and Culture in the Caribbean and Central America.* Belize City, Belize: Angelus Press, 1997.

Bongo Jerry. "Mabrak." In *The Penguin Book of Caribbean Verse in English.* Edited by Paula Burnett, 69–71. London: Penguin Books, 1986.

Bradley, Lloyd. *This Is Reggae Music: The Story of Jamaica's Music.* New York: Grove Press, 2001.

Braithwaite, Edward. *The Development of Creole Society in Jamaica, 1770–1820.* Oxford: Clarendon Press, 1971.

Brandon, George. *Santería from Africa to the New World: The Dead Sell Memories.* Bloomington: Indiana University Press, 1993.

Breathett, George, "Catholic Missionary Activity and the Negro Slave in Haiti," *Phylon* 23, no. 3 (3rd Qtr., 1962): 278–85.

Brereton, Bridget. *Race Relations in Colonial Trinidad (1870–1900).* New York: Cambridge University Press, 1979.

———. *A History of Modern Trinidad 1783–1962.*Oxford: Heinemann, 1981.

Brown, David H. "Annotated Glossary for Fernando Ortiz's 'The Afro-Cuban Festival Day of the Kings.'" In *Cuban Festivals: An Illustrated Anthology.* Edited by Judith Bettelheim, 49–98. New York: Garland, 1993.

———. *Santería Enthroned: Art, Ritual, and Innovation in an Afro-Cuban Religion.* Chicago: University of Chicago Press, 2003.

Burgess, Stanley, and Eduard M. Van der Maas, eds. *The New International Dictionary of Pentecostal and Charismatic Movements.* Revised and expanded. Grand Rapids, MI: Zondervan, 2002.

Cabrera, Lydia. *La Sociedad Secreta Abakuá.* Miami: Ediciones CR, 1970.

———. *Reglas de Congo: Palo Monte Mayombe.* Miami: Peninsular Printing, 1979.

———. "Religious Syncretism in Cuba." *Journal of Caribbean Studies* 10, no. 1–2 (Winter 1994-Spring 1995): 84–94.

Caldecott, Alfred. *The Church in the West Indies.* London: Frank Cass, 1970 [originally published 1898].

Campo Lacasa, Cristina. *Historia de la Iglesia en Puerto Rico (1511–1802).* Barcelona, Spain: Artes Gráficas Medinaceli, 1977.

Castellanos, Jorge, and Isabel Castellanos, *Cultura Afrocuban.* Vol. 1: *El Negro en Cuba, 1492–1844.* Miami: Ediciones Universal, 1988.

Castellanos, Isabel. "From Ulkumí to Lucumí: A Historical Overview of Religious Acculturation in Cuba." In *Santería Aesthetics in Contemporary Latin America Art.* Edited by Arturo Lindsay, 39–50. Washington, DC: Smithsonian Institution Press, 1996.

Chevannes, Barry. *Rastafari: Roots and Ideology*. Syracuse, NY: Syracuse University Press, 1994.

———. "Introducing the Native Religions of Jamaica." In Rastafari and Other African-Caribbean Worldviews. Edited by Barry Chevannes. New Brunswick, NJ: Rutgers University Press, 1998.

Chevannes, Barry, ed. *Rastafari and Other African-Caribbean Worldviews*. New Brunswick, NJ: Rutgers University Press, 1998.

Christian, William A. *Local Religion in Sixteenth-Century Spain*. Princeton: Princeton University Press, 1981.

Clark, James A. *The Church and the Crisis in the Dominican Republic*. Westminster, MD: Newman Press, 1967.

Clark, Mary Ann. "Godparenthood in the Afro-Cuban Religious Tradition of Santería." *Religious Studies and Theology* 22, no. 1 (2003): 45–62.

———. *Where Men Are Wives and Mothers Rule: Santería Ritual Practices and Their Gender Implications*. Gainesville: University Press of Florida, 2005.

Cleary, Edward L., and Hannah W. Stewart-Gambino, eds. *Power, Politics, and Pentecostals in Latin America*. Boulder, CO: Westview Press, 1997.

Conniff, Michael L., and Thomas J. Davis. *Africans in the Americas*. New York: St. Martin's Press, 1994.

Corse, Theron. *Protestants, Revolution, and the Cuba-U.S. Bond*. Gainesville: University of Florida Press, 2007.

Corten, André, and Ruth Marshall-Fratani, eds. *Between Babel and Pentecost: Transnational Pentecostalism in Africa and Latin America*. Bloomington: Indiana University Press, 2001.

Cosentino, Donald J. "Introduction: Imagine Heaven." In *Sacred Arts of Haitian Vodou*. Edited by Donald J. Cosentino. Los Angeles: UCLA Museum of Cultural History, 1995.

Cros Sandoval, Mercedes. *Worldview, the Orichas, and Santería: Africa to Cuba and Beyond*. Gainesville: University of Florida Press, 2006.

Cummins, Alissandra. "European Views of the Aboriginal Population." In *Indigenous People of the Caribbean*. Edited by Samuel M. Wilson. Gainesville: University Press of Florida, 1997

Curry, Mary C. *Making the Gods in New York: The Yoruba Religion in the African American Community*. New York: Routledge, 1997.

Dabydeen, David, and Brinsley Samaroo, eds. *India in the Caribbean*. London: Hansib, 1987.

———. *Across the Dark Waters: Ethnicity and Indian Identity in the Caribbean*. Basingstoke: Macmillan Caribbean, 1996.

Davis, Kortright. *Emancipation Still Comin': Explorations in Caribbean Emancipatory Theology*. Maryknoll, NY: Orbis Books, 1990.

Deive, Carlos Esteban. *Vodou y Magia en Santo Domingo*. Santo Domingo, Dominican Republic: Taller, 1975.

De la Fuente, Alejandro. "The New Afro-Cuban Cultural Movement and the Debate on Race in Contemporary Cuba." Journal of Latin American Studies 40 (2008): 697–720.

de las Casas, Bartolomé. *History of the Indies*. Translated by Andrée Collard. New York: Harper and Row, 1971.

———. *Bartolomé de las Casas: A Selection of His Writings*. Translated and edited by George Sanderlin. New York: Knopf, 1973.

De Mello e Souza, Laura. *The Devil and the Land of the Holy Cross: Witchcraft, Slavery, and Popular Religion in Colonial Brazil.* Translated by Diane Grosklaus Whitty. Austin: University of Texas Press, 2006.

De Nieves, Julián. *The Catholic Church in Colonial Puerto Rico (1898–1964).* Río Piedras, Puerto Rico: Edittorial EDIL, 1982.

Desmangles, Leslie G. *The Faces of the Gods: Vodou and Roman Catholicism in Haiti.* Chapel Hill: University of North Carolina Press, 1992.

Desmangles, Leslie G., Stephen D. Glazier, and Joseph M. Murphy. "Religion in the Caribbean." In *Understanding the Contemporary Caribbean.* Edited by Richard S. Hillman and Thomas J. D'Agostino, 263–304. Boulder, CO: Lynne Rienner, 2003.

Dianteill, Erwan. "Kongo À Cuba: Transformations d'une religion africaine." *Archives de Sciences Sociales des Religion* 117 (January-March 2002): 59–80.

Diaz, María Elena. *The Virgin, the King, and the Royal Slaves of El Cobre: Negotiating Freedom in Colonial Cuba, 1670–1780.* Stanford: Stanford University Press, 2000.

Diouf, Silviane. *Servants of Allah: African Muslims Enslaved in the Americas.* New York: New York University Press, 1998.

Dodson, Jualynne E. *Sacred Spaces and Religious Traditions in Oriente Cuba.* Albuquerque: University of New Mexico Press, 2008.

Dubois, Laurent. "Filming the *Lwa* in Haiti." *Caribbean Studies* 36, no. 1 (January-June 2008): 215–19.

Eastman, Rudolph, and Maureen Warner-Lewis. "Forms of African Spirituality in Trinidad and Tobago." In *African Spirituality: Forms, Meanings, and Expressions.* New York: Crossroad, 2000.

Edmonds, Ennis Barrington, *Rastafari: From Outcasts to Culture Bearers.* New York: Oxford University Press, 2003.

Erskine, Noel Leo. *Decolonizing Theology: A Caribbean Perspective.* Maryknoll, NY: Orbis Books, 1981.

Falola, Toyin, and Matt D. Childs, eds. *The Yoruba Diaspora in the Atlantic World.* Bloomington: Indiana University Press, 2004.

Farris Thompson, Richard. *Flash of the Spirit: African and Afro-American Art and Philosophy.* New York: Random House, 1983.

———."Kongo Influences on African American Artistic Culture." In *Africanisms in American Culture.* Edited by Joseph E. Holloway, 283–325 Bloomington: Indiana University Press, 2005.

Fernández Olmos, Margarite, and Lizabeth Paravisini-Gebert, eds. *Sacred Possessions: Vodou, Santería, Obeah, and the Caribbean.* New Brunswick, NJ: Rutgers University Press, 1997.

———. *Creole Religions of the Caribbean: An Introduction from Vodou and Santería to Obeah and Espiritismo.* New York: New York University Press, 2003.

———. *Healing Cultures: Art and Religion as Curative Practices in the Caribbean and Its Diaspora.* New York: Palgrave, 2001.

Fleurant, Gerdès. "The Music of Haitian Vodou." In *African Spiritualities: Forms, Meanings, and Expressions.* Edited by Jacob K. Olupona, 416–49. New York: Crossroad, 2000.

Floyd-Thomas, Stacey M. and Anthony B. Pinn, eds. *Liberation Theologies in the United States: An Introductory Reader.* New York: New York University Press, 2010.

Frazier, E. Franklin. *The Negro Family in the United States.* Chicago: University of Chicago Press, 1940.

Fuentes Guerra, Jesús, and Grisel Gómez Gómez. *Cultos afrocubanos: Un estudio etno-lingüístico.* Havana, Cuba: Editorial de Ciencias Sociales, 1996.

Galembo, Phyllis, *Vodou Visions and Voices of Haiti.* Berkeley, CA: Ten Speed Press, 2005.

Gardner, W. J. *A History of Jamaica from Its Discovery by Christopher Columbus to the Year 1872.* London: Frank Cass, 1873.

Garvey, Marcus Mosiah, *Philosophy and Opinions of Marcus Garvey: Africa for the Africans,* 2nd ed. Edited by Amy Jacques Garvey. New York: Routledge, 1967.

Gates, Brian, ed. *Afro-Caribbean Religions.* London: Ward Locke Educational, 2980.

Gaustad, Edwin, and Leigh Schmidt. *The Religious History of America.* San Francisco: HarperSanFrancisco, 2002.

Giovannetti, Jorge L. "Jamaican Reggae and the Articulation of Social and Historical Consciousness in Musical Discourse." In *Contemporary Caribbean Cultures and Societies in Global Context.* Edited by Franklin W. Knight and Teresita Martinez-Vergne, 211–32. Chapel Hill: University of North Carolina Press, 2005.

Glazier, Steven. *Perspectives on Pentecostalism: Case Studies from the Caribbean and Latin America.* Washington, DC: University Press of America, 1980.

———. "African Cults and Christian Churches in Trinidad: The Spiritual Baptists Case." *Journal of Religious Thought* 39, no. 2 (Fall-Winter 1982): 17–25.

———. *Marchin' the Pilgrims Home: A Study of the Spiritual Baptists of Trinidad.* Salem, WI: Sheffield, 1983.

———. "Embedded Truths: Creativity and Context in Spiritual Baptist Music." *Latin American Music Review/Revista de Musica Latinamericana* 18, no. 1 (Spring-Summer 1997): 44–56.

———. "Contested Rituals of the African Diaspora." In *New Trends and Developments in African Religions.* Edited by Peter B. Clarke, 105–20. Westport CT: Greenwood, 1998.

Gomez, Michael A. "African Identity and Slavery in America." *Radical History Review* 75 (1999): 111–20.

———. *Black Crescent: The Experience and Legacy of African Muslims in the Americas.* New York: Cambridge University Press, 2005.

———. *Reversing Sail: A History of the African Diaspora.* New York: Cambridge University Press, 2005.

González, Justo. *The Development of Christianity in the Latin Caribbean.* Ann Arbor, MI: University Microfilms International, 1969.

Gonzalez, Michelle A. *Afro-Cuban Theology: Race, Religion, Culture, and Identity.* Gainesville: University Press of Florida, 2006.

González, Ondina E., and Justo L. González. *Christianity in Latin America: A History.* New York: Cambridge University Press, 2008.

Gossai, Henchand, and Nathaniel Samuel Murrell, eds. *Religion, Culture, and Tradition in the Caribbean.* New York: St. Martin's Press, 2000.

Greene, Anne. *The Catholic Church in Haiti: Political and Social Change.* Ann Arbor, MI: University Microfilms, 1993.

Hall, Douglas. *The Caribbean Experience: An Historical Survey, 1450–1960.* Kingston, Jamaica: Heinemann Educational Books, 1982.

Hall, Linda B. *Mary, Mother and Warrior: The Virgin in Spain and the Americas*. Austin, TX: University of Texas Press, 2004.

Ham, Adolfo. "Caribbean Theology: The Challenge of the Twenty-First Century." In *Caribbean Theology: Preparing for the Challenges Ahead*. Edited by Howard Gregory. Kingston, Jamaica: Canoe Press, 1995.

Ham Reyes, Adolfo. "An Ecumenical Perspective on the Cuban Protestant Missionary Heritage." *International Review of Mission* 74: 295 (July 1985): 327–36.

Hamilton, J. Taylor, and Kenneth G. Hamilton. *History of the Moravian Church: The Renewed Unitas Fratrum, 1722–1957*. Winston-Salem, NC: Interprovincial Board of Christian Education, Moravian Church of America, 1967.

Harricharan, John T. *The Catholic Church in Trinidad: 1498–1852*. Port of Spain, Trinidad: Inprint Caribbean Ltd., 1981.

Henry, Frances. *Reclaiming African Religions in Trinidad: The Socio-Political Legitimation of the Orisha and Spiritual Baptist Faiths*. Kingston, Jamaica: University of the West Indies Press, 2003.

Herskovits, Melville J., and Frances S. Herskovits. *Trinidad Village*. New York: Knopf, 1947.

Hernández-Hiraldo, Samiri. *Black Puerto Rican Identity and Religious Experience*. Gainesville: University of Florida Press, 2006.

Hess, David J. *Spirit and Scientists: Ideology, Spiritism, and Brazilian Culture*. University Park: Pennsylvania State University Press, 2001.

Heywood, Linda M., ed. *Central Africans and Cultural Transformations in the American Diaspora*. New York: Cambridge University Press, 2002.

Highfield, Arnold R. "Some Observations on the Taino Language." In *The Indigenous People of the Caribbean*. Edited by Samuel M. Wilson. Gainesville: University Press of Florida, 1997.

Hintzen, Percy C. "The Caribbean: Race and Creole Ethnicity." In *Cultural Identity and Creolization in National Unity: The Multiethnic Caribbean*. Edited by Prem Misir. Latham, MD: University Press of America, 2006.

Houk, James T. *Spirit, Blood and Drums: The Orisha Religion in Trinidad*. Philadelphia: Temple University Press, 1995.

Howard, Philip A. *Changing History: Afro-Cuban Cabildos and Societies of Color in the Nineteenth Century*. Baton Rouge: Louisiana State University Press, 1998.

Hunte, Keith "Protestantism and Slavery in the British Caribbean." In *Christianity in the Caribbean: Essays on Church History*. Edited by Armando Lampe. Kingston, Jamaica: University of the West Indies Press, 2001.

Hurbon, Laënnec. "Religious Movements in the Caribbean." In *New Religious Movements and Rapid Social Change*. Edited by James A. Beckford, 146–76. Beverly Hills, CA: Sage, 1986.

———. *Vodoo, Search for the Spirit*. New York: Abrams, 1995.

Keegan, William F. "'No Man [or Woman] Is an Island': Elements of Taino Social Organization." In *The Indigenous People of the Caribbean*. Edited by Samuel M. Wilson. Gainesville: University Press of Florida, 1997.

Kirk, John M. *Between God and the Party: Religion and Politics in Revolutionary Cuba*. Tampa: University of South Florida Press, 1989.

Knight, Franklin W., and Colin A. Palmer. "The Caribbean: A Regional Overview." In *The Modern Caribbean*. Edited by Franklin W. Knight and Colin A. Palmer. Chapel Hill: University of North Carolina Press, 1989.

Korom, Frank J. *Hosay Trinidad: Muharram Performances in an Indo-Caribbean Diaspora.* Philadelphia: University of Pennsylvania Press, 2003.

Laguerre, Michel S. *Voodoo and Politics in Haiti.* New York: St. Martin's Press, 1989.

La Guerre, John Gaffa ,ed. *Calcutta to Caroni: The East Indians of Trinidad.* Jamaica: Logman Caribbean, 1974

Lake, Obigale. "Religion, Patriarchy, and the Status of Rastafarian Women." In *New Trends and Developments in African Religions.* Edited by Peter B. Clarke, 141–58. Westport, CT: Greenwood, 1998.

Lalive d'Epinday, Christian, "Dependance Sociale et Religion: Pasteurs et Protestantismes Latino-Americains." *Archives de Sciences Sociales de Religions* 26 (July-September 1981): 85–91.

Lampe, Armando. "Christianity in the Caribbean." In *The Church in Latin America, 1492–1992.* Edited by Enrique Dussel, 201–16. Maryknoll, NY: Orbis Books, 1992.

Lampe, Armando, ed. *Christianity in the Caribbean: Essays in Church History.* Kingston, Jamaica: University of the West Indies Press, 2001.

LeGrace, Benson. "Some Observations on West African Islamic Motifs and Haitian Religious Art." *Journal of Caribbean Studies* 9, no. 1–2 (Winter 1992-Spring 1993): 59–66.

———. "'Quismat' of the Names of Allah in Haitian Vodou." *Journal of Haitian Studies* 8, no. 2 (Fall 2002): 160–64.

Lindsay, Arturo. *Santería Aesthetics in Contemporary Latin American Art.* Washington, DC: Smithsonian Institution Press, 1996.

Littlewood, Roland. "From Mimesis to Appropriation in Shouter Baptism and Shango: The Earth People of Trinidad." In *New Trends and Developments in African Religions.* Edited by Peter B. Clarke, 121–39. Westport, CT: Greenwood, 1998.

Livi-Bacci, Massimo. "Return to Hispaniola: Reassessing the Demographic Catastrophe." *Hispanic American Historical Review* 83, no. 1(2003): 3–52.

Lovelace, Earl. *The Wine of Astonishment.* London: Heineman, 1982, and New York: Vintage, 1984.

Mack, Douglas R. A. *From Babylon to Rastafari: Origin and History of the Rastafarian Movement.* Chicago: Research Associates School Times Publications, 1999.

Malloch, Theodore. "Rastafarianism: A Radical Caribbean Movement/Religion." Center Journal 4, no. 4 (Fall 1985): 67–89.

Martin, David. *Tongues of Fire: The Explosion of Protestantism in Latin America.* Cambridge, MA: Blackwell, 1990.

Martínez-Fernández, Luis. *Protestantism and Political Conflict in the Nineteenth-Century Hispanic Caribbean.* New Brunswick, NJ: Rutgers University Press, 2002.

Mathieu, Suze Marie. *The Transformation of the Catholic Church in Haiti.* Ann Arbor, MI: University Microfilms, 1991.

Maza Miquel, Manuel, S.J. *El alma del Negocio y el negocio del alma: testimonies sobre la iglesia y la sociedad en Cuba, 1878–1894.* Santiago, Dominican Republic: PUCMM, 1990.

McClure, Marian. *The Catholic Church and Rural Social Change: Priests, Peasant Organizations, and Politics in Haiti.* Ann Arbor, MI: University Microfilms, 1986.

McDaniel, Lorna. "Memory Spirituals of the Ex-Slave American Soldiers in Trinidad's 'Company Villages.'" *Black Music Research Journal* 14, no. 2 (Autumn 1994): 119–43.

Midlo Hall, Gwendolyn. *Slavery and African Ethnicities in the Americas.* Chapel Hill: University of North Carolina Press, 2005.

Miller, Ivan. "A Secret Society Goes Public: The Relationship between Abakua and Cuban Culture." *African Studies Review* 43, no. 1 (April 2000): 161–88.

Mintz, Sidney W. *Worker in the Cane: A Puerto Rican Life History.* New Haven: Yale University Press, 1960.

Mintz, Sidney W., and Sally Price, eds. *Caribbean Contours.* Baltimore: Johns Hopkins University Press, 1985.

Misir, Prem. "Introduction." In *Cultural Identity and Creolization in National Unity: The Multiethnic Caribbean.* Edited by Prem Misir. Latham, MD: University Press of America, 2006.

Moore, Carlos. "Afro-Cubans and the Communist Revolution." In *African Presence in the Americas.* Edited by Carlos Moore, Tanya R. Saunders, and Shawna Moore. Trenton, NJ: Africa World Press, 1995.

Murphy, Joseph, *Santeria: African Spirits in America.* Boston: Beacon Press, 1993

Murphy, Joseph M., and Mei-Mei Sanford, eds. *Òsun across the Waters: A Yoruba Goddess in Africa and the Americas.* Bloomington: Indiana University Press, 2001.

Murrell, Nathaniel Samuel, William David Spencer, and Adrian Anthony McFarlane, eds. *Chanting Down Babylon: The Rastafarian Reader.* Philadelphia: Temple University Press, 1998.

Nettleford, Rex. *Mirror Mirror: Identity, Race and Protest in Jamaica.* Kingston, Jamaica: Collins and Sangster, 1970.

Oliver, José R. "The Taino Cosmos." In *The Indigenous People of the Caribbean.* Edited by Samuel M. Wilson. Gainesville: University Press of Florida, 1997.

Olupona Jacob K., and Terry Rey, eds. *Orisa Devotion as World Religion.* Madison: University of Wisconsin Press, 2008.

Orozco, Román, and Natalia Bolivár Aróstegui. *Cuba Santa: Comunistas, Santeros, y Cristianos en la Isla de Fidel Castro.* Madrid: El País Aguilar, 1998.

Ortiz, Fernando. *Los cabildos y la fiesta afrocubano del Dia de los Reyes.* Havana, Cuba: Editorial de Ciencias Sociales, 1992.

———. "La Fiesta Afro-Cubana del 'Dia de Reyes,'" *Revista Bimestre Cubana* 15, no. 1 (January-February 1921): 5–26.

———. *Los Negros brujos.* Miami, FL: Ediciones Universal, 1973.

Osborne, Francis, S.J. *History of the Catholic Church in Jamaica.* Bucks, U.K: Ginn and Company, 1977.

Palmié, Stephan. "Against Syncretism: Africanizing and Cubanizing Discourses in North American Òrìsà Worship." In *Counterworks: Managing the Diversity of Knowledge.: Uses of Knowledge.* Edited by Richard Fardon, 73–104. London: Routledge, 1995.

———. *Wizards and Scientists: Explorations in Afro-Cuban Modernity and Tradition.* Durham, NC: Duke University Press, 2002.

Pané, Fray Ramón. *An Account of the Antiquities of the Indians.* Edited by José Juan Arrom and translated by Susan C. Griswold. Durham, NC, and London: Duke University Press, 1999.

Perera Pintado, Ana Celia, "Religion and Cuban Identity in a Transnational Context" *Latin American Perspectives* 32 (2005): 147–73.

Pérez, Jr., Louis A. *On Becoming Cuban: Identity, Nationality, and Culture.* Chapel Hill: University of North Carolina Press, 1999.

Pérez Mémen, Fernando. *La iglesia y el estado en Santo Domingo (1700–1853).* Santo Domingo, Dominican Republic: Editorial de la UASD, 1984.

Pérez y Mena, Andrés I. "Cuban Santería, Haitian Vodun, Puerto Rican Spiritualism: A Multiculturalist Inquiry into Syncretism." *Journal for the Scientific Study of Religion* 37, no. 1 (1998): 15–27.

———. "Understanding Religiosity in Cuba." *Journal of Hispanic/Latino Theology* 7, no. 3 (2000): 6–34.

Phillippo, James M. *Jamaica: Its Past and Present State*. Freeport, NY: Books for Library Press, 1971 [1843].

Pollard, Velma. *Dread Talk: The Language of Rastafari*. Kingston, Jamaica: Canoe Press, 1994.

Portuondo Zúñiga, Olga. *La Virgen de la Caridad del Cobre: Simbolo de la Cubanía*. Rev. ed. Madrid, Spain: Agualarga Editores, 2002.

Premdas, Ralph R. *Identity, Ethnicity, and Culture in the Caribbean*. Kingston, Jamaica: University of the West Indies, 1998.

Quezada, Noemí, ed. *Religiosidad Popular: México y Cuba*. México, D.F.: UNAM, 2004.

Ramos, Marco Antonio. *Panorma del Protestantismo en Cuba: La presensia de los protestantes o evangélicos en la historia de Cuba desde la colonización española hasta la revolución*. San Jose, Costa Rica; Editorial Caribe, 1986.

Ramos, Miguel "Willie." "Afro-Cuban Orisha Worship." In *Santería Aesthetics in Contemporary Latin America Art*. Edited by Arturo Lindsay, 51–76. Washington, DC: Smithsonian Institute Press, 1996.

———. "La division de la Habana: Territorial Conflict and Cultural Hegemony in the Followers of Oyo Lukumí Religion, 1850s–1920s." *Cuban Studies* 34 (2003): 38–69.

Ramsey, Kate. "Legislating 'Civilization' in Postrevolutionary Haiti." In *Race, Nation, and Religion in the Americas*. Edited by Henry Goldschmidt and Elizabeth MacAlister, 231–58. New York: Oxford University Press, 2004.

Reid-Salmon, Delroy A. *Home Away from Home: The Caribbean Diasporan Church in the Black Atlantic Tradition*. London: Equinox, 2008.

———. "Sin of Black Theology: The Omission of the Caribbean Diasporan Experience from Black Theological Discourse." *Black Theology* 6, no. 2 (2008): 154–73.

Rey, Terry. *Our Lady of Class Struggle: The Cult of the Virgin Mary in Haiti*. Trenton, NJ: Africa World Press, 1999.

———. "The Politics of Patron Sainthood in Haiti: 500 Years of Iconic Struggle." *Catholic Historical Review* 88, no. 3 (2002): 519–45.

Righter, Elizabeth. "Ceramics, Art, and Material Culture of the Early Ceramic Period in the Caribbean Islands." In *The Indigenous People of the Caribbean*. Edited by Samuel M. Wilson. Gainesville: University Press of Florida, 1997.

Rivera-Pagán, Luis. "Doing Pastoral Theology in a Post-Colonial Context: Some Observations from the Caribbean." *Journal of Pastoral Theology* 17, no. 2 (Fall 2007): 1–27.

Rodriguez, Miguel. "Religious Beliefs of the Saladoid People." In *The Indigenous Peoples of the Caribbean*. Edited by Samuel A. Wilson. Gainsville: University Press of Florida, 1997.

Roget, Henry Petijean. "Notes on Ancient Caribbean and Mythology." In *The Indigenous People of the Caribbean*. Edited by Samuel M. Wilson. Gainesville: University Press of Florida, 1997.

Román, Reinaldo L. "Spiritists versus Spirit-Mongers: Julía Vazquez and the Struggle for Progress in 1920s Puerto Rico." *Centro Journal* 14, no. 2 (Fall 2002): 27–47.

————. *Governing Spirits: Religion, Miracles, and Spectacles in Cuba and Puerto Rico, 1898–1956.* Chapel Hill: University of North Carolina Press, 2007.

Rommen, Timothy. "Nationalism and the Soul: Gospelypso as Independence." *Black Music Research Journal* 22, no. 1 (2002): 37–63.

————. "Protestant Vibrations? Reggae, Rastafari, and Conscious Evangelicals." *Popular Music* 25, no. 2 (2006): 235–63.

Rouse, Irving. *The Tainos: Rise and Decline of the People Who Greeted Columbus.* New Haven: Yale University Press, 1992.

Rout, Jr. Leslie B. *The African Experience in Spanish America.* Princeton: Marcus Wiener, 2003; 1976.

Ryman, Cheryl. "Kumina: Stability and Change." *ACIJ Research Review* 1 (1984): 81–128.

Saez, José Luis, S.J. *Cinco siglos de la iglesia dominicana.* Santo Domingo, República Dominicana:Editora Amigo del Hogar, 1987.

————. *La iglesia y el negro esclavo en Santo Domingo: Una historia de tres siglos.* Santo Domingo, República Dominicana: Patronato de la Ciudad Colonial de Santo Domingo, 1994.

Samaroo, Brinsley. "India and the Indian Diaspora: The Continuing Links." In *Cultural Identity and Creolization in National Unity: The Multiethnic Caribbean.* Edited by Prem Misir. Latham, MD: University Press of America, 2006.

Samaroo, Brinsley, and Ann Marie Bissessar, eds. *The Construction of an Indo-Caribbean Diaspora.* St. Augustine: Trinidad and Tobago: University of the West Indies, 2004.

Samuel, Hewlester A. Sr. *The Birth of the Village of Liberta, Antigua.* Antigua: Hewlester Samuel, 2007.

Schuler, Monica. "Myalism and the African Religious Tradition in Jamaica." In *Africa and theCaribbean: The Legacies of a Link.* Edited by Margaret E. Crahan and Franklin W. Knight. Baltimore: Johns Hopkins University Press, 1979.

————. *"Alas, Alas, Kongo": A Social History of Indentured African Migration to Jamaica, 1841–1865.* Baltimore: Johns Hopkins University Press, 1980.

Sernett, Milton C., ed. *African American Religious History: A Documentary Witness.* 2nd. ed. Durham, NC: Duke University Press, 1999.

Silva Gotay, Samuel. *Protestantismo y Política en Puerto Rico: 1898⊠1930.* San Juan, Puerto Rico: Editorial de la Universidad de Puerto Rico, 1990.

————. "Historia social de las iglesias en Puerto Rico." In *Historia general de la Iglesia en America Latina,* vol. 4: *Caribe.* Edited by Johannes Meier et al., 251–80. Salamanca, Spain: Ediciones Sígueme, 1995.

Simpson, George Eaton. "Baptismal 'Mourning' and 'Building' Ceremonies of the Shouters in Trinidad." *Journal of American Folklore* 79, no. 314 (October-December 1966): 537–50.

————. *Black Religions in the New World.* New York: Columbia University Press, 1978.

Singh, Kelvin, *Bloodstained Tombs: The Muhurram Massacre 1884.* London: Macmillan Caribbean, 1988.

Smith, Ashley, "Mainline Churches in the Caribbean: Their Relationship to the Cultural and Political Process," *Caribbean Journal of Religious Studies* 9 (1998): 27–40.

Smith, M. G. "Social and Cultural Pluralism." *Annals of the New York Academy of Science* 83 (January 1960): 763–785.

————. *The Plural Society in the British West Indies.* Berkeley: University of California Press, 1965.

Smith, M. G., Roy Augier, and Rex Nettleford. *The Rastafari Movement in Kingston, Jamaica*. Mona, Jamaica: Institute of Social and Economic Research, 1960.

Smith, Robert Worthington. "Slavery and Christianity in the British Caribbean." *Church History* 19, no. 3 (September 1950): 171–86.

Stevens-Arroyo, Anthony M. "The Contribution of Catholic Orthodoxy to Caribbean Syncretism: The Case of la Virgen de la Caridad del Cobre in Cuba." *Des Sciences Sociales des Religion* 117 (January-March 2002): 37–58.

Stewart, Dianne M. *Three Eyes for the Journey: African Dimensions of the Jamaican Religious Experience*. New York: Oxford University Press, 2005.

———. "Womanist Theology in the Caribbean Context: Critiquing Culture, Rethinking Doctrine, and Expanding Boundaries." *Journal of Feminist Studies in Religion* 20, no. 1 (Spring 2004): 61–82. Stoll, David. *Is Latin America Turning Protestant? The Politics of Evangelical Growth*. Berkeley: University of California Press, 1990.

Suárez Polcari, Ramón. *Historia de la Iglesia Católica en Cuba*. 2 vols. Miami: Ediciones Universal, 2005.

Taylor, Patrick, ed. *Nation Dance: Religion, Identity, and Cultural Difference in the Caribbean*. Bloomington: Indiana University Press, 2001.

Thomas, Eudora. *A History of the Shouter Baptists in Trinidad and Tobago*. Tacarigua, Trinidad: Calaloux, 1987.

Thornton, John. "The Development of an African Catholic Church in the Kingdom of Kongo, 1491–1750." *Journal of African History* 25, no. 2 (1984): 147–67.

———. "On the Trail of Voodoo: African Christianity in Africa and the Americas." *The Americas* 44 (1988): 261–78.

Turner, Victor. *The Ritual Process: Structure and Anti-Structure*. New York: Aldine, 1969.

Tweed, Thomas. *Our Lady of the Exile: Diasporic Religion at a Cuban Catholic Shrine in Miami*. New York: Oxford University Press, 1997.

Tyler, S. Lyman. *Two Worlds: The Indian Encounter with the European, 1492–1509*. Salt Lake City: University of Utah Press, 1988.

Underhill, Edward Bean. *The West Indies: Their Social and Religious Condition*. Westport, CT: Negro Universities Press, 1970 [1862].

Young, Jason R. *Rituals of Resistance; African Atlantic Religion in Kongo and the Lowcountry South in the Era of Slavery*. Baton Rouge: Louisiana State University Press, 2007.

Vertovec, Steven. *Hindu Trinidad: Religion, Ethnicity and Socio-Economic Change*. Hong Kong: Macmillan Caribbean, 1992.

———. *The Hindu Diaspora: Comparative Patterns*. New York: Routledge, 2000.

Walker, D. J. R. *Columbus and the Golden World of the Island Arawaks: The Story of the First Americans and Their Caribbean Environment*. Lewes, Sussex: The Book Guild, 1992.

Warner-Lewis, Maureen. *Central Africa in the Caribbean: Transcending Time, Transforming Cultures*. Kingston, Jamaica: University of the West Indies Press, 2003.

Westmeier, Karl-Wilhelm. *Protestant Pentecostalism in Latin America: A Study in the Dynamics of Missions*. Cranbury, NJ: Associated University Presses, 1999.

Williams, Lewin. *Caribbean Theology*. New York: Peter Lang, 1994.

Wipfler, William Louis. *The Churches of the Dominican Republic in the Light of History: A Study of the Root Causes of Current Problems*. Cuernavaca, Mexico: Sondeos, 1966.

Wright, Irene. "Our Lady of Charity." *Hispanic American Historical Review* 5 (1922): 709–17.

Yaremeko, Jason M. *U.S. Protestant Missions in Cuba: From Independence to Castro*. Gainesville: University Press of Florida, 2000.

Young, Jason R. *Rituals of Resistance; African Atlantic Religion in Kongo and the Lowcountry South in the Era of Slavery*. Baton Rouge: Louisiana State University Press, 2007.

Index

Abakuá (religion), 107–9, 215, 218, 232n40
ABC Islands, 66–68. *See also* Aruba;
   Bonaire; Curaçao
Acculturation, 103
Act of Toleration, 72, 83
Act of Uniformity, 77
Adefunmi, Nana Oseijeman, 101–2
Adrián, Trajana, 170
Afonso (king of Congo), 59
African culture, 8–11; Afro-Christian,
   121–54; Afro-Cuban, 50–51, 98–102,
   155–57, 203–4; Afro-Jamaican, 131–38,
   184–85; Afro-Trinidadian, 138–54; *cabildos* and, 98–100, 103, 227n9; creolization
   and, 93–119, 121; drumming and, 51, 58,
   96, 211; music and, 210–11; re-African-
   ization, 154. *See also specific ethnicities*
African Methodist Episcopal Church, 133–34
African people: African Americans,
   146–47, 161–62, 207–8; in Cuba, 98–102;
   demographics of, 55–56; diaspora of, 47,
   119, 142, 158, 175, 185, 194, 204, 206, 208,
   215, 218; indentureship of, 81, 122, 129,
   141; population estimates for, 98, 112,
   138; Roman Catholicism and, 43, 50–52,
   59–64. *See also* Slavery
Afroz, Sultana, 182
Agriculture, 18–19
Ahye, Molly, 142
Albear, Timotea "Latuán," 99
Alexander VI (pope), 34
Alvaranga, Philmore, 194
Álvarez, Adalberto, 214
Americanization: in Cuba, 163, 165; of
   Puerto Rico, 160–61
American Revolution, 75, 80–81, 84, 146

Amerindians, 2–3; atrocities against,
   37–39; de las Casas and, 36, 42–43, 57;
   population estimates for, 37; slavery of,
   39; social conventions of, 17–22; Spanish
   Catholics and, 15–43. *See also specific
   ethnicities*
Anacaona, 21, 38
Ancestor worship: Ciboneys and, 22;
   Kumina and, 130; Myal and, 125; Tainos
   and, 24–25
Animal sacrifice, 130, 152
Antigua, 67, 70, 80
Antoine, Robert, 145
Apostles of Infinite Love, 215
Arawak people (Caiquetos), 16, 56, 67–68,
   139
Arieto (ceremonial dance), 22, 29
Aristide, Jean-Bertrand, 115–16
Arnaz, Desi, 215
Aroyinde, Christine, 118
Art, and Yoruba traditions, 214
Aruba, 2, 66–67
Arya Samaj (religion), 180
Ashanti people, 182
Assembly of God Church, 169–70, 172–73
Atabeira/Atabey, 23, 28
Atheism, 164
Atrocities, against Amerindians, 37–39
Augier, Roy, 193
Austin-Broos, Diane, 218
Auto-sacramentals, 49–50
Ayorinde, Christine, 204
Azor (band), 214

Babalawos (high priests), 95–96, 204–5, 218
Babalu-Ayé (spirit), 95, 215

Hausa, Muhammad, 183
Hausa traditions, 122
Hawkins, John, 66
Healing rituals, 129, 147–48; by healer, 132–34, 145, 152; herbal, 103, 111, 123–25; magical, 123, 125; by spirits, 144–45
Henry, Claudius, 191–92
Henry, Frances, 143
Henry, Ronald, 192
Herbal healing rituals, 103, 111, 123–25
Hernández González, Francisco, 170
Hernández-Hiraldo, Samiri, 159
Herne, Vital, 172
Hibbert, Joseph Nathaniel, 186
Hinds, Robert, 186–87
Hinduism, 140, 142, 150, 177–80, 201
Hip-hop music, 214
Hispaniola, 2, 15, 31, 58, 67
Hojeda, Alonso, 36
Holiness Church, 136–37, 158, 168, 173
Homiak, John P., 187
Hopkins, Dwight, 208
Houk, James T., *Spirit, Blood and Drums: The Orisha Religion in Trinidad*, 145, 147, 150
House of Youth Black Faith (HYBF), 187–89
Howell, Leonard Percival, 186, 188, 199
Hoyos, Juan de, 156
Hoyos, Rodrigo de, 156
Hudson, Henryu, 173
Huguenots, 65, 71
Hunte, Keith, 86
Hunter-gatherer culture, 18
Hurbon, Laënnec, 168, 206, 215
HYBF. *See* House of Youth Black Faith
Hyperventilation shouting, 135, 146–47, 152, 153

Ifá Iranlowo (priests' association), 204
I-gelic House, 187–89
Illegal trading, 65–66
Indentureship, 12; of Africans, 81, 122, 129, 141; of South Asians, 88, 129, 138, 177–78
Indian Arrival Day, 149
Indians. *See* Amerindians; South Asians; *specific ethnicities*

Initiation: in Abakuá, 107–9; in Palo Monte, 103, 105; in Vodou, 110
Inman, Samuel Guy, 161, 163
Inquisition, 61
Irrigation, 19
Isabella (queen of Spain), 30–31, 33–35, 39, 53
Islam, 177–83, 201; Columbus, C., and, 180–81; in Jamaica, 182; marriage in, 179; Sunni v. Shi'ah, 182; in Trinidad, 182–83; Yoruba traditions and, 181

Jamaica, 2; Afro-Jamaican culture, 131–38, 184–85; Baptist Church in, 81–83, 86–88, 126–27, 131; Church of England in, 83, 85; Democratic Socialism in, 4; England and, 67, 70; Islam in, 182; Jamaica Labor Party, 187; Methodist Church in, 80; Obeah in, 122–24; Pentecostal churches in, 173–74. *See also* Rastafarianism
Jehovah's Witnesses, 215–16
Jerry, Bongo, 189
Jerry, Jah, 196
Jesuit order, 63
Jesús Miranda, José Luis de, 171
Jews, European, 3, 67, 71, 77
Jorge, Silvestre, 170
Joseph, Paulceus, 172
Judaism, 140
Julius II (pope), 41

Kabbalah, 140, 142, 145, 150
Kardec, Allan. *See* Rivail, Hippolyte Léon, Denizard
Kebra Nagast (Ethiopian epic), 183
Kenney, Edward, 163–64
Kersuzan, François-Marie, 53, 64, 158
Kikongo traditions, 122
Kimbisa (religion), 103
Kirk, John, 57
Kirkland, Colonel, 81
Kluzit, John, 172
Kluzit, Stephanie, 172
Knibb, William, 81–82
Knight, Franklin W., 5
Kongo. *See* Congo

Mowatt, Judy, 200
Murphy, Joseph, 94, 157
Music: African culture and, 210–11; gospelypso, 213; hip-hop, 214; in Pentecostal churches, 212–13; reggae, 196, 198–201, 211–12; ska, 196; in Vodou, 213–14
Muslims. *See* Islam
Myal (religion), 122–28, 130–31

National Council of Orisha Elders, 143
Nation dance, 12
Native Baptists, 126–28, 131
Neble, Stirling Augustus, 164
Negro Education Grant, 86
Neoculturation, 103
Netherlands. *See* Dutch settlements
Nettleford, Rex, 7, 11, 193
Nevis, 67, 70, 80, 224n1
New Testament Church of God, 136–37
Nganga (priests), 61, 104–6
Nicholas V (pope), 182
Niewindt, Matinus J., 68–69
Nitchmann, David, 78
Nkisi (magical object), 104, 106, 130
Nkrumah, Kwame, 194
Nkuyu (ancestors), 130
Noirism (black consciousness), 115
Nonconformists, 71, 77–85, 87
Notre Dame du Perpétuel Secours, 157–58
Nutall, Enos, 90
Nyabinghi Issembly, 192–93, 196–99
Nzaambi Mpungu (God), 130
Nzinga (king of Congo), 59

Obeah (religion), 122–28, 140
Ocasio, Rafael, 51
Oever, Ten, 69
Offshore operations, 6
Ogun (spirit), 62, 94, 141, 144, 214
Ojeda, Alonso de, 67
Oliver, José R., 26–27
Olodumare (creator), 94, 141
Olson, George, 136
Olson, Nellie, 136
Orishas (deities), 51, 94–97, 106, 139–45, 214
Orisha tradition, 101, 139–45, 147, 150, 179

Ortíz, Fernando, 50
Oshun (orisha), 9, 94, 96, 141, 157
Ovando, Nicolas de, 21, 38–39, 42
Oyo Kingdom, 97

La Palma Sola (religion), 215–16
Palmer, Colin A., 5
Palo Monte: baptism in, 103; initiation in, 103, 105; rituals of, 103, 105–6; syncretism in, 102; Yoruba traditions in, 102–4
Pané, Ramón, 18, 22–27, 41
Papiamento language, 3
Parham, Charles, 167
Parkinson, James M, 136
Patronal festivals, 49–50
Patterson, Orlando, 8, 122
Patwa. *See* English patois
Paul, Thomas, 162
Peninsulares, 10
Pentecostal churches, 166–69; in Cuba, 171; in Dominican Republic, 170–71; Espiritismo and, 168; gender issues in, 218; in Haiti, 172; in Jamaica, 173–74; music in, 212–13; in Puerto Rico, 158–59, 169–70; revivalism and, 135–38, 200; Revival Zion and, 122, 133; United Pentecostal Church, 172
People's Nation Party (Jamaica), 187, 198
Péralte, Charlemagne, 115
Pérez, Juan, 31
Perrault, Lawrence, 172
Pétion, Alexandre, 114
Petit, Andrés Facundo Cristos de los Dolores, 103, 107–8
Petroglyphs, 22, 28
Phillippo, James, 81, 123
Phillips, Raglan, 136
Pichardo, Ernesto, 219
Pietism, 78
Pigmentocracy, 58
Pilgrimages, 152, 204
Pinn, Anthony, 208
Piracy, 66, 70
Planno, Mortimo, 194–95, 199
Plantation societies, and slavery, 5, 8–9
Pluralism, social, 9–11

Pollard, Velma, 188
Population estimates: for Africans, 98, 112, 138; for Amerindians, 37; for Rastafarians, 201
Possession rituals, 129, 131, 134–35, 142, 144
Presbyterian Church, 77, 86–88, 131, 160, 209
Primitivism, 100
Privateers, 66
Protestantism: in Barbados, 67, 70–71, 75, 77; in colonial era, 65–92; in Cuba, 163–66; in Haiti, 64, 162; after 1900, 155–75; Roman Catholicism and, 158–66, 210; slavery and, 75–77
Protestant Reformation, 49, 53
Puerto Rico, 2, 118–19, 158–61, 169–70, 210
Pukumina (religion), 132
Purchas, Samuel, 65
Purification spirit rituals, 152–53
Puritans, 71, 77

Quakers, 71, 77, 162, 166

Racial stratification: in Cuba, 156, 214, 220; in Haiti, 58
Ramirez, Miguel, 41
Ramsey, Kate, 64
Ras Tafari (king of Ethiopia), 183–84
Rastafarianism, 14, 177, 183–201; cooptation of, 198–99; diaspora of, 200–201; drumming in, 192–93, 211; gender issues and, 217–18; history of, 184–86, 193–98; influence of, 199–201, 206; population estimates for, 201; repatriation and, 191, 194–95; social conventions of, 187–90, 217
Rasvelt, Wigbold, 69
Re-Africanization, 154
Reformation, Protestant, 49, 53
Reggae music, 196, 198–201, 211–12
Reggae Sunsplash (festival), 212
Regla Congo. See Palo Monte
La Regla de Palo Monte. See Palo Monte
Regla Lucumí, 93, 99
Reid, Victor, 194
Reid-Salmon, Delroy A., 208

Religion(s): Afro-Christian, 121–54; Afro-Trinidadian, 138–54; folklorization of, 115; government support for, 89–90; legitimation of, 203–6; *religion cruzada*, 102; of Tainos, 22–30; theoretical perspectives on, 8–14. *See also specific religions*
Remittances, 6
Renteria, Pedro de, 42
Repartimeintos (redistribution of land), 39
Repatriation, and Rastafarianism, 191, 194–95
Revivalism, 135–38, 168, 187, 200
Revival Zion, 121–22, 131–38, 147
Rey, Terry, 52–53, 62
Rivail, Hippolyte Léon, Denizard, 116–19; *Book of the Spirits*, 117; *The Gospel According to Spiritism*, 119
Rivera-Pagán, Luis, 209
Roatán Island, 2, 17
Roberts, James Deotis, 208
Rodney, Melvina, 142–43
Rodney, Walter, 197
Rodríguez, Miguel, 27
Rodríguez Rivera, Juan Francísco, 27
Rodríguez y Lorenzo, Isidoro, 56
Roget, Henry Petijean, 28
Rojas Torres, Bernardo, 100
Román, Reinaldo L., 117–18
Roman Catholicism: Africans and, 43, 50–52, 59–64; *cabildos* and, 50–51, 157; in colonial era, 45–64; Columbus, C., and, 40; in Congo, 52, 58–62; in Cuba, 54, 98–99, 103; in Dominican Republic, 55–57, 162; England and, 63; Espiritismo and, 47; in Haiti, 57–64; institutional aspect of, 51–52; Marian devotions in, 46–48, 52–53, 175; medieval, 46–48; after 1900, 155–58; Orisha and, 139–40, 143; Protestantism and, 158–66, 210; Santería and, 204; slavery and, 57, 68–69, 113; Spanish Crown and, 45–46, 52; syncretism and, 46, 61, 158, 203; Tainos and, 22–23, 34–35, 39–40; vernacular religious practices and, 45–46, 150; Vodou and, 53, 61–64, 111–12; Yoruba traditions and, 58, 219

About the Authors

ENNIS B. EDMONDS is Associate Professor of Religious Studies at Kenyon College and author of *Rastafari: From Outcasts to Culture Bearers*.

MICHELLE A. GONZALEZ is Assistant Professor of Religious Studies at the University of Miami and author of *Afro-Cuban Theology: Religion, Race, Culture, and Identity*.